The Cornwallis Papers

The Campaigns of 1780 and 1781

in

The Southern Theatre of the American Revolutionary War

Volume VI

Arranged and edited by

Ian Saberton

The Naval & Military Press Ltd

Published by
The Naval & Military Press Ltd

Unit 10 Ridgewood Industrial Park,
Uckfield, East Sussex,
TN22 5QE England

Tel: +44 (0) 1825 749494
Fax: +44 (0) 1825 765701

www.naval-military-press.com
www.military-genealogy.com
www.militarymaproom.com

ISBN Volume I   9781845747923
ISBN Volume II   9781845747916
ISBN Volume III 9781845747909
ISBN Volume IV   9781845747893
ISBN Volume V   9781845747886
ISBN Volume VI   9781845747879

Printed and bound in Great Britain by
CPI Antony Rowe, Chippenham and Eastbourne

CONTENTS

PART TWELVE
THE LAST DAYS OF CORNWALLIS IN VIRGINIA
HIS RETURN TO NEW YORK
20th October to 18th November 1781

PART THIRTEEN
CORNWALLIS IN NEW YORK
19th November to 14th December 1781

HIS PASSAGE TO ENGLAND
15th December 1781 to 17th January 1782

PART FOURTEEN
SUPPLEMENTARY PAPERS

Editorial method

Subject to the following modifications, the editorial method remains the same as described in volume I.

Omitted papers

Though belonging to the period covered by this volume, the following papers in the series PRO 30/11/- are omitted on the ground that they do not relate to the southern campaigns or are too inconsequential: 6(1); 7(19) and (32); 58(1); 71(28); 74(143); 92(49) and (51); 94(5); 102(8); 105(53); 270(7); and 275(13).

Footnotes

As a general rule biographical footnotes on persons who are not the subject of such notes in this volume will be found in one of the preceding volumes.

Titles of works cited in abbreviated form in footnotes

Appletons'
 Appletons' Cyclopædia of American Biography (New York, 1888-)

Army Lists
 A list of the general and field officers... (London, 1754-77), together with *A list of all the officers of the army...* (London, 1778-)

Bass, *The Green Dragoon*
 Robert D Bass, *The Green Dragoon: The Lives of Banastre Tarleton and Mary Robinson* (Sandlapper Press Inc, 1973)

Boatner, *Encyclopedia*
 Mark Mayo Boatner III, *Encyclopedia of the American Revolution* (D McKay Co, 1966)

Charnock, *Biographia Navalis*
 John Charnock, *Biographia Navalis: or Impartial Memoirs of the Lives and Characters of Officers of the Navy of Great Britain from the Year 1660 to the Present Time* (London, 1794-98)

Clark, *Loyalists in the Southern Campaign*
 Murtie June Clark, *Loyalists in the Southern Campaign of the Revolutionary War*, volume I (Genealogical Publishing Co, 2003)

Clinton, *The American Rebellion*
 Sir Henry Clinton, *The American Rebellion,* edited by William B Willcox (Yale University Press, 1954)

Coldham, *Loyalist Claims*
    Peter Wilson Coldham, *American Loyalist Claims* (National Genealogical Society, 1980)

DAB
    Dictionary of American Biography (New York, 1928-1958)

Davies ed, *Docs of the Am Rev*
    K G Davies ed, *Documents of the American Revolution 1770-1783,* volumes XVIII and XX (Irish Academic Press, 1978 and 1979)

DCB
    Dictionary of Canadian Biography (University of Toronto, 1967; also available on internet)

DeMond, *Loyalists in NC*
    Robert O DeMond, *The Loyalists in North Carolina during the Revolution* (Duke University Press, 1940)

Garden, *Anecdotes* (1st Series)
    Alexander Garden, *Anecdotes of the Revolutionary War* (Charleston, 1822)

Garden, *Anecdotes* (2nd series)
    Alexander Garden, *Anecdotes of the American Revolution, Second Series* (Charleston, 1828)

The Greene Papers
    The Papers of General Nathanael Greene, volumes VI-X, edited by Richard K Showman, Dennis M Conrad, Roger N Parks, et al (University of North Carolina Press, 1991-8)

Gwathmey, *Historical Register*
    John H Gwathmey, *Historical Register of Virginians in the Revolution 1775-1783* (The Dietz Press, 1938)

Hay ed, *Soldiers from NC*
    Gertrude Sloan Hay ed, *Roster of Soldiers from North Carolina in the American Revolution* (Reprint, Genealogical Publishing Co Inc, 1988)

Heitman, *Historical Register*
    Francis B Heitman, *Historical Register of the Officers of the Continental Army during the War of the Revolution* (Reprint, Clearfield Publishing Co Inc, 2000)

James, *Marion*
    William Dobein James, *A Sketch of the Life of Brig Gen Francis Marion* (Reprint, Continental Book Co, Marietta GA, 1948)

Johnson, *Traditions*
    Joseph Johnson, *Traditions and Reminiscences chiefly of the American Revolution in the South* (Charleston, 1851)

Johnston, *Commissioned Officers in the Medical Service*
William Johnston, *Roll of Commissioned Officers in the Medical Service of the British Army: 20 June 1727 to 23 June 1898* (Reprint, The Wellcome Historical Medical Library, 1968)

Lambert, *SC Loyalists*
Robert Stansbury Lambert, *South Carolina Loyalists in the American Revolution* (University of South Carolina Press, 1987)

Lee, *Memoirs*
Henry Lee, *Memoirs of the War in the Southern Department of the United States* (Revised edition, New York, 1869)

McCowen Jr, *Charleston, 1780-82*
George Smith McCowen Jr, *The British Occupation of Charleston, 1780-82* (University of South Carolina Press, 1972)

McCrady, *SC in the Rev 1775-1780*
Edward McCrady, *The History of South Carolina in the Revolution 1775-1780* (The Macmillan Co, New York, 1901)

McCrady, *SC in the Rev 1780-1783*
Edward McCrady, *The History of South Carolina in the Revolution 1780-1783* (The Macmillan Co, New York, 1902)

Moss, *SC Patriots*
Bobby Gilmer Moss, *Roster of South Carolina Patriots in the American Revolution* (Genealogical Publishing Co Inc, 1983)

Moultrie, *Memoirs*
William Moultrie, *Memoirs of the American Revolution* (New York, 1802)

ODNB
Oxford Dictionary of National Biography (Oxford University Press, 2004)

Raymond, 'British American Corps'
W O Raymond, 'Roll of Officers of the British American or Loyalist Corps', *Collections of the New Brunswick Historical Society*, ii, 1899

Robinson, *NC Guide*
Blackwell P Robinson ed, *The North Carolina Guide* (University of North Carolina Press, 1955)

Ross ed, *Cornwallis Correspondence*
Charles Ross ed, *Correspondence of Charles, First Marquis Cornwallis*, volume I (London, 1859)

Sabine, *Biographical Sketches*
> Lorenzo Sabine, *Biographical Sketches of Loyalists of the American Revolution* (Boston, 1864)

Stevens, *Clinton-Cornwallis Controversy*
> Benjamin Franklin Stevens, *The Campaign in Virginia 1781: the Clinton Cornwallis Controversy* (London, 1887-8)

Syrett and DiNardo ed, *The Commissioned Sea Officers*
> David Syrett and R L DiNardo ed, *The Commissioned Sea Officers of the Royal Navy 1660-1815* (Navy Records Society, 1994)

Tarleton, *Campaigns*
> Banastre Tarleton, *A History of the Campaigns of 1780 and 1781 in the Southern Provinces of North America* (London, 1787)

Tyler, *Encyclopedia*
> Lyon Gardiner Tyler, *Encyclopedia of Virginia Biography* (New York, 1915)

Va Military Records
> *Virginia Military Records* (Genealogical Publishing Co Inc, 1983)

Valentine, *The British Establishment*
> Alan Valentine, *The British Establishment, 1760-1784: An Eighteenth-Century Biographical Dictionary* (University of Oklahoma Press, 1970)

Wheeler, *Reminiscences*
> John Hill Wheeler, *Reminiscences and Memoirs of North Carolina and Eminent North Carolinians* (Reprint, Genealogical Publishing Co, 1966)

Wickwire, *Cornwallis*
> Franklin and Mary Wickwire, *Cornwallis: The American Adventure* (Houghton Mifflin Co, 1970)

The Cornwallis Papers

CHAPTER 57

Introduction

In this final volume we see in part the tragic sequence of events that ended in the disaster at Yorktown.

As Part Eleven opens, Cornwallis advises Clinton on 26th July that he, his engineer and the sea captains had examined Old Point Comfort and that they all agreed it was quite unsuitable for a post to cover large ships lying in Hampton Road. 'This being the case,' he continued, 'I shall in obedience to the spirit of your Excellency's orders take measures with as much dispatch as possible to seize and fortify York and Gloucester, being the only harbour in which we can hope to be able to give effectual protection to line of battle ships. I shall likewise use all the expedition in my power to evacuate Portsmouth and the posts belonging to it, but untill that is accomplished, it will be impossible for me to spare troops, for York and Gloucester from their situation command no country and a superiority in the field will not only be necessary to enable us to draw forage and other supplies from the country but likewise to carry on our works without interruption.' He had nonetheless gone some way in warning that they would be 'dangerous defensive posts'.

Cornwallis occupied Yorktown and Gloucester on 1st and 2nd August, the evacuation of Portsmouth was completed on the 18th, and four days later he was joined by the remaining troops from there.

Meanwhile momentous events were taking place elsewhere. On 14th August, while posted with Washington on the Hudson, de Rochambeau, the commander of the French expeditionary troops, received notice from de Grasse that he would quit Santo Domingo on the 13th for the Chesapeake, bringing with him 25 to 29 ships of war, over 3,000 troops, 10 field pieces, and a number of siege cannon and mortars. He would return with the troops on 15th October.

Displaying a decisiveness that does them great credit, Washington and de Rochambeau decided in concert to abandon their plans for taking New York City and to strike south for Virginia as soon as possible. On 21st August their march began, with 2,000 Continental and 4,000 French troops, and was conducted in such a way as to mislead Clinton that an attack on Staten Island was in prospect. It was not until 2nd September, when the Continentals were passing through Philadelphia, that Clinton received intelligence that the allied forces were bound for Virginia. Even if he had known a few days sooner, there would have been no window of opportunity to fit out a troop reinforcement for Cornwallis in time to reach him before the French naval blockade of the Chesapeake began.

To conceal his destination as long as possible de Grasse took an indirect route through the Bahama Channel, arriving off the Capes of Virginia on 29th August, the date on which he was spotted by HMS *Guadeloupe*, which promptly reported his presence to Cornwallis. According to a detailed note of his fleet appearing later in this volume[1], he had brought 37 men of war, all but three of which were of 64 guns or more, and 8 frigates. He proceeded to anchor in Lynnhaven Bay and on 1st September dispatched 40 boats with troops to Jamestown Island, where they joined up with Lafayette in attempting to bottle up Cornwallis on the landward side of Williamsburg Neck. All that was needed to complete the naval armament was the arrival of a convoy of siege artillery from Newport, Rhode Island, escorted by de Barras and 8 ships of the line.

On 5th September, as he rode south through Chester, Washington received news of de Grasse's arrival, and on the 6th his Continentals reached the Head of Elk, a short distance from the northern point of Chesapeake Bay. Two days later they were joined by de Rochambeau's men.

What, in the meantime, had become of the Royal Navy? On 3rd May Rodney, the naval commander in the West Indies, had warned his counterpart at New York that de Grasse might visit the coast of North America, 'in which case I shall send every assistance in my power'. On learning of de Grasse's projected departure, he detached Sir Samuel Hood after him, but unaware of the strength of de Grasse's armament, he assigned to the squadron only 14 men of war, 3 frigates and a fire-ship. Following a more direct route, Hood reached the Chesapeake four days before de Grasse, but not finding him there, he sailed onward to New York. It was only then that Graves was acquainted with de Grasse's approach, though not with his overwhelming strength. Seized of the need to take immediate action, he united 5 of his 7 men of war with Hood's reinforcement, and assuming overall command, he set sail on 31st August for the Chesapeake, hoping to pre-empt or contest de Grasse's occupation of the Bay or at least to prevent de Barras, of whose departure he was aware, from joining up with de Grasse. In none of these objectives was Graves successful. Finding de Grasse had already arrived, he attempted to dislodge him, but in the Battle of the Chesapeake Capes on 5th September he came off worse against a superior French fleet and two or three of his ships were badly damaged. After the two fleets had manœuvred for a further five days, de Barras passed safely within the Capes, de Grasse re-entered the Bay, and shortly afterwards Graves, outnumbered and outgunned, sailed for New York to repair the damage to his ships.

To consolidate the entrapment of Cornwallis all that now remained was for Washington's and de Rochambeau's men to join up with Lafayette's and the French naval troops on Williamsburg Neck. From the Head of Elk the artillery and stores were embarked in transports while the main body of the troops marched on to Baltimore and Annapolis. By

---

[1] See pp 103-4.

18th September they had boarded vessels there, and by the 26th all had been set ashore at landings in James River near to Williamsburg. Washington assumed command of the entire land forces while de Rochambeau, who was nominally under him, had also arrived to command those of the French.

From Cornwallis's perspective events from the arrival of de Grasse to the capitulation are set out in his correspondence with Clinton during the siege and after. It is unnecessary to elaborate here, save to apportion blame for the disaster.

Undoubtedly the navy was in part responsible. No allowance was made for a worst-case scenario with the result that its men of war were too few to repulse de Grasse and remain in control of North American waters. Nor might its culpability end there. There is reason to suspect that the repairs to the ships damaged in the Battle of the Chesapeake Capes may not have been progressed as rapidly and as urgently as the critical situation demanded. Had they been completed a week sooner, Cornwallis might well have been saved. As it was, the date of departure was constantly put back, the fleet was not ready to convoy Clinton and 7,000 troops until 19th October – the day of the capitulation, and they did not arrive off the Capes of Virginia until five days later.

After the capitulation we are treated to the distasteful spectacle of Cornwallis and Clinton attempting to offload on to each other responsibility for the disaster, whereas in reality both were in part to blame. As explained in Chapter 44[2] and amplified in Chapter 49[3], Cornwallis for his part ought never to have marched into Virginia in the first place, while Clinton, once Cornwallis was there, brought undue pressure on him to return to Williamsburg Neck, tacitly acquiescing, despite Cornwallis's reservations, in the choice of Yorktown as the only place there to protect line of battle ships. The danger to such a post, if command of the Chesapeake was lost, it did not take an accomplished strategist to see[4] — and Clinton was aware that de Grasse was expected in the hurricane season[5].

With hindsight it is easy to question decisions taken by Cornwallis immediately before and during the siege, but it would be harsh to do so, as they are perfectly understandable under the circumstances then obtaining. After the French naval troops had joined up with Lafayette's men on 1st September, he could have attacked them before the arrival of Washington's and de Rochambeau's reinforcement and hopefully broken out, whether to retire to the Carolinas or to proceed to the north. Alternatively, he could have broken out on the Gloucester side and attempted by rapid marches to reach New York. Yet either option would have involved the abandonment of numerous sick, artillery, stores and shipping, and under these circumstances it was entirely reasonable that he should have preferred to await news from Clinton of his intentions. In mid September Clinton's dispatches arrived, in which he

---

[2] See vol IV, p 101.

[3] See vol V, pp 5-6.

[4] See, for example, Clinton to Cornwallis, 29th May and 1st June, vol V, p 120.

[5] See Clinton to Cornwallis, 19th June, vol V, p 135.

undertook to embark with a reinforcement as soon as possible, and with this assurance Cornwallis, again quite reasonably, forsook for the time being all thoughts of breaking out.

Cornwallis has been criticised for abandoning his outer line of defence, about a half a mile beyond the inner, on the night of 29th September as the enemy began to invest Yorktown. If it could have been held, if only for a few days, defence of the post would have been protracted. Yet, observing that the enemy were taking measures that could not fail to turn his left flank in a short time, and having just received word from Clinton that there was every reason to expect his departure on 5th October, Cornwallis did not hesitate in withdrawing within his inner works, conscious that he could hold out until Clinton's anticipated arrival. It is idle to try and second-guess his judgement now.

In his *Campaigns* Tarleton makes out a seemingly convincing case for breaking out on the Gloucester side soon after Major Cochrane arrived on 10th October with Clinton's dispatch of the 30th. In it Clinton indicated that his departure had fallen back at the earliest to the 12th but that even that date was subject to disappointment. Yes, the chances of a break-out would have markedly improved if Cornwallis had acted promptly as Tarleton suggests, but in the circumstances in which he found himself it is perfectly understandable that, for the same reason as he had not abandoned his post earlier, Cornwallis should have decided to wait for relief until matters became critical. By the 16th they had become so and on that night he attempted to transfer his fit troops to the Gloucester side, but fate in the form of a squall intervened, his boats were dispersed, and the attempt came to nought. He was then left with no option but to capitulate.

As far as Washington is concerned, he emerges from his campaign as a decisive, resolute commander with keen strategic awareness, but his success was due less to concentrating his forces in an exemplary way than preponderantly to chance circumstances: Cornwallis's absurd decision to march into Virginia, the occupation of Yorktown against his better judgement, its coincidence with the arrival of de Grasse, the failure of the Royal Navy to cater adequately for command of North American waters, Cornwallis's decision not to break out at once from Yorktown, and ultimately the squall which put paid to his doing so at the close of the siege. '*Est-il heureux?*' Napoleon was wont to ask of a prospective general. 'Is he lucky?' In Washington's case, the answer, incontrovertibly, is: 'Yes, in spades!'

According to Johnston, the besiegers numbered 5,500 Continentals, 7,500 French, and 3,000 militia – a total of 16,000, and he calculates the besieged to be 7,500, though they were in fact 225 fewer. Of those that capitulated, the return of 18th October appearing later in this volume lists 5,950 rank and file, and when we extrapolate by using a factor of 17.5% to cater for officers, serjeants and drummers, we arrive at a figure of 6,991 for all ranks. If, from the return of 27th October appearing in Johnston, we subtract the staff of the public departments, followers of the army, pioneers, and odds and sods not listed in the former return, the figure is 6,949 for all ranks, so that the two returns correlate, as it is reasonable to assume that some of the severely wounded had died in the interval before the later return was prepared. Not accounted for in the above figures are some 800 marines engaged on land on each side.

Writing in 1902, Fortescue concluded, 'The blow was, on the whole, perhaps the heaviest that has ever fallen on the British Army.' It would have been difficult at that time to disagree with him.

The main body of the prisoners was marched off to camps in Virginia and Maryland under guard of militia. After being wined and dined by Washington, de Rochambeau and other revolutionary or French officers, Cornwallis and his officers were paroled and permitted to go to New York, Charlestown or Europe. One field officer per 50 men remained behind to reside with the rest of the prisoners.

The period from the capitulation till Cornwallis's departure for England is chiefly notable for the beginning of the Clinton-Cornwallis controversy, in which each sought to absolve himself of blame for the disaster. Clinton's letter of 2nd and 10th December is in particular misleading, where he asserts that his promises of relief, held out in his letters of 2nd and 6th September, might have been frustrated by the navy, though no such assertions were made at the time. It was reasonable for Cornwallis to assume, as he did, that Clinton was speaking in the name of both services. In the same letter Clinton attempts to muddy the waters by stating that Cornwallis had implied that on the arrival of Washington's troops he had been prevented from breaking out by Clinton's letter of 24th September, but Cornwallis had made no such implication. It was Clinton's letters of the 2nd and the 6th, received in mid September, that had led Cornwallis to continue with his decision not to break out when Washington's troops arrived.

Cornwallis set sail for England on 15th December aboard the *Robust*, a 74-gun man of war convoying home a fleet of 120 merchantmen. The passage was not entirely without incident. On the 25th the *Robust* sprang a leak and began to make for the West Indies, its pumps constantly working. On the 28th, when 113 leagues east of Bermuda, Cornwallis had no option but to transfer to the *Greyhound* transport for his onward journey, but ill luck tempered by good fortune would continue to befall him. On 14th January, as the *Greyhound* raced up the English Channel, she was captured by the *Boulogne* privateer out of St-Malo in Brittany. Unable to make land there from the violence of the weather, and conscious how dangerous it would be to approach elsewhere the coast of France or to remain at sea, her captain agreed to his prize putting into an English port, having entered into a certificate with his captives that she would be treated as such and that they would consider themselves as prisoners on parole. On or about the 22nd Cornwallis arrived in London.

As Cornwallis would have realised, Yorktown had effectively ended the revolutionary war. On 4th March the House of Commons resolved that 'it would consider as enemies to His Majesty and the Country all those who should advise or by any means attempt the further prosecution of offensive war on the Continent of North America for the purpose of reducing the revolted colonies to obedience by force'. Commissioners were appointed by the warring parties and on 30th November 1782 they signed provisional articles. It was not, however, until 3rd September 1783 that the Treaty of Paris was formally signed recognising the independence of the United States.

The Cornwallis Papers end as they begin — with South Carolina and Georgia.

§ - §

Principal papers and works consulted in the writing of this chapter

Mark Mayo Boatner III, *Encyclopedia of the American Revolution* (D McKay Co, 1966)

The Cornwallis Papers (UK National Archives, Kew)

Sir John Fortescue, *A History of the British Army*, volume III (Macmillan and Co Ltd, 1902)

Henry P Johnston, *The Yorktown Campaign and the Surrender of Cornwallis 1781* (Harper & Bros, 1881)

Benjamin Franklin Stevens, *The Campaign in Virginia 1781: the Clinton Cornwallis Controversy*, volume I (London, 1887)

Banastre Tarleton, *A History of the Campaigns of 1780 and 1781 in the Southern Provinces of North America* (London, 1787)

Sir George Otto Trevelyan Bt, *The History of the American Revolution*, volume VI (Longmans, Green, and Co, 1915)

Christopher Ward, *The War of the Revolution* (The Macmillan Co, NY, 1952)

§ - §

PART ELEVEN

Evacuation of Portsmouth

Occupation and siege of Yorktown and Gloucester

23rd July to 19th October 1781

CHAPTER 58

Letters to or from New York

---

1 - Between Cornwallis and Clinton

Cornwallis to Clinton, 24th July 1781[1]

74(47): ADf

Portsmouth
Virginia
July 24th 1781

His Excellency Sir Henry Clinton KB etc etc etc

Sir

I find by your Excellency's letter of the 29th of May[2], delivered to me by Lt Colonel Macpherson on the 12th of this month, that neither my march from Cross Creek to Wilmington or from thence to Petersburgh meets with your approbation. The move from Cross Creek to Wilmington was absolutely necessary. Such was the situation and distress of my troops and so great were the sufferings of the sick and wounded that I had no option left. I tried many methods of informing Lord Rawdon of it; they all failed. I had left such a force in South Carolina that, if Lord Rawdon could have had timely notice of the probability of General Greene's moving towards that province and could have called in Lt Colonel Watson, General Greene would not have ventured to have placed himself before Camden.

---

[1] Published in Stevens, *Clinton-Cornwallis Controversy*, ii, 88. There are no material differences.

[2] *letter..*: see vol V, p 118.

On the 22nd of April I received a dispatch from Lt Colonel Balfour[3] inclosing a letter from Lord Rawdon of the 13th apprizing him of General Greene's approach and saying that he could not hope to get Lt Colonel Watson to him in time and that he had then at least fifteen days' provision. The fate of the garrison of Camden must have been decided before I could have hoped to have reached the Pedee or Waggamaw. I had then no certainty of being able to get vessels in time to assist in passing the latter. From Wilmington to the Waggamaw is a perfect desert, and indeed in all that low country it is impossible to subsist in the summer for want of water to turn the mills.

Had a misfortune happened to Lord Rawdon's corps, I knew that the whole country east of Santee and Pedee would be in arms against us. I therefore did not think that I could with about thirteen hundred infantry and 200 cavalry undertake such a march and the passage of two such rivers as the Pedee and Santee without exposing the corps under my command to the utmost hazard of disgrace and ruin. If, on the contrary, Lord Rawdon should have effected his retreat from Camden and have assembled his whole force west of Santee, I was convinced that General Greene could do no effectual mischief but overrunning the Back Country, which I should arrive too late to prevent, and which different corps of the rebels have constantly done ever since the 1st Battle of Camden, exclusive only of the ground on which our forts were constructed. I should therefore have carried back my army to South Carolina, giving every advantage to General Greene's movement, in order to commence a defensive war on the frontiers of that province, which I have long since declared both to yourself and to the Minister to be in my opinion impracticable against the rebellious inhabitants supported by a Continental army. In the measure which I pursued I neither risked my own corps or Major General Phillips's, being determined to return to Wilmington from Halifax unless I heard from that officer that I could join him with safety. The great quantity of provisions which I was credibly informed I should find at Halifax would easily enable me to return. Major General Phillips could be in no danger as I had written expressly to him to take no measures in consequence of my letter that could expose his corps to hazard, and indeed I cannot help observing that in this instance your Excellency seems to think the force of Virginia rather more formidable than you have done on some other occasions. With the warmest zeal for the service of my King and country I am conscious that my judgement is liable to error. Perhaps, in the difficult situation I was in at Wilmington, the measure which I adopted was not the best[4], but I have at least the satisfaction to find by the intercepted letter

---

[3]   *a dispatch..*: of 20th April. It was received by Cornwallis late on the 29th of that month and answered the following day. See vol IV, pp 170-6.

[4]   This clause is substituted for: 'Perhaps, in the difficult choice I had to make at Wilmington, I adopted the most objectionable measure'. This latter clause, together with the rest of the passage from 'With the warmest zeal' to the end of the letter, was previously substituted for: 'The reinforcement which you say you fortunately ordered to the Chesapeak in consequence of my letter of the 24th April, altho' I see it had been previously requested by General Phillips, did not contribute much to the safety of the move, as I had joined General Arnold before its arrival in Chesapeak Bay.

'Whether the move was judicious or not the impartial world must judge. I flatter myself that it has been attended with more good consequences than bad ones, and by the intercepted letter of the 14th of May from General Greene to Baron Steuben I have the satisfaction to find that it was not the move he wished for.'

of the 14th of May from General Greene to Baron Steuben[5] that it was not agreeable to his wishes that I came into Virginia.

[I have the honour to be etc

CORNWALLIS]

Cornwallis to Clinton, 26th July 1781[6]

74(51): C

Portsmouth
Virginia
26th July 1781

His Excellency Sir Henry Clinton KB etc etc etc

Sir

I received your cyphered letter of the 11th instant[7] on the 20th, in consequence of which the expedition was detained, and on the 21st I was honoured with your dispatches of the 8th and 11th instant[8] delivered by Captain Stapleton, the contents of which, I will confess, were to me as unexpected as I trust they are undeserved.

As a subordinate officer I think it my duty to obey positive orders or, in exercising discretionary powers, to act as much as possible conformable to the apparent wishes of my superior officer, combined with the evident good of the service; and in my late conduct I hope I have not deviated from those principles, for permit me to remark that I cannot discover in the instructions to General Phillips[9] and the substance of private conversation with him[10] (extracts of which I take the liberty to inclose), to which I am referred, nor in our former correspondence any trace of the extreme earnestness that now appears to secure a harbour for ships of the line; and your assent to my engaging in operations in the upper Chesapeake, if I could have brought myself to think them expedient, would, if I had doubted before, have convinced me that securing a harbour for line of battle ships was not with you a primary and

---

5   *the intercepted letter..*: see vol V, p 107.

6   A draft of this letter (74(61)) is annotated: 'Dispatched by Captain Stapleton, 28th July 1781'. The letter as sent was dated the 27th and is published without enclosure (1) in Stevens, op cit, ii, 104. There are no other material differences.

7   *your cyphered letter..*: see vol V, p 139.

8   *your dispatches..*: see vol V, pp 140-3.

9   *the instructions..*: see vol V, p 7.

10   *the substance..*: see vol V, p 55.

immediate object. In my letter of the 26th of May[11] I informed your Excellency that after destroying the stores at Richmond and the adjoining country I should move back to Williamsburgh, keeping the army in readiness to comply with your further instructions. I arrived at that place on the 25th, and on the 26th of June I received from Ensign Amiel your dispatches of the 11th and 15th of the same month[12], being the first letters that I had received from you since my arrival in Virginia. In the first you tell me that New York is threatened to be attacked by a very numerous enemy and, therefore wishing to concentrate your force, you recommend to me to send a body of troops to you as I can spare them in the order mentioned in a list unless I have engaged in operations in the upper Chesapeake; and in the dispatch of the 15th, taking for granted that I have not engaged in those operations, you require that the embarkation of those troops may begin with the greatest dispatch. After a full compliance with this requisition the force left under my command would have been about two thousand and four hundred rank and file fit for duty as will appear by the returns, which in a post adapted to that number I hoped would be sufficient for a defensive and desultory water expeditions. You mention Williamsburgh and York in your letter of the 11th as defensive stations, but only as being supposed healthy, without deciding on their safety. Williamsburgh, having no harbour and requiring an army to occupy the position, would not have suited us. I saw that it would require a great deal of time and labour to fortify York and Gloucester, both of which are necessary to secure a harbour for vessels of any burthen; and to effect it assistance would have been wanted from some of the troops then under embarkation orders, which, when New York was in danger, I did not think myself at liberty to detain for any other purpose than operations in the upper Chesapeake; and supposing both places fortified, I thought they would have been dangerous defensive posts, either of them being accessible to the whole force of this province, and from their situation they would not have commanded an acre of country. I therefore, under these circumstances, with the most earnest desire to comply with what I thought were your present wishes and to facilitate your intended future operations in Pensylvania, did not hesitate in deciding to pass James River and to retire to Portsmouth that I might be able to send you the troops required. And I was confirmed in the propriety of the measure when, upon passing James River, I received your dispatch[13] informing me that for essential reasons you had resolved to make an attempt on Philadelphia and directing me to embark with the greatest expedition the same body of troops with stores etc for that purpose. Having likewise executed this order with the utmost exertion and alacrity, I must acknowledge I was not prepared to receive in the next dispatch from your Excellency[14] a severe censure of my conduct.

Immediately on the receipt of your cyphered letter[15] I gave orders to the engineer to examine and survey Point Comfort and the channels adjoining to it. I have likewise visited

---

11 *my letter..*: see vol V, p 88.

12 *your dispatches..*: see vol V, pp 95-8.

13 *your dispatch*: of 28th June, vol V, p 114.

14 *the next dispatch..*: of 8th July, vol V, p 140.

15 *your cyphered letter*: of 11th July, vol V, p 139.

it with the captains of the King's ships now lying in Hampton Road. I have the honour to inclose to you copies of the report of the engineer and of the opinions of the captains of the navy on that subject, with which my own entirely concurs, and I likewise transmit a survey[16] of the peninsula made by Lieutenants Sutherland and Straton, from all which your Excellency will see that a work on Point Comfort would neither command the entrance nor secure His Majesty's ships at anchor in Hampton Road. This being the case, I shall in obedience to the spirit of your Excellency's orders take measures with as much dispatch as possible to seize and fortify York and Gloucester, being the only harbour in which we can hope to be able to give effectual protection to line of battle ships. I shall likewise use all the expedition in my power to evacuate Portsmouth and the posts belonging to it, but untill that is accomplished, it will be impossible for me to spare troops,[17] for York and Gloucester from their situation command no country and a superiority in the field will not only be necessary to enable us to draw forage and other supplies from the country but likewise to carry on our works without interruption.

Your Excellency having been pleased to disapprove of my going to South Carolina, I have sent General Leslie, who sailed on the 25th instant in the *Carysfort* to take the command there.

I have the honour to be with great respect, sir,
Your most obedient and most humble servant

CORNWALLIS

Enclosure (1)
Extracts from the Phillips Papers etc   74(57): C

Instructions to Major General Phillips, 10th March

'If the Admiral, disapproving of Portsmouth and requiring a fortified station for large ships in the Chesapeak, should propose York Town or Old Point Comfort, if possession of either can be acquired and maintained without great risk or loss, you are at liberty to take possession thereof, but if the objections are such as you think forcible, you must, after stating those objections, decline it 'till solid operation take place in the Chesapeak.'

Substance of conversations etc, 26th April

'With regard to a station for the protection of the King's ships, I know of no place so proper as York Town if it could be taken possession of, fortified and garrisoned with 1,000 men, as, by having 1,000 men more at a post somewhere in Elizabeth River, York and James

---

[16] *a survey*: no copy.

[17] The rest of the sentence is substituted for: 'for York and Gloucester from their situation commanding no country, I cannot support the cavalry and other horses of the army, nor maintain any intercourse with the country, without a superiority in the field.'

Rivers would be ours and our cruizers might command the waters of the Chesapeak. Troops might likewise be spared from these posts to carry on expeditions during the summer months when probably nothing can be risked in that climate but water movements. But if the heights of York and those on Gloucester side cannot be so well and so soon fortified as to render that post *hors d'insulte* before the enemy can move a force etc against it, it may not be adviseable to attempt it. In that case something may possibly be done at *Old Point Comfort* to cover large ships lying in Hampton Road (which is reckoned a good one and not so liable to injury from gales at north-east as that of York, particularly in winter). If neither can be secured, we must content ourselves with keeping the Chesapeak with frigates' etc.

Sir Henry Clinton to Lord Cornwallis, 11th June, received 26th June

'Respecting my opinions of stations in James and York Rivers I shall beg leave to refer your Lordship to my instructions to and correspondence with Generals Phillips and Arnold' etc.

Enclosure (2)
Engineer's report, 25th July 1781[18]

74(55): LS

Billy ordnance transport
Hampton Road
July 25th 1781

Lt General Earl Cornwallis etc etc etc

My Lord

Agreeable to your orders I have examined the ground on Old Point Comfort with as much accuracy as I possibly could, and for your Lordship's better information I have made a survey of the ground, upon which is lay'd down the width and soundings of the channel.

I beg leave to offer what appears to me respecting the situation of a work on that spot.

The ground where the ruins of Fort George lay is the fittest for a work but at the same time must be attended with many inconveniences.

The level of the ground there is about two feet higher than the high water mark, which from its very short distance to the deep water must soon be destroyed by a naval attack.

The great width and depth of the channel give ships the advantage of passing the fort with very little risque. I apprehend fifteen hundred yards is too great a distance for batteries to stop ships, which is the distance here. Ships that wish to pass the fire of the fort have no occasion to approach nearer.

---

[18] Published in Stevens, op cit, ii, 95. There are no differences.

Nor do I imagine a fort built there could afford any great protection to an inferior and weak fleet anchored near the fort against a superior fleet of the enemy, which must have it in their power to make their own disposition and place our fleet between them and the fort, the channel affording no bay for the security of ships under cover of a fort.

The time and expence to build a fort there must be very considerable from the low situation of the ground, which must necessarily cause the soil to be moved from a great distance to form the ramparts and parapets, and every other material must be carried there, as the timber on the peninsula is unfit for any usefull purpose.

These are the remarks which have occur'd to me on examining the ground and situation of a work on Old Point Comfort for the protection of the harbour and fleet, which I humbly submit to your Lordship.

I have the honor to be with the greatest respect
Your Lordship's most obedient and very humble servant

ALEX SUTHERLAND
Lieutenant of Engineers

Enclosure (3)
Naval report, 26th July 1781[19]   *74(59): LS*

Richmond
Hampton Road
the 26th July 1781

Rt Hon Lt General Earl Cornwallis
Commander in Chief etc etc etc

My Lord

In consequence of a requisition that your Lordship received from the Commanders in Chief of His Majesty's troops and ships relative to a post being established at Old Point Comfort for the protection and security of the King's ships that may occasionally be sent to the Chesapeak, we whose names are hereunto subscribed have taken as accurate a survey of that place as possible and are unanimously of opinion from the width of the channel and depth of water close to it that any superior enemy's force coming in may pass any work that can be established there with little damage or destroy it with the ships that may be there under its protection.

---

[19] Published in Stevens, op cit, ii, 101. There are no differences.

We have the honor to be, my Lord,
Your Lordship's most obedient very humble servants

CHARLES HUDSON
THO[S] SYMONDS
CHA[S] HOLMES EVERITT[20]
RALPH DUNDAS[21]

Cornwallis to Clinton, 27th July 1781   *72(80): ADfS*

Portsmouth
July 27th 1781

His Excellency Sir Henry Clinton KB etc etc etc

Sir

I see by the orders that your Excellency has been pleased to promote Captain Campbell of the 33rd Regiment to be Major of the 71st from his very gallant behaviour in the actions of the 16th of August and 15th of March. I have no doubt of his proving himself worthy of your favour.

I beg leave to recommend Captain Lieutenant George Anson Nutt to succeed to Captain Campbell's company and (as Lieutenant Warde, who is the eldest, is obliged by his ill state of health to think of retiring from the service) Lieutenant Salwin for the captain lieutenantcy and eldest Ensign Ralph Gore for the lieutenantcy (both these gentlemen were severely wounded in the action of the 15th of March), and I likewise take the liberty of adding my recommendation of my nephew, Mr Charles Madan, for the ensigncy.

I have the honour to be with great respect
Your most obedient and most humble servant

CORNWALLIS

---

[20] Commissioned a lieutenant in the Royal Navy on 20th October 1772, Charles Holmes Everitt (?-1807) had been promoted to commander on 11th November 1776 and to post-captain ten months later. He was now commanding the *Solebay*, a 28-gun frigate launched at Newcastle in 1763. He died an admiral of the blue, having in later life assumed the surname of Calmady. (Syrett and DiNardo eds, *The Commissioned Sea Officers*, 69; Michael Phillips, 'Ships of the Old Navy 2' (Internet, 27th July 2006))

[21] Ralph Dundas (?-1787) of Ochtertyre, Kincardine-in-Menteith, Perthshire, had been commissioned a lieutenant in the Royal Navy on 1st November 1757 and promoted to commander on 3rd April 1779, a rank which carried with it the courtesy title of captain. For the past two years he had been commanding the sloop of war *Bonetta*. He would rise no higher in the service. (Syrett and DiNardo eds, op cit, 136)

York in Virginia
August 12th 1781

His Excellency Sir Henry Clinton KB etc etc etc

Sir

I received the enclosed letter last night from Governour Bruere. One to the same effect arrived two days ago from him directed to the commanding officer of the navy and was immediately forwarded to the Admiral by the officer stationed near the Capes.

I embarked the 80th Regiment in boats and went myself on board of the *Richmond* very early in the morning of the 29th, but we were so unfortunate in winds as to be four days on our passage. The 80th landed on the night of the 1st at Glocester, and the troops which were in the transports on the morning of the 2nd at this place. I have since brought the 71st and Legion hither and sent the Regiment du Prince Hereditaire to Glocester. The works on the Glocester side are in some forwardness and I hope in a situation to resist a sudden attack. Brigadier General O'Hara is hastening as much as possible the evacuation of Portsmouth. As soon as he arrives here I will send to New York every man that I can spare consistent with the safety and subsistence of the force in this country.

[I have the honour to be etc

CORNWALLIS]

Enclosure
Bruere to Cornwallis etc, 3rd August 1781   *6(344): LS*

Bermuda
Government House
St George's
3rd August 1781

The Rt Hon the Earl of Cornwallis or the officer
    commanding His Majesty's forces in Virginia

My Lord

I think it my duty to give your Lordship the earliest intelligence possible of a supposed inimical fleet.

Various accounts from the West Indies announce the departure of the French fleet from Martinico steering for Cape François, but by many supposed bound for North America, and

---

[22] Published without the enclosure in Stevens, op cit, ii, 124. There are no other differences.

yesterday from twenty five to thirty sail of large ships were discovered to the eastward of these islands and within sight thereof, steering north-westerly, and Captain Parker of the privateer brigg *Hammond* with a prize in company was close aboard of them at one o'clock yesterday morning and with difficulty got to windward of them by day light, then in sight of land. Captain Parker took them to be a fleet of men of war.

Captain Basden of the sloop *Hope* is charged with this letter. These isles are in want of indian corn and provisions, which, if circumstances permit, I request your Lordship he may be allowed to load with.

I have the honor to be with the utmost respect
Your Lordship's most humble and obedient servant

GEORGE BRUERE
Lt Governor

Clinton to Cornwallis, 15th July 1781[23]

68(52): LS

New York
July 15th 1781

Lt General Earl Cornwallis

My Lord

Until I had the honor to receive your Lordship's letter of the 8th instant[24] I had flattered myself that upon reconsidering the general purport of our correspondence and General Phillips's papers in your possession you would at least have waited for a line from me in answer to your letter of the 30th ultimo[25] before you finally determined upon so serious and mortifying a move as the repassing James River and retiring with your army to Portsmouth. And I was the more induced to hope that this would have been the case as we both seemed to agree in our opinion of the propriety of taking a healthy station on the neck between York and James Rivers for the purpose of covering a proper harbor for our line of battle ships. And I am persuaded your Lordship will be sensible that in all my letters I clearly leave you at full liberty to detain any part or even the whole of the troops I solicited you to send me, should your Lordship have determined on any solid operation of your own in Virginia or elsewhere, or should you have adopted the one I had recommended in the upper Chesapeak, or even should you have judged their continuance with you necessary untill the stations you might think proper to take were rendered respectably defensive.

Your letter of the 30th ultimo, in which your Lordship was pleased to intimate this intention, did not leave the Chesapeak before the 5th instant, and as soon as I consulted the

---

[23]   Received on or shortly before 16th August and published with no differences in Stevens, op cit, ii, 73.

[24]   *your Lordship's letter..*: see vol V, p 116.

[25]   *your letter..*: see vol V, p 104.

Admiral at the Hook upon its contents, I lost no time in dispatching my answer[26] to your Lordship both by a ship of war and one of my runners, but as I now find your Lordship has decided, I shall say no more upon the subject. And I sincerely congratulate you upon the success of your well concerted plan against the Marquis de la Fayette, hoping that, amongst other good effects which may be expected from it, it will prevent his giving you disturbance in the execution of what I recommended to your Lordship in my letter of the 11th instant, a duplicate of which accompanies this. I likewise request your Lordship will be pleased to communicate to Lt Colonels Dundas, Simcoe and Tarleton (whom you have particularised, the first for his conduct and gallantry in the action of James Town, and the two others for their active services on your march thro' Virginia) and to all the other officers and soldiers under your command the high sense I have of their spirit and good behaviour, for which I desire their acceptance of my thanks.

As your Lordship is again pleased to recall my serious attention to the question of the utility of a defensive post in Virginia, which you say cannot have the smallest influence on the war in Carolina and which only gives us some acres of an unhealthy swamp, I must in answer beg leave again to repeat to your Lordship that it never was my intention to continue a post on Elizabeth River any longer than until the commencement of solid operation in the Chesapeak nor to have there more troops than what might be capable of defending a small work on that river, and that all the general officers who have commanded in the Chesapeak have had my consent to change that station for one more healthy if they judged it proper to do so, to which I will moreover add that it ever has been, is, and ever will be my firm and unalterable opinion that it is of the first consequence to His Majesty's affairs on this Continent that we take possession of the Chesapeak and that we do not afterwards relinquish it. I beg leave also, my Lord, to dissent from the opinion you have given me of a defensive post in Chesapeak, and that desultory expeditions there may be undertaken from New York with as much ease and more safety, for I cannot but suppose that a defensive station in Chesapeak with a corps of at least 4,000 regular troops for its protection and desultory water movements during the summer months, wherein land operation may be impracticable, would have the most beneficial effects on more distant districts for the reasons I have already had the honor to give your Lordship. Nor do I recollect that in any of my letters to your Lordship I have suggested an idea that there was a probability of the enemy's having a naval superiority in these seas for any length of time, much less for so long a one as two or three months. But with respect to the unhealthiness of the station at Portsmouth, my letters to General Phillips on that subject (wherein I say God forbid I should wish to bury the elite of my army in Nansemond and Princess Ann) will satisfy your Lordship that we are both of one opinion.

With regard to your Lordship's returning to Charlestown (for which you say you wait my approbation), tho' I allow your Lordship to be the best judge where your presence may be most required, yet as I cannot conceive that offensive operation will be carried on in Carolina for some months, I must beg leave to recommend it to you to remain in Chesapeak, at least until the stations I have proposed are occupied and established and your Lordship favors me with your opinion of the number of men you can afterwards spare from their defence until the first week in October, about which time it is my intention, as I have before told your Lordship, to recommence operation in the Chesapeak, but whether in Virginia according to

---

[26] *my answer*: of 11th July, vol V, p 139, supplemented by a later letter of that date, vol V, p 142.

your Lordship's plan, or in the upper Chesapeak according to my own, I shall then determine. If in the first, I shall request the favor of your Lordship to conduct it, as you must be a better judge than I can from the local knowledge you have acquired in your march thro' great part of the country and your being from thence capable of judging how far it is connected with the southern provinces. If in the last, I shall probably assume the direction of it myself, and I shall in that case be glad to have your Lordship's assistance, but if you should prefer returning to Carolina, I shall after that no longer restrain your Lordship from following your inclinations.

Now, my Lord, I have only to repeat what I have already said in all my letters, that you are at full liberty to employ all the troops under your immediate command in Chesapeak if you are of opinion they may be wanted for the defence of the stations you shall think proper to occupy, securing to us at least a healthy one from whence we may start at the proper time for beginning operation and for the carrying on in the interim such desultory water expeditions as you may think of any utility. I should indeed have hoped that even in the season for active operation 7,000 men would have been quite sufficient, considering the force which the enemy can bring against you; in this, however, your Lordship seems to think differently. Should nothing, therefore, happen to induce you to alter your opinion, or should any object cast up of importance enough to be undertaken at this inclement season, you are at liberty to keep the whole, but before you finally decide, I request your Lordship will recollect the very bare defensive I am reduced to in this post, whilst I have opposed to me Washington's army, which is already 8 or 10,000 men, the French 4,000, besides the large reinforcements expected to them; and I scarce need mention to your Lordship, who is so well acquainted with their disposition, the effect which such an appearance will have on the numerous and warlike militia of the five neighbouring provinces.

I have the honor to be
Your Lordship's most obedient and most humble servant

H CLINTON

Clinton to Cornwallis, 26th July 1781[27]

68(57): LS

New York
July 26th 1781

Lt General Earl Cornwallis

My Lord

I had the honor to receive your Lordship's letter of the 17th instant[28] by Major Damer, who arrived here the 22nd. And as it is possible that my dispatches of the 11th[29] may not

---

[27] Received on or shortly before 16th August and published with no differences in Stevens, op cit, ii, 98.

[28] *your Lordship's letter..*: see vol V, p 137.

[29] *my dispatches..*: see note 26 above.

have reached you before the troops under General Leslie sailed from Portsmouth, and lest any change of arrangement your Lordship may have judged proper in consequence may be thereby prevented, I immediately dispatched a runner to cruise for the fleet off the Delaware with orders for the troops in that case to return immediately to you and wait your further commands; but if you had received my letters by Captain Stapleton[30] before they sailed and had notwithstanding directed them to proceed according to their original destination, they are ordered to come to the Hook to receive mine.

What I said to your Lordship in my letter of the 19th instant[31] respecting the continuance of the three European regiments in Carolina was only on a supposition that your Lordship thought they would be wanted there. But as that appears not to be the case from your having ordered two of them to join me, if you should still be of opinion that they can be spared during the inactive summer months, I hope your Lordship will think proper to renew your order for their coming here, as I shall probably want them, as well as the troops you may be able to spare me from the Chesapeak, for such offensive or defensive operations as may offer in this quarter, untill the season will admit of their acting in yours, where I propose collecting in the beginning of October all the force which can be spared from the different posts under my command. But if your Lordship wishes that Brigadier General Gould should command in Carolina upon the departure of Lord Rawdon, I shall have no objection to his remaining behind for that purpose.

I have the honor to be
Your Lordship's most obedient and most humble servant

H CLINTON

Clinton to Cornwallis, 11th August 1781[32]   68(70): LS

New York
August 11th 1781

Earl Cornwallis

My Lord

I am honored with your Lordship's dispatches of the 24th and 27th ultimo[33], which were delivered to me by Captain Stapleton on the 1st instant, which I shall defer answering to a safer opportunity.

---

[30] *my letters..*: of 8th and 11th July, vol V, pp 140-3.

[31] *my letter of the 19th instant*: ultimo. See vol V, p 135.

[32] Published with inconsequential differences in Stevens, op cit, ii, 123.

[33] *your Lordship's dispatches..*: see pp 11 and 13, together with note 6.

I have the pleasure to inform you that the *fleet from Bremelehe is* this *day arrived with* about *two thousand five hundred German recruits* etc.

I hope before this reaches your Lordship you will have *so far established yourself on the Williamsburg Neck* as to have *been able to embark the troops you can spare me for operation here*, in which case I have no doubt *Captain Hudson* will have *given every assistance to forward* them *to us as soon as possible*. And if they are not *already sailed*, I beg that the *Queen's Rangers* may be the *second corps you send me* and that your Lordship will please to recollect my wish *to have* such a *proportion* of General *Arnold's boats* and *artillery men* and stores *as you can spare*. And as you have *three engineers*, I beg that *Lieutenant* Sutherland may be sent to this place, as also Captain Fage of the artillery. *The French and rebels shewed themselves* the other day *in front* of our *lines* to the *amount* of 11,000.

A man goes from hence *thro' the country* to your Lordship with a proposal *to liberate the Convention troops*, for which he says he will only want a *frigate* and some *transports to receive them*. Lest any accident should happen to the runner that carries this, a duplicate of it is sent by *him in cypher*.

HC

Cornwallis to Clinton, 16th August 1781[34]   74(68): C

York Town
16th August 1781

Sir

This morning I received your cyphered letter of the 11th instant by the runner.

I did not imagine that my letter of the 26th July would have given your Excellency reason to be so sanguine as to hope that by this time any detachment could have been made from hence. The evacuation of Portsmouth has employed one engineer and a number of labourers and artificers, and with every exertion by land and water I do not expect that business to be compleated before the 21st or 22nd instant. Since our arrival we have bestowed our whole labour on the Gloucester side, but I do not think the works there (after great fatigue to the troops) are at present, or will be for some time to come, safe against a coup de main with less than 1,000 men.

After our experience of the labour and difficulty of constructing works at this season of the year, and the plan for fortifying this side not being entirely settled, I cannot at present say whether I can spare any troops, or if any, how soon. But when the garrison of Portsmouth arrives and the engineer's plan is compleated, I shall apply to Captain Hudson for a frigate to carry my report of the state of things here and to bring your Excellency's commands upon it. I have received your Excellency's dispatches of the 15th and 26th ultimo, which I shall answer by the first safe opportunity. I beg that your Excellency will be pleased to order it to be notified to the port of New York that Portsmouth is evacuated to prevent vessels from

---

[34] Published with no differences in Stevens, op cit, ii, 127.

going into that harbour.

I have the honour to be, sir, etc

CORNWALLIS

Cornwallis to Clinton, 20th August 1781[35]

74(70): C

York Town
Virginia
20th August 1781

His Excellency Sir Henry Clinton KB etc etc etc

Sir

I have been honoured with your Excellency's dispatches of the 15th and 26th ultimo.

I beg leave to assure your Excellency that before I resolved to pass James River to enable me to comply with your requisition of troops, I had very maturely considered the general tenor of your dispatches to General Phillips as well as those to me of the 11th and 15th of June[36] delivered on the 26th by Ensign Amiel; and when I decided upon that measure, I sufficiently felt how mortifying it was to me personally and how much the reputation of His Majesty's arms would suffer by it in this province.

But your Excellency was pleased to give me to understand in your dispatch of the 11th that you wished to concentrate your force, being threatened with an attack at New York by General Washington with 20,000 men at least, besides an expected French reinforcement and the numerous militia of the five neighbouring provinces; and in your dispatch of the 15th, supposing that I had not thought it expedient to engage in operations in the upper Chesapeak and that those I had undertaken in this province would be finished, you require that part of the troops mentioned in a list contained in the former dispatch should be embarked to be sent to New York with all possible dispatch, notifying to me at the same time that you would in proper time sollicit the Admiral to send more transports to the Chesapeak, in which you desired that I would send the remaining troops that I judged could be spared from the defence of the posts that I might occupy, as you did not think it adviseable to leave more troops in this unhealthy climate at this season of the year than what were absolutely wanted for a defensive and desultory water excursions.

My own operations being finished, and being of opinion that, with the force under my command and circumstanced as I was, in a variety of respects, it would have been highly inconsiderate in me and dangerous for the King's Service to engage in operations in the upper

---

[35] Published with no differences in Stevens, op cit, ii, 130.

[36] *those to me..*: see vol V, pp 95-8.

Chesapeak, I thought it incumbent upon me to take effectual measures to enable me to obey so explicit an order without loss of time. To this end, as I could not discover in your instructions to General Phillips, or in your paper containing the substance of private conversations with him, or in your dispatches to me, any earnestness for immediately securing a harbour for line of battle ships, I thought myself under the necessity of being contented with the post at Portsmouth such as it was, for I did not imagine myself at liberty to exercise my discretionary power by changing that post for another, which I knew would have required so great a part of the troops under my command for many weeks for the purposes of covering, subsisting and fortifying it that any offensive or defensive plans of yours which depended upon material reinforcement from hence might thereby have been totally frustrated.

My resolution to pass James River was just executed when I received your dispatch of the 28th of June[37] ordering the expedition for the attempt upon Philadelphia. That order being likewise positive unless I was engaged in any important move of my own or in operations in the upper Chesapeak, I felt a particular satisfaction that my decision on your first order had enabled me to comply so expeditiously with this, and I own that, instead of blame, I hoped to have merited approbation.

I was clearly convinced when I received those orders, and I cannot yet see any cause to alter my opinion, that, having a sufficient force remaining for a defensive in the post that I had resolved to occupy and for desultory water excursions, if I had detained the troops required and specified in your list for any other reason than that of being engaged in an important move of my own or in operations in the upper Chesapeak, and if in the mean time a misfortune had happened at New York or you had been disappointed of any material object at Philadelphia, my conduct would have been highly and deservedly censured. But I acknowledge I never apprehended, even though it might afterwards appear that the danger at New York was not imminent nor the attempt upon Philadelphia expedient, that I should be subject to blame for passing James River, a step rendered indispensably necessary by an obedience of your orders and for the safety of the troops remaining under my command.

Your Excellency, after mentioning your intention of recommencing operation in the Chesapeak about the beginning of October, is pleased to say that you will then determine whether you will act in Virginia according to my plan or in the upper Chesapeak according to your own.

It is true that it is my opinion that while we keep a naval superiority Virginia is by its navigable rivers extremely accessible, and that if we have force to accomplish it the reduction of the province would be of great advantage to England on account of the value of its trade to us, the blow that it would be to the rebels, and as it would contribute to the reduction and quiet of the Carolinas. But in my subordinate situation, being unacquainted with the instructions of administration, ignorant of the force at your command from other services, and without the power of making the necessary arrangements for execution, I can only offer my opinions for consideration, certainly not as plans. I am thoroughly sensible that plans which essentially affect the general conduct of the war can only come from your Excellency as being in possession of the requisite materials for framing them and of the power of arranging the

---

[37] *your dispatch..*: see vol V, p 114.

means for their execution. But whatever plan you may think proper to adopt for operations in the Chesapeak, I shall be most sincerely concerned if your Excellency should be so circumstanced as not to be able to undertake the execution of it in person, for the event must be of great importance to our country, and not only the military operations would be best directed by your superior abilities but your weight and authority as Commissioner might have the happiest effects in the civil and political regulation of the country, without which military success would not be attended with solid consequences. However, if your Excellency should find it necessary to direct me to undertake the execution of any plan that may be fixed upon by you, I shall make the best use in my power of the force put under my command, but as my acting differently from your ideas or wishes might in many instances be attended with great detriment to the King's Service, I shall, if employed, hope to be honoured with explicit instructions from your Excellency on all points that will admit of them.

I shall by the first opportunity acquaint General Leslie that if he can spare troops from the service in South Carolina, you wish them to be sent to New York, but being ignorant of the present state of affairs and knowing well that since the surrender of Charlestown the seasons of the year have not occasioned military inactivity in that quarter, I cannot judge whether your Excellency may expect any reinforcement from thence.

As there appears to be little chance of co-operation from hence with the troops in that province, and as my communication with it is extremely precarious, I submit it to your Excellency's consideration whether it would not be most expedient to transmit your commands relating to the affairs of that country directly to General Leslie.

I have the honour to be with great respect, sir, etc

CORNWALLIS

Cornwallis to Clinton, 22nd August 1781[38] *74(74): Df*

York Town
Virginia
22nd August 1781

His Excellency Sir Henry Clinton etc etc etc

Sir

Portsmouth having been compleatly evacuated without any interruption from the enemy, General O'Hara arrived here this day with the stores and troops, and a great number of refugees have accompanied him from the counties of Norfolk, Suffolk and Princess Anne.

The engineer has finished his survey and examination of this place and has proposed his plan for fortifying it, which, appearing judicious, I have approved of and directed to be executed.

---

[38] Published with an inconsequential difference in Stevens, op cit, ii, 137.

The works at Gloucester are now in such forwardness that a smaller detachment than the present garrison would be in safety against a sudden attack, but I make no alteration there, as I cannot hope that the labour of the whole will compleat that post in less than five or six weeks.

My experience there of the fatigue and difficulty of constructing works in this warm season convinces me[39] that all the labour that the troops here will be capable of, without ruining their health, will be required at least for six weeks to put the intended works at this place in a tolerable state of defence. And as your Excellency has been pleased to communicate to me your intention of recommencing operation in the Chesapeak about the beginning of October, I will not venture to take any step that might retard the establishing of this post; but I request that your Excellency will be pleased to decide whether it is more important for your plans that a detachment of a thousand or twelve hundred men, which I think I can spare from every other purpose but that of labour, should be sent to you from hence or that[40] the whole of the troops here should continue to be employed in expediting the works.

[41]My last accounts of the enemy were that the Marquis de la Fayette was encamped in the fork of the Pamunky and Matapony with his own detachment of Continentals, a considerable body of eighteen months' men and two brigades of militia under Stevens and Lawson, that he had armed 400 of the 700 Virginia prisoners lately arrived from Charlestown and expected to be joined in a short time by General Smallwood with 700 eighteen months' men from Maryland, and that Generals Wayne and Morgan, having returned from the other side of James River, were likewise on their march to join him.

There being only four eighteens and one 24 pounder here, more heavy guns will be wanted for the sea batteries at this place, and we are likewise in want of many other artillery and engineer's stores, the returns of which[42] I take the liberty to inclose.

It is proper to mention to your Excellency, that[43] you may make your arrangements accordingly, that there are only about 600 stand of spare arms in the Chesapeak and that our consumption of provisions is considerably increased by a number of refugees lately come to us and by Negroes that are employed in different branches of the publick service.

---

[39] 'convinces me' is substituted for 'induces me to coincide in opinion with the engineer'.

[40] *that*: the meaning is 'whether'. As in modern French, a subordinate conjunction, if repeated in 18th-century English, was often replaced by 'that'.

[41] The following words are deleted at the beginning of this paragraph: 'Our information from the country is not frequent and seldom good'.

[42] *the returns..*: no copies.

[43] *that*: used in the sense of 'so that'.

[I have the honour to be etc

CORNWALLIS]

Cornwallis to Clinton, 31st August 1781[44]

74(78): C

York Town in Virginia
31st August 1781

His Excellency Sir Henry Clinton KB etc etc etc

Sir

A French ship of the line with two frigates and the *Loyalist*, which they have taken, lie at the mouth of this river.

A lieutenant of the *Charon*, who went with an escort of dragoons to Old Point Comfort, reports that there are between thirty and forty sail within the Capes, mostly ships of war, and some of them very large.

I have the honour to be etc

CORNWALLIS

Cornwallis to Clinton, 1st September 1781[45]

74(80): C

York
1st September 1781

Sir Henry Clinton

An enemy's fleet within the Capes, between 30 and 40 ships of war, mostly large.

CORNWALLIS

[*Superscribed*:]

Written in cypher on a Congress note.

---

[44] Published with an inconsequential difference in Stevens, op cit, ii, 146.

[45] Published with no differences in Stevens, op cit, ii, 147.

Cornwallis to Clinton, 2nd September 1781[46]

74(82): C

York Town
Virginia
2nd September 1781

His Excellency Sir Henry Clinton KB etc etc etc

Sir

Comte de Grasse's fleet is within the Capes of the Chesapeak. Forty boats with troops went up James River yesterday and four ships lie at the entrance of this river.

I have the honour to be etc

CORNWALLIS

Cornwallis to Clinton, 4th September 1781[47]

74(84): C

York Town
Virginia
4th September 1781

His Excellency Sir Henry Clinton KB etc etc etc

Sir

Comte de Grasse's fleet is within the Capes of the Chesapeak. Forty boats with troops went up James River on the 1st instant, which are landed, as I am informed, at James City Island, and four ships lie at the entrance of this river.

I have the honour to be etc

CORNWALLIS

---

[46] Published with no differences in Stevens, op cit, ii, 148.

[47] Published with no differences in Stevens, op cit, ii, 151.

York Town in Virginia
8th September 1781

His Excellency Sir Henry Clinton KB etc etc etc

Sir

I have made several attempts to inform your Excellency that the French West India fleet under Monsieur de Grasse entered the Capes the 29th ultimo. I could not exactly learn their number; they report twenty five or twenty six sail of the line. One of 74 and two of 64 and one frigate lay in the mouth of this river. On the 6th the 74 and frigate turned down with a contrary wind, and yesterday the two others followed. My report dated last evening from a point below, which commands a view of the Capes and bay, says that there were within the Capes only seven ships, two of which were certainly ships of the line and two frigates. Firing was said to be heard off the Capes[49] the night of the 4th, morning and night of the 5th, and morning of the 6th.

The French troops landed at Jamestown are said to be 3,800. Washington is said to be shortly expected and his troops are intended to be brought by water from the Head of Elk under protection of the French ships. The Marquis de la Fayette is at or near Williamsburgh. The French troops are expected there but were not arrived last night. As my works were not in a state of defence, I have taken a strong position out of the town.[50] I am now working hard at the redoubts of the place. The army is not very sickly[51]. Provision for six weeks[52]. I will be very carefull of it.

I have the honour to be with great respect, sir,
Your most obedient and most humble servant

[CORNWALLIS]

---

[48] This dispatch was enciphered. It is published with no material differences in Stevens, op cit, ii, 154.

[49] *Firing..*: the action between Graves and de Grasse. The British fleet was badly mauled and returned to New York.

[50] This sentence is substituted for: 'I have taken a position which covers some country and is by the help of two days' work a strong defensive to receive an attack'.

[51] The following words are deleted: 'and work with the greatest'.

[52] The following words are deleted: 'and rum for three.'

Clinton to Cornwallis, 2nd and 4th September 1781[53]   *68(77): CS*

New York
September 2nd 1781

Earl Cornwallis

My Lord

By intelligence which I have this day received, it would seem that Mr *Washington is moving an army to the southward* with an appearance of *haste* and *gives out* that he *expects the cooperation of a considerable French armament.* Your Lordship, however, may be assured *that if this should be the case I shall either endeavor to reinforce the army under your command by all the means within the compass of my power* or make *every possible diversion in your favor.*

Captain Stanhope[54] of His Majesty's Ship *Pegasus*, who has just arrived from *the West Indies, says that on Friday last in latitude* 38 *about* 60 *leagues from the coast he was chased by eight ships of the line which he took to be French and that one of the victualers* he had under *his convoy had counted upwards of* 40 *sail more.* However, as Rear Admiral Graves, after being *joined by Sir Samuel Hood*[55] *with fourteen coppered ships of the line, sailed from hence on the* 31st *ultimo with a fleet of nineteen sail* besides some *fifty gun ships*, I flatter myself *you will have little to apprehend from that* of the French.

---

[53] Published in Stevens, op cit, ii, 149, with material differences in the punctuation of the postscript.

[54] Commissioned a lieutenant in the Royal Navy on 15th October 1762, John Stanhope (1744-1800) had been promoted to commander on 4th June 1774 and to post-captain some five years later. As Clinton states, he was now commanding the frigate *Pegasus*. He died a rear admiral of the red. He is not to be confused with Henry Edwyn Stanhope (1754-1814), who, as captain of the 74-gun man of war *Russell*, would take part in the Battle of Frigate Bay off St Kitts in January 1782. (Syrett and DiNardo eds, *The Commissioned Sea Officers*, 418)

[55] Entering the Royal Navy in 1741, Sir Samuel Hood Bt (1724-1816) saw service as a post-captain during the Seven Years' War and was promoted to rear admiral of the blue on 26th September 1780. Two months later, having hoisted his flag on the 98-gun *Barfleur*, he departed with eight sail of the line to join Rodney as second in command in the West Indies, where on 29th April he had an inconclusive engagement with de Grasse off Martinique. In anticipation that de Grasse would go to North America for the hurricane season (but not with his entire fleet) Hood was detached on 10th August with fourteen sail of the line and reached the Chesapeake first. Not finding de Grasse there or in the Delaware, he continued on to New York, where he joined Thomas Graves as his second in command. With him he took part in the failed attempt to defeat de Grasse off Virginia and has been criticised for failing to involve Graves' rear division, which he commanded, in the action of 5th September. Seven weeks later he would return with Graves and Clinton to the Chesapeake but arrive too late to relieve Cornwallis. Back in the West Indies by early 1782, he conducted a brilliant operation against the odds in an unsuccessful attempt to save St Kitts and in April captured de Grasse and his flagship, the 110-gun *Ville de Paris* — events which led to his being created an Irish peer. After the war he entered the Commons as the Member for Westminster, served on the Board of Admiralty, and was briefly Commander-in-Chief in the Mediterranean. By 1796 his active service had ended, and vacating his parliamentary seat at the general election, he was elevated to a viscountcy in the English peerage. An admiral of the red, he died at Bath and was buried beside his wife at Greenwich Hospital, of which he had been appointed Governor in 1796. (*ODNB*; Boatner, *Encyclopedia*, 510-11; Syrett and DiNardo eds, op cit, 226-7)

I have the honor to be
Your Lordship's most obedient and most humble servant

H CLINTON

PS

Washington, 'tis said, was to be at Trentown this day and means to go *in vessels to Christian Creek, from thence by Head of Elk down Chesapeak in vessels* also, if that *navigation is not interrupted.* If he should go *by land from Baltimore*, your Lordship can best judge *what time it will require* — I should suppose at least *three weeks from Trenton. Washington has about* 4,000 *French and* 2,000 *rebel troops with him.*

HC

September 4th

To this triplicate, and by this very uncertain conveyance, I shall only add to your Lordship that I have had the honor to receive this morning a duplicate, and this evening a triplicate, of your letter of the 31st ultimo.

HC

Clinton to Cornwallis, 6th September 1781[56]   *68(81): LS*

New York
September 6th at noon 1781

Earl Cornwallis

My Lord

As I find by your letters that Le Grasse has got into the Chesapeak and *I can have no doubt that Washington is moving with at least six thousand French* and *rebel troops against you, I think the best way to relieve you is to join you as soon as possible with all the force that can be spared from hence, which is about* 4,000 *men. They are already embarked* and *will proceed the instant I receive information from the Admiral that we may venture or that from other intelligence the Commodore*[57] and *I shall judge sufficient to move upon.*

---

56 Published with inconsequential differences in Stevens, op cit, ii, 154.

57 The Commodore was Edmund Affleck (1727-1788), the naval officer commanding at New York in the absence of Thomas Graves, who was away engaging de Grasse off Virginia. Commissioned a lieutenant in the Royal Navy on 25th July 1746, he had been promoted to commander on 5th June 1756 and to post-captain some nine months later. After an almost uneventful naval career he had come out to North America as part of Graves' squadron, arriving at New York on 13th July 1780 in command of the 74-gun man of war *Bedford*. Ten months later he was promoted to the rank of an established commodore. After the catastrophe at Yorktown he would repair to the West

By accounts from Europe we have every reason to expect Admiral Digby hourly on the coast.

Commodore Johnston[58] has beat a superior French fleet at St Iago and proceeded the day after for the place of his destination.

I beg your Lordship will let me know as soon as possible your ideas how the troops embarked for the Chesapeak may be best employed for your relief, according to the state of circumstances when you receive this letter. I shall not, however, wait to receive your answer should I hear in the mean time that the passage is open.

I have the honor to be
Your Lordship's most obedient and most humble servant

H CLINTON

PS

I have just received your Lordship's dispatch by the *Dundas* galley — *from Master Cary*.

Cornwallis to Clinton, 16th September 1781[59]   *74(89): ADf*

York
September 16th 1781

His Excellency Sir Henry Clinton KB etc etc etc

Sir

I have received your letters of the 2nd and 6th. The enemy's fleet has returned. Two line of battle ships and one frigate lie at the mouth of this river, and three or four line of battle

---

Indies, where he distinguished himself in an encounter off St Kitts and in the defeat of de Grasse, events which led to his being created a baronet. On his return to England at the peace he struck his pennant, and although later promoted to flag rank, he never again had an active command. For the rest of his life he served in Parliament as the Member for Colchester but made little impression. He died at his house in Queen Anne Street East, Colchester. (John Charnock, *Biographia Navalis*, vi, 209-214; Syrett and DiNardo eds, *The Commissioned Sea Officers*, 2; Valentine, *The British Establishment*, 11)

[58] A former naval officer and sometime Governor of West Florida, George Johnstone (1730-1787) had gone on to become an MP and a member of Carlisle's peace mission to America. In 1779, having vilified the North ministry for years, he accepted a commodoreship in the navy and returned to active service, alleging that France's entry into the war had transformed the conflict. After serving in the Channel and on the Portuguese station, he took command in 1781 of a naval squadron, transports and East Indiamen on what was supposed to be a secret mission to seize the strategically important Dutch colony at the Cape of Good Hope. Discovering what was afoot, the French dispatched Admiral Pierre André de Suffren to foil the attempt. He caught up with Johnstone in the Cape Verde islands, where Johnstone was anchored at the port of Praia on Saõ Tiago island. Suffren damaged the British fleet enough to hinder an effective reply and ruined all chance of the Cape being surprised and captured. Johnston died at Hotwells, Bristol, possibly of Hodgkin's disease. (*ODNB*)

[59] Published in Stevens, op cit, ii, 156. Note 62 below refers to the only material difference.

ships, several frigates and transports went up the bay on the 12th and 14th. I hear Washington arrived at Williamsburgh on the 14th. Some of his troops embarked at Head of Elk and the others arrived at Baltimore on the 12th.

If I had no hopes of relief, I would rather risk an action than defend my half finished works, but as you say Digby is hourly expected and promise every exertion to assist me, I do not think myself justified in putting the fate of the war on so desperate an attempt. By examining the transports with care and turning out useless mouths, my provisions will last at least six weeks from this day if we can preserve them from accidents. The cavalry must, I fear, be all lost. I am of opinion that you can do me no effectual service but by coming directly to this place.

Lieutenant Conway[60] of the *Cormorant* is just exchanged. *He assures me that* since the Rhode Island squadron has joined *they have 36 sail of the line. This place is in no state of defence.*[61] *If you cannot relieve me very soon, you must be prepared to hear the worst.*[62]

I have the honour to be with great respect, sir,
Your most obedient and most humble servant

CORNWALLIS

Clinton to Cornwallis, 24th September 1781[63]

68(83): LS

New York
September 24th 1781

Earl Cornwallis

My Lord

I was honored yesterday with your Lordship's letter of the 16th and 17th instant, and *at a meeting of the general and flag officers held this day it is determined that above* 5,000 *men, rank and file, shall be embarked on board the King's ships and the joint exertions of the navy and army made in a few days to relieve you and afterwards cooperate with you.*

---

[60] Apart from belonging to the *Cormorant*, a 14-gun sloop of war captured by de Grasse's fleet on 24th August, David Conway has not been identified. No officer with his name is recorded by Syrett and DiNardo. (Michael Phillips, 'Ships of the Old Navy' (Internet, 2nd August 2006))

[61] After 'defence' are deleted the words: 'I have been on the point of determining to remain in my outward position'.

[62] In the letter as sent this paragraph forms a postscript dated 17th September.

[63] Published with no differences in Stevens, op. cit., ii, 159.

The fleet *consists of 23 sail of the line, three of which are three deckers*. There is every reason *to hope we start from hence the* 5th *October*[64]. I have received your Lordship's letter of the 8th instant.

I have the honor to be
Your Lordship's most obedient and most humble servant

H CLINTON

PS

Admiral Digby is this moment arrived at the Hook with three sail of the line.

At a venture, without knowing whether they can be *seen by us, I request that if all is well, upon hearing a considerable firing towards the entrance of the Chesapeak, three large separate smokes may be made parallel to it*, and if you *possess the post of Gloucester, four*.

I shall send *another runner soon*.

H CLINTON

Cornwallis to Clinton, 29th September 1781[65]   *74(93): ADf*

York Town in Virginia
September 29th 1781 10 pm

His Excellency Sir Henry Clinton KB etc etc etc

Sir

I have ventured these last two days to look General Washington's whole force in the face in the position on the outside of my works, and I have the pleasure to assure your Excellency that there was but one wish throughout the whole army, which was that the enemy would advance.

I have this evening received your letter of the 24th, which has *given me the greatest satisfaction. I shall retire this night within the works* and *have no doubt, if relief arrives in any reasonable time, York and Glocester will be both in possession of His Majesty's troops*.

I believe your Excellency must depend more on the *sound of our cannon* than the *signal of smokes for information*. However, *I will attempt it on the Glocester side. Medicines are wanted*.

---

[64] In the copy of this letter (68(85)), which was left undeciphered, there is substituted 'about the 5th October' for 'the 5th October'.

[65] Published with no differences in Stevens, op cit, ii, 169.

I have the honour to be with great respect, sir,
Your most obedient and most humble servant

CORNWALLIS

Clinton to Cornwallis, 25th September 1781[66]   68(87): CS

New York
September 25th 1781

Earl Cornwallis

My Lord

My letter of yesterday will have informed your Lordship of the _number of ships and troops we can bring with us_. It is supposed the _necessary repairs of the fleet will detain us here to the_ 5th _October_, and your Lordship must be sensible _that unforeseen accidents may lengthen it out a day or two longer. I therefore entreat you to lose no time in letting me know by the bearer your real situation_ and _your opinion how upon our arrival we can best act to form a junction with you_, together with _the exact strength of the enemy's fleet_ and what _part of the Chesapeak they appear to be most jealous of_.

I have the honor to be
Your Lordship's most obedient and most humble servant

H CLINTON

PS

As your Lordship must have better intelligence than we can possibly have, I request you will send a trusty person to each of the Capes about the 7th _of next month with every information respecting the force_ and _situation of the enemy you may judge necessary_ and _directions to continue there until our arrival, when small vessels will be sent to bring off any person they may find there._

H CLINTON

---

[66] Published with inconsequential differences in Stevens, op cit, ii, 163.

York Town
Virginia
3rd October 1781

His Excellency Sir Henry Clinton KB etc etc etc

Sir

I received your letter of the 25th September last night. The enemy are encamped about two miles from us. On the night of the 30th September they broke ground and made two redoubts about 1,100 yards from our works, which, with some works that had been constructed to secure our exterior position, occupies a gorge between two creeks which nearly embrace this post. They have finished those redoubts and I expect they will go on with their works this night. From the time that the enemy have given us and the uncommon exertions of the troops our works are in a better state of defence than we had reason to hope.

I can see no means of forming a junction with me but by York River, and I do not think that any diversion would be of use to us. Our accounts of the strength of the French fleet have in general been that they were *35 or 36 sail of the line.* They have frequently changed their position. Two ships of the line and one frigate lye at the mouth of this river and our last accounts were *that the body of the fleet lay between the Tail of the Horse Shoe and York Spit.* And it is likewise said *that four line of battle ships lay a few days ago in Hampton Road. I see little chance of my being able to send persons to wait for you at the Capes, but I will if possible.*

I have the honour to be with great respect, sir, etc

CORNWALLIS

Clinton to Cornwallis, 30th September 1781[68]   **68(91): CS**

New York
30th September 1781

Earl Cornwallis

My Lord

Your Lordship *may be assured that I am doing every thing in my power to relieve you by a direct move* and *I have reason to hope from the assurances given me this day by Admiral Graves that we may pass the bar by the* 12th *October if the winds permit* and *no unforeseen*

---

[67] Published with inconsequential differences in Stevens, op cit, ii, 174.

[68] Published with no differences in Stevens, op cit, ii, 172.

accident happens. This, however, is subject to dissappointment. Wherefore if I hear from you, your wishes will of course direct me and I shall persist in my idea of a direct move even to the middle of November should it be your Lordship's opinion that you can hold out so long. But if, when I hear from you, you tell me that you cannot and I am without hopes of arriving in time to succour you by a direct move, I will immediately make an attempt upon Philadelphia by land, giving you notice if possible of my intention. If this should draw any part of Washington's force from you, it may possibly give you an opportunity of doing something to save your army, of which, however, you can best judge from being upon the spot.

I have the honor to be
Your Lordship's most obedient and most humble servant

H CLINTON

Cornwallis to Clinton, 11th and 12th October 1781[69]   74(101): C

York Town
Virginia
12 m[70], 11th October 1781

His Excellency Sir Henry Clinton KB etc etc etc

Sir

Cochran arrived yesterday.[71] I have only to repeat what I said in my letter of the 3rd,

---

[69] This letter was enciphered. It is published with one inconsequential difference in Stevens, op cit, ii, 175.

[70] *m*: midday.

[71] The Hon Charles Cochrane (1749-1781) was a younger son of the Earl of Dundonald. Entering the 25th Regiment as an ensign, he went on to serve as a lieutenant in the 7th Regiment (Royal Fusiliers) before arriving in Boston in 1774 as a captain in the 4th (The King's Own) Regiment. After later transferring for a short time to the 1st Regiment of Foot Guards (the Grenadier Guards), he was taken on to the Provincial establishment in 1778, when he became a major in command of the infantry of the British Legion. On 10th June 1780, having until then participated in the Legion's actions in the south, he obtained Cornwallis's leave to take passage home on personal business, but not before gaining in South Carolina an abiding reputation for rapacity. According to an adversary, 'There was not a marauder in the army... more distinguished for sagacity in discovering the secret deposits of plate, and appropriating all that came within his grasp, than... Cochran: and he is much belied by the reports of his military friends if he did not ship to Europe several barrels filled with the article to revive at a future day the recollection of the toils endured in procuring it.' On reaching New York, he was entrusted with Clinton's dispatches and arrived in London in mid October. Having spent part of his time in trying to expedite the procurement of much needed cavalry appointments for America, he returned to New York by mid June. Now, in October, he had just delivered to Cornwallis Clinton's letter of 30th September, slipping through the blockading French fleet in a runner. Almost immediately he was to come to an untimely end. In the words of Captain Samuel Graham of the 76th Highlanders, who was present at the siege, 'The Hon Major Cochrane of the Legion, who... was appointed to act as an aid-de-camp to Lord Cornwallis, being led by zeal to fire a gun from behind the parapet in the horn work "en ricochet", and anxious to see its effect, looked over to observe it, when his head was carried off by a cannon ball.' (Margaret Baskin, 'Charles Cochrane (1749-1781)' (www.banastretarleton.org, 30th June

that nothing but a direct move to York River, which includes a successfull naval action, can save me. The enemy made their first parallel on the night of the 6th at the distance of 600 yards and have perfected it and constructed places of arms and batteries with great regularity and caution. On the evening of the 9th their batteries opened and have since continued firing without intermission with about 40 pieces of cannon, mostly heavy, and 16 mortars from 8 to 16 inches. We have lost about 70 men and many of our works are considerably damaged. With such works on disadvantageous ground, against so powerfull an attack we cannot hope to make a very long resistance.

I have the honour to be etc

CORNWALLIS

PS

5 pm, October 11th

Since the above was written we have lost 30 men.

October 12th, 7 pm

Last night the enemy made their second parallel at the distance of 300 yards.

We continue to lose men very fast.

Cornwallis to Clinton, 15th October 1781[72]   74(103): C

York Town
Virginia
15th October 1781

His Excellency Sir Henry Clinton KB etc etc etc

Sir

Last evening the enemy carried my two advanced redoubts on the left by storm, and during the night have included them in their second parallel, which they are at present busy in perfecting. My situation now becomes very critical. We dare not shew a gun to their old batteries and I expect that their new ones will open tomorrow morning. Experience has shewn that our fresh earthen works do not resist their powerfull artillery, so that we shall soon be exposed to an assault in ruined works, in a bad position, and with weakened numbers.

2005); Garden, *Anecdotes* (1st series), 263n; Garden, *Anecdotes* (2nd series), 103; *Memoir of General Graham...*, edited by his son, Colonel James John Graham (Edinburgh, 1862), 60)

[72] Published with no differences in Stevens, op cit, ii, 188.

The safety of the place is therefore so precarious that I cannot recommend that the fleet and army should run great risque in endeavouring to save us.

I have the honour to be etc

CORNWALLIS

§ - §

2 - Cornwallis to Graves

Cornwallis to Graves, 26th July 1781[73]   **88(50): C**

Portsmouth
26th July 1781

Rear Admiral Graves etc etc etc

Sir

I was honoured with your letter of the 12th July[74] by the *Solebay*, in which you mention a desire of having a harbour secured in the Chesapeake for line of battle ships. I immediately ordered the engineers to examine Old Point Comfort and went thither myself with the captains of the navy on this station. You will receive a copy of the engineer's report[75], with a sketch of the peninsula, and the opinion of the officers of the navy[76] relative to the occupying and fortifying of that post.

The Commander in Chief having signified to me in his letter of the 11th instant[77] that he thought a secure harbour for line of battle ships of so much importance in the Chesapeake that he wished me to possess one even if it should occupy all the force at present in Virginia, and as it is our unanimous opinion that Point Comfort will not answer the purpose, I shall immediately seize and fortify the posts of York and Gloucester and shall be happy at all times to concur in any manner which may promote the convenience and advantage of His Majesty's Navy.

---

[73]   Published with one inconsequential difference in Stevens, op cit, ii, 100.

[74]   *your letter..*: see vol V, p 145.

[75]   *engineer's report*: see p 16.

[76]   *the opinion..*: see p 17.

[77]   *his letter..*: see vol V, p 142.

I have the honour to be etc

CORNWALLIS

§ - §

3 - Clinton to Leslie

Clinton to Leslie, 23rd July 1781   *97(14): CS*

Head Quarters
New York
July 23rd 1781

Hon Lt General Leslie etc etc etc

Sir

Should the *Solebay* frigate have arrived in the Chesapeak before you sailed from thence and Lord Cornwallis have received from Captain Stapleton my letter of the 11th instant[78] sent by that opportunity, and should his Lordship notwithstanding have thought proper to direct you to proceed according to your original destination, you will be pleased in that case to come with the troops under your command to Sandy Hook and, coming to an anchor within the Hook, there wait my further orders. But if the *Solebay* had not arrived in Chesapeak and Lord Cornwallis had not received the letter I sent by her before your departure, you will be pleased upon the receipt of this immediately to return to Portsmouth and follow such further directions as you may receive from his Lordship.

As corresponding directions with these will be sent to Captain Hudson or the officer commanding the King's ships that compose your convoy by Commodore Affleck, who commands His Majesty's ships at New York in the absence of Rear Admiral Graves, you will of course receive from him every assistance you want in carrying these orders into execution.

I have the honor to be, sir,
Your most obedient and most humble servant

H CLINTON

§ - §

---

[78] *my letter..*: see vol V, p 142.

CHAPTER 59

Letters between British officers in Virginia

---

1 - Between Cornwallis and O'Hara

Cornwallis to O'Hara, 2nd August 1781[1]

89(1): C

York Town
August 2nd 1781

Brigadier General O'Hara

My dear Charles

After a passage of four days we landed here and at Gloucester without opposition.

The position is bad, and of course we want more troops, and you know that every senior general takes without remorse from a junior and tells him that he has nothing to fear. I send nine boats for the Regiment of Prince Hereditaire, and as your Portsmouth boats must by this time be put to rights, I wish you would send me the 71st or, if that regiment is too strong for the boats, either the 23rd or 33rd. You will judge how many trips may be absolutely necessary for the horse vessels; the first must be the Legion. Pray send them as soon as possible; we are in great want of them. The cattle drivers are absolutely necessary; we cannot do without them. We are likewise in the greatest want of engineer's tools and labouring Negroes. The transports will be sent as soon as possible for the removal of every thing. Adieu, my dear Charles. I shall be happy to embrace you on the delightfull banks of York River.

---

[1]   A brief extract is published in Ross ed, *Cornwallis Correspondence*, i, 111.

Yours very sincerely

[CORNWALLIS]

[*Subscribed*:]

Order the *Spitfire* Quarter Master General's vessel to return with the boats. Use all expedition.

Cornwallis to O'Hara, 4th August 1781[2]   89(5): C

York Town
August 4th 1781

Dear Charles

I write to Tarleton relative to the mode of his joining me. He will shew you my letter[3]. I am not easy about my post at Gloucester and am in great want of Negroes to work, as the heat is too great to admit of the soldiers doing it. I fear the horse vessels must make at least three trips. If Tarleton comes by Hampton, it will save much time. The transports set off this day. If you hear of no enemy your way, perhaps you may be able to send one more regiment, besides those destined for the boats, in transports under convoy of one of the Quarter Master General's vessels. The *Guadaloupe* is stationed off the Horse Shoe. Nothing but horses can make your business very long and I think you must not admit of more than two trips besides Tarleton's even if regulation allowed it. Cattle drivers and commissaries are much wanted and I should wish to have them sent as soon as possible. Perhaps England could find some sort of boat that might bring the cattle drivers and their horses with Tarleton in case he comes by the short passage.

I am etc

[CORNWALLIS]

O'Hara to Cornwallis, 5th August 1781   70(12): ALS

Portsmouth
the 5th of August 1781

Earl Cornwallis etc etc etc

My dear Lord

I send you the Hereditary Prince's Regiment with their guns and the 71st Regiment. We have been able to send you *50 Negroes* only, as I am obliged to keep about 50 more to assist

---

2   A brief extract is published in Ross ed, op cit, i, 112.

3   *my letter..*: see p 59.

in embarking the victualling and other stores, which I am affraid will be a very heavy, tiresome business. What will you have done with the hundreds of wretched Negroes that are dying by scores every day?

All the engineer's tools are sent. Whenever the horse vessells come, I propose embarking the Legion at *Sewell's Point* and mean they shall land at Hampton. I shall do the same with all the horses without I receive contrary orders. Our numbers of sick are nearly the same. In every other respect we are exactly as you left us. I am affraid that we shall have so much to do in embarking the enormous quantitys of stores, and the means of doing it so feeble, that I am persuaded I shall spend my Christmas here. Patience — no exertions shall be wanting on our side.

God bless you, my Lord.

Yours most affectionately

C O'HARA

[*Subscribed*:]

We have not the means of sending the cattle drivers' horses.

Cornwallis to O'Hara, 6th August 1781   *89(9): C*

York
August 6th 1781

Dear Charles

The boats with the two regiments are just arrived safe. I wrote to you on the 4th, desiring that the Legion might land at Hampton, but I was not aware that you would propose sending any other horses that way. There are some lurking people in arms about Hampton, and as we do not here command the Neck, militia might get down without our knowledge, so that nothing can land and march up without escort. If you please after the Legion has passed, you may send one other cargo of horses and desire Tarleton to leave Captain Champaigne[4] with the two companies to bring them to us. I then hope that the horse vessels will be able to bring at one time all the necessary horses. The transports have sailed for Portsmouth above 48 hours and have not advanced above three leagues. I have ordered all the cartel vessels, except one, from James Town to Hampton Road. Be so kind as desire Captain Aplin to send them to you as they will be of great use to you. My accounts say that Lafayette was yesterday at Newcastle and that Wayne has repassed James River. I shall be glad to have

---

[4] Forbes Champaigne had been serving as a captain in the 23rd Regiment (Royal Welch Fusiliers) since 24th April 1779. At the beginning of June he had been involved in the Charlottesville raid, when he and seventy of his men were mounted and formed part of the troops under Tarleton's command. Cornwallis's present letter suggests that they were still attached to the Legion. (WO 65/164(8) (National Archives, Kew): Bass, *The Green Dragoon*, 178)

either the 23rd or 33rd before your final evacuation. Captain Campbell tells me that England wishes to have some of the boats back. If I can, I will send three or four.

Yours, my dear Charles, etc

[CORNWALLIS]

[*Subscribed*:]

I hope you will get the cattle drivers' horses or at least some of them over to Hampton. I should likewise wish that you would send a victualler and a commissary of provisions.

Cornwallis to O'Hara, 7th August 1781   *89(11): C*

York
August 7th 1781

Brigadier General O'Hara

Dear Charles

I return you the four batteaux which I think you must want.

By an agreement between the commissaries of prisoners to the southward all militia men taken in arms before the 18th of June are to be released. You will please to give orders accordingly to the commissary of prisoners at Portsmouth and send him here by the first opportunity.

It is shocking to think of the state of the Negroes, but we cannot bring a number of sick and useless ones to this place. Some flour must be left for them and some person of the country appointed to take charge of them to prevent their perishing. Brown and Frazer must draw only for those that can work and that will be usefull to us here.

Simcoe is very anxious to get some horses of his that were left at Portsmouth. If it is possible to get them to Hampton and if they are worth bringing, I should be glad that it might be done.

Most earnestly wishing to see you here, I am, dear Charles, etc

[CORNWALLIS]

Portsmouth
the 7th of August 1781

Lt General Earl Cornwallis etc etc etc

My dear Lord

I have wrote to Captain Aplin to order the cartel vessells to Portsmouth.

The Legion are now embarking at Sewell's Point and likewise the cattle drivers. That is a very tedious opperation as they carry off the horses above one mile before they can be put into the horse vessells. The engineer with the tools, Browne and 150 Negroes, Weir the commissary, and the baggage of the *80th*, Hereditary Prince, Legion and Yagers left us last night.

The transports are not yet arrived. We have no victuallers here. I have wrote to Tarlton to leave Champaign for the purposes you directed.

I will send you the 23rd Regiment the moment I have the means of doing it.

As I had concluded your position at York, in the absence of Fayette and Wayne, compleatly covered the Neck in your rear, I had not dreamt of danger in landing horses at Hampton. Your letter to Tarlton shewed me I had, as I often do, concluded wrong. I wish we may be able to leave this place so soon as I am affraid you seem to think we shall. We will do our best.

Yours most affectionately

C O'HARA

[*Subscribed*:]

It is strongly reported here that Lord Rawdon has given Greene another thrashing.

O'Hara to Cornwallis, 9th August 1781   *70(16): ALS*

Portsmouth
the 9th of August 1781

Lt General Earl Cornwallis etc etc etc

My dear Lord

The second trip of horses was render'd incompleat by the wind changing before the whole of the horse vessells got to Sewell's Point. No more arrived than could carry the remainder of the Legion and the cattle drivers. They are gone under the escort of Champignée. The navy officer tells me that all the horse vessells must come to Portsmouth to water before they can make another trip, which gives me time to ask you wether it would be safe to send the 23rd Regiment (now at *Norfolk*) with the *third* trip of horses to *Newport Nuse* (where Tarlton landed) and escort them to York — if you should approve of the 23rd being employed as I point out. I will send the *fourth trip* of horses with a detachment of *100* men from hence likewise to Newport Nuse to join you, and the *fifth trip*, which will rid us of all the horses, shall come round with the transports to York. Send me your immediate orders upon this business. The transports are within two miles of this place. The moment they arrive at the wharfs, we shall begin to ship our victualling and military stores. The refugees from Princess Ann and Norfolk Countys are very numerous, but I can't refuse taking them as they are affraid of being hanged if they remained at home. I shall venture, till I receive your positive instructions to the contrary, to victual the *sick Negroes*, above 1,000 in number. They would inevitably perish if our support was withdrawn from them. The people of this country are more inclined to fire upon than receive and protect a Negroe whose complaint is the small pox. The abandoning these unfortunate beings to disease, to famine, and, what is worse than either, the resentment of their enraged masters I should conceive ought not to be done if it can possibly be avoided, or in as small a degree as the case will admit.

I am, my dear Lord,
Your most affectionate faithfull servant

CHAS O'HARA

Cornwallis to O'Hara, 10th August 1781

89(15): C

York
August 10th 1781

Brigadier General O'Hara etc etc etc

Dear Charles

I have just received yours of yesterday's date. It will be perfectly safe to send the horses as you propose. We are now so strong in cavalry that nothing can venture into the Neck. The 23rd and the subsequent detachment must be, I believe, two days on the road and must take provisions accordingly. I am told that if you embarked the horses at the Distillery you would get them much quicker on board than at Sewell's Point. Of that, however, you will be better informed.

I leave it to your humanity to do the best you can for the poor Negroes, but on your arrival here we must adopt some plan to prevent an evil which not only destroys a great quantity of provisions but will certainly produce some fatal distemper in the army.

I have made Gloucester pretty secure, so that I do not feel so uneasy at being *à cheval*. The Marquis is said to be still somewhere about Newcastle.

Yours, my dear Charles, most faithfully

CORNWALLIS

We are in great want of artillery men. I beg you will send as many as you can conveniently spare by the first opportunity.

O'Hara to Cornwallis, 11th August 1781   70(18): ALS

Portsmouth
the 11th of August 1781

My dear Lord

I have this moment read your letter of yesterday.

Enquiry shall be made about the Distillery immediately. Horses are now embarking at Sewell's Point. They shall be landed at Newport Nuse and the 23rd Regiment with two days' provisions sent with them – the detachment in the same manner with the fourth trip of horses. A detachment from our artillery shall be sent with the 23rd Regiment, which will rather distress us as their assistance is much wanted in embarking the artillery stores etc etc etc, but we will spare all we can. We are become extremely sickly. I propose, if I can get a convoy, to send you the hospital patients immediately with another victualler. I wish I could tell you that we make great dispatch in embarking the stores but we have very few Negroes that are able to work. In a *fortnight*, I am affraid not sooner, we shall be able to leave this place and bury the last atom of confidence the people of America will ever place in English *proclamations* and *declarations*.

I am, my dear Lord, most faithfully

C O'HARA

[*Subscribed*:]

I enclose you a state of our prisoners[5] and wish you would send me your orders relative to them. I conclude you would make as large a jail delivery as possible before we leave this place.

Are you ready to receive the French if they make you a visit?

England, that is now reading your letter, tells me that the objection to the Distillery is the difference of two[6] tydes between that place and Sewell's Point. Loss of time is every thing against us.

---

5   *a state of our prisoners*: not extant.

6   *two*: alternatively, 'low'.

Cornwallis to O'Hara, 14th August 1781   *89(21): C*

York
14th August 1781

Brigadier General O'Hara etc

Dear Charles

I am sorry to find by your letter of the 11th that you are growing sickly and that it will be so long before you can get away. I can only say come as soon as you can.

The 23rd Regiment and the horses arrived safe this morning.

All militia men prisoners of war taken before the 18th of June are to be released, and I would have all those taken by Tarleton dismissed on parole, unless some particular crime is alledged against them. I would have you detain all prisoners charged with heinous offences and the very violent people of Princess Ann and the neighbourhood of Portsmouth, who may be some security to those who have been more favourable to us.

The fleet reported to be seen off Bermuda[7], by the course it was steering, does not appear to be bound to any part of America.

I should wish the commissary of prisoners to be sent the first opportunity.

Yours, my dear Charles, most faithfully

CORNWALLIS

O'Hara to Cornwallis, 15th August 1781   *70(20): ALS*

Portsmouth
15th of August 1781

Earl Cornwallis etc etc etc

My dear Lord

Your directions respecting the prisoners shall be immediately complied with.

The *fourth trip* of horses are now embarking, and with them (as I understand there is no danger between Newport Nuse and York) I send you all our rubbish — *Hamilton* and his

---

[7] *The fleet..*: See Bruere to Cornwallis, 3rd August, p 19.

corps, Colonels *Branson* and *Hunter*[8], *Jolliffe's*[9], *Stewart's*[10], *Maxey's*[11], and other respectable[12] Provincial corps, with their suites, which you know are not tryfling, and about *400 Negroes*.

I hope to get quit of this very usefull detachment in the course of to morrow.

Our leaving this place will in a great measure depend upon the return of the horse vessells to take of the remainder of our horses. We are in much greater forwardness here than I thought practicall. By Saturday next or Sunday at farthest we shall, I hope, be able to quit this cursed place.

Ever, my dear Lord, most faithfully

C O'HARA

[*Subscribed*:]

I have sent you Grant[13] with all the hospital patients. My first object was to send them away from this very unhealthy place.

It is unavoidable — I am bringing you all the inhabitants of Princess Ann and Norfolk Countys. What a cursed scrape those unfortunate people are in!

---

[8] *Colonels Branson and Hunter*: O'Hara is contemptuously referring to Captain Eli Branson (see vol I, p 186, note 8), who commanded the North Carolina Independent Company, and Captain N N Hunter, who commanded one or two companies called the North Carolina Volunteers (not to be confused with the Royal North Carolina Regiment). Branson's company had recently been raised on the Provincial establishment during the winter campaign, whereas Hunter and his men had belonged to Samuel Bryan's irregular militia and were not uniformed or provided for as Provincial corps were. During the forthcoming siege Hunter would come to an untimely end at Gloucester. (Clark, *Loyalists in the Southern Campaign*, i, 417; Nan Cole and Todd Braisted, 'An Introduction to North Carolina Loyalist Units' (*The On-Line Institute for Advanced Loyalist Studies*, 17th April 2006))

[9] *Jolliffe's*: a company called the Virginia Volunteers and commanded by Richard Jolliffe of Norfolk County. It appears to have been a militia company rather than one raised on the Provincial establishment. Jolliffe was captured at Yorktown and settled after the war in Nova Scotia. (Todd Braisted to the editor, 17th April 2006; information from Paul Gifford, 17th August 2002; AO 13/26(202) (National Archives, Kew))

[10] *Stewart's*: a company commanded by James Stewart, who had come to North America in 1773, having been 'born in' the Coldstream Regiment of Foot Guards. He too was captured at Yorktown. (Todd Braisted to the editor, 17th April 2006)

[11] *Maxey's*: not identified.

[12] *respectable*: used ironically.

[13] Alexander Grant (?-1817) had begun serving in North America when he was appointed a staff surgeon at Boston in February 1775. At some time during the revolutionary war he became Inspector of Field Hospitals for North America and retired on half pay at the peace. (Johnston, *Commissioned Officers in the Medical Service*, 46)

Portsmouth
the 17th of August 1781

Lt General Earl Cornwallis etc etc etc

My dear Lord

The last trip of horses sails this day from Sewell's Point under the convoy of the *Defiance*.

I shall leave this place to morrow and shall not leave behind me any thing I conceive can be of the smallest service. I wish I could add that all I have sent you was serviceable. We shall be obliged to leave near *400* wretched Negroes. I have passed them all over to the Norfolk side, which is the most friendly quarter in our neighbourhood, and have begg'd of the people of Princess Ann and Norfolk Countys to take them. We have left with them *fifteen days' provisions*, which time will either kill or cure the greatest number of them. Such as recover will by that time be free from the small pox, which is the invincible objection the people here have to these miserable beings.

Yours most affectionately

CHAS O'HARA

[*Subscribed*:]

Only one, *The Two Brothers*, of the cartel vessells have yet appear'd.

§ - §

2 - Between Cornwallis and the Royal Navy

Cornwallis to Hudson, 24th July 1781   *88(48): ADf*

Portsmouth
July 24th 1781

Sir

I have directed Lieutenant Sutherland of the Corps of Engineers to wait upon you with the draft of Point Comfort and the soundings and with his report to me[14] relative to the

---

[14] *his report to me*: see p 16.

practicability and utility of erecting a work upon it. I likewise transmit to you a copy of a letter which I received from Rear Admiral Graves of the 12th instant[15].

You will oblige me very much if you will assemble the commanding officers of His Majesty's ships under your orders and be pleased to give me your joint opinions whether such a work as we could construct would answer the purpose specified in the Admiral's letter.

[CORNWALLIS]

Cornwallis to Hudson, 27th July 1781

88(54): ADfS

Portsmouth
July 27th 1781

Charles Hudson Esq
Commanding His Majesty's ships in Chesapeak Bay

Dear Sir

I propose doing myself the honour of waiting upon you on board the *Richmond* very early on the morning of the 29th, at which time I should be glad, if wind and tide suit, that the fleet should get under way to proceed to Yorktown, leaving one or two men of war in Hampton Road. Most of the new boats here are reported to me to be unserviceable. I have therefore thought it necessary to order up six of those boats which are with the fleet in order to carry the 80th Regiment to Glocester. As that regiment will employ eight boats, I shall be much obliged to you if you will please to order fifty six seamen to man them at the rate of seven to each boat.

My dispatches for New York[16] go down by this opportunity, and I have no farther occasion to detain the *Solebay* and hope she will proceed to sea immediately.

I am with the greatest esteem and regard, dear sir,
Your most obedient and faithfull servant

CORNWALLIS

---

15   *a letter..*: see vol V, p 145.

16   *My dispatches..*: of 24th, 26th (27th as sent), and 27th July to Clinton, pp 11-18, and of 26th July to Graves, p 41.

York Town
2nd August 1781

Charles Hudson Esq
Commanding His Majesty's ships in the Chesapeak

Dear Sir

Nothing can be more desireable in our present situation than the hastening the evacuation of Portsmouth and bringing the troops, stores etc to this place. I therefore shall be much obliged to you if you will order the nine boats under the command of a lieutenant of the navy with a petty officer and fourteen men in each boat to proceed as soon as possible to Portsmouth to bring such troops as Brigadier General O'Hara can send to us. The Quarter Master General's vessell *Defiance*, I am informed, can go with them over the *Horse Shoe*. I must likewise request that the *Swift* sloop should proceed with all the horse vessels with the utmost expedition to Portsmouth to bring the Legion. I am so well convinced of your zeal for His Majesty's Service and your personal goodwill to me that I am sure you will put this business in the way of being most speedily executed. I think if the *Guadaloupe* or any other ship of war which you may think most proper was to anchor at the point of the *Horse Shoe* it would add much to the safety of our communication. As soon as the transports can be got ready, I should wish them to proceed to Portsmouth under such convoy as you may think proper to bring every thing from that port. Your expediting the boats and horseships will greatly oblige me.

I am, dear sir, with great regard etc

[CORNWALLIS]

Cornwallis to Hudson, 5th August 1781   *89(7): C*

York Town
August 5th 1781

Charles Hudson Esq
Commanding His Majesty's ships in Chesapeak Bay

Dear Sir

As I find but few of our prisoners are expected to be sent from the country to James Town, I have ordered all the transports that brought the prisoners from Charlestown, except one, to fall down to Hampton Road and receive directions from the commanding officer of His Majesty's ships. If they should arrive in Hampton Road previous to the evacuation of Portsmouth, which I should apprehend would certainly be the case, I must desire that you will please to direct the commanding officer in Hampton Road to order them immediately to Portsmouth, where they will be very serviceable.

I am, sir, etc

[CORNWALLIS]

[*Subscribed*:]

A boat which came from Portsmouth is returning this morning, but I don't believe it will be a safe conveyance. Perhaps the best way will be to send the order by Lieutenant Robertson, the agent, who has not proceeded very far.

Hudson to Cornwallis, 5th August 1781   6(340): ALS

Richmond
York River
the 5th August 1781

The Rt Hon Lt General Earl Cornwallis etc etc etc

My Lord

In consequence of your letter just now to me directed, I have ordered Captain Robinson of the *Guadaloupe* to fulfill your Lordship's wishes, which I flatter myself will be effectually comply'd with.

I have the honor to be, my Lord,
Your Lordship's most obedient very humble servant

CHARLES HUDSON

Enclosure
Hudson to Robinson, 5th August 1781   6(342): ACS

By Charles Hudson,
Commander of His Majesty's Ship *Richmond*
and senior officer etc etc etc

Captain Robinson
Commander of HMS *Guadaloupe*

In consequence of a requisition from the Rt Hon Lt General Earl Cornwallis etc etc etc relative to transports that brought the prisoners from Charles Town to James Town in that river in order to have them regularly exchanged, which the rebels have not complied with, and as his Lordship has ordered them to Hampton Road and wishes the said transports should be immediately sent to Portsmouth, where they may be of use, you are therefore hereby required and directed to order such of them that may arrive there during your stay at that anchorage up to Portsmouth that are not crowded with troops that may have been exchanged, and should you sail from that port prior to the *Fowey*, you are to direct her captain or the commanding officer there to put the above orders in execution, as I apprehend from my Lord's letter that the transports now under your orders are not adaquate to accomplish the total evacuation of that garrison.

Given under my hand on board His Majesty's Ship *Richmond*
York River
5th August 1781

CHARLES HUDSON

Cornwallis to Hudson, 9th August 1781[17]   89(13): C

York
9th August 1781

Charles Hudson Esq
Commanding His Majesty's ships in Chesapeak Bay

Dear Sir

I shall be much obliged to you if you will be pleased to lend six 12 pounders from the *Richmond* to be placed on the works at Gloucester. I should be glad to have them landed this day if possible.

Lt Colonel Dundass will likewise want assistance to man them. Perhaps, if you dislike the men's remaining on shore, it may be time enough to send them in case of an alarm, which might be communicated by signal from Lt Colonel Dundass.

I am etc

CORNWALLIS

Hudson to Cornwallis, 8th August 1781   6(354): ALS

Richmond
8th August 81

Rt Hon Lt General Earl Cornwallis etc etc etc

My Lord

I am just now honored with your Lordship's letter relative to the landing of six 12 pounders from this ship. Every requisition of your Lordship's to me shall upon every occasion be comply'd with and your present wishes shall be executed without delay.

---

[17]   Either this letter or Hudson's reply is misdated.

I have the honor to be, my Lord,
Your Lordship's obedient and faithfull humble servant

CHARLES HUDSON

Hudson to Cornwallis, 13th August 1781

6(357): ALS

Richmond
York River
the 13th August 1781

The Rt Hon Lt General Earl Cornwallis etc etc etc

My Lord

The master of the *Fidelity*, lately a cartel that was up James River and landed the few people that he brought down with him from thence at Portsmouth and, since that, brought Negroes and baggage round here, informs me that the Deputy Quarter Master General has ordered him to proceed without a moment's loss of time back to Portsmouth. That ship in consequence of being a cartel is totally unarmed and her master thinks that he runs a very great risk in going from hence without a protection. I shall be glad to know your Lordship's sentiments on this subject, and I have the honor to be, my Lord,

Your Lordship's most obedient very faithful humble servant

CHARLES HUDSON

Cornwallis to Hudson, 13th August 1781

89(17): C

York
13th August 1781

Charles Hudson Esq
Commanding His Majesty's ships in Chesapeake

Dear Sir

As Captain Campbell, Deputy Quarter Master General, did not consider the passage between this port and Portsmouth unsafe, he gave directions to the master of the *Fidelity* to proceed thither, but as the master thinks he runs a very great risk without a protection, he may defer it for two days, when the *Spitfire* armed brig will be in readiness to convoy him.

I have the honour to be etc

CORNWALLIS

Charon
York River
29th August 1781

Earl Cornwallis

My Lord

As His Majesty's ships under my command will in a few days be in immediate want of provisions, especially bread, I am to request your Lordship will be pleased to order such a supply as you shall think proper and can be conveniently spared.

I have the honor to be
Your Lordship's most obedient and most humble servant

THO^S SYMONDS

Cornwallis to Symonds, 29th August 1781   *89(33): C*

York
August 29th 1781

Captain Symonds
Commanding His Majesty's ships in Chesapeak Bay

Dear Sir

Whenever the King's ships are in want of provisions they shall be supplied from the magazines of the army as long as there is any thing in them. I must, however, desire that you will order the pursers to purchase all that can be collected from the merchants here, especially rum, of which we have no great stock and of which I understand there is a considerable quantity to be sold. We have no bread, but you shall have flour. Let me hear what quantity of the different species you think it necessary to receive at present and I will give the order.

I am with great regard etc

[CORNWALLIS]

§ - §

3 - To Tarleton, Vallancey or von Fuchs

Cornwallis to Tarleton, 4th August 1781[18]   *89(6): C*

York Town
August 4th 1781

Dear Tarleton

We had a passage of four days but made good our landing without opposition on either side. I have no positive accounts of the enemy. Fayette is said to be marching towards the Pamunky and I am not quite easy about our post at Gloucester. Wayne had certainly advanced to Goode's Bridge but I suppose he will be now recalled. Simcoe himself is ill, and his horses by being so long on board are in wretched condition. According to the present appearance of things it will certainly be much the best way for you to land at Old Point Comfort and march by Hampton to this place, which will nearly insure your not being above one day on board. You must in that case make your horses leap out in deep water and swim on shore. We practised that method here without any accident. I do not at present see any thing that cou'd endanger your march from Hampton hither, nor do I think it probable that Fayette can come near us with a superior force before your arrival. You must, however, see that I cannot well march out from hence, as I must leave at Gloucester and this place such a force as would render me too weak to wish to fight. They assure me that there is no carriage road from Williamsburgh to Hampton that does not pass within five miles of us. Should circumstances alter, I think I could inform you in time by an express boat. After having said this, I leave it to your discretion, and if you see difficulty and danger in joining me by the short way of Point Comfort, I would have you go round, but if you prefer the short passage it should be kept very secret. Your baggage should come round and what you are most in want of you may by my authority put into any of the Quarter Master General's armed vessels and send round immediately. You will communicate the contents of this to General O'Hara, to whom I write by this opportunity.

I am with great regard, [dear Tarleton,
Most faithfully yours

CORNWALLIS]

---

[18]   Published with inconsequential differences in Tarleton, *Campaigns*, 411.

Haldane to Vallancey, 25th August 1781

89(23): C

Head Quarters
25th August 1781

Captain Vallancey
Assistant Deputy Quarter Master General

Sir

I layed the inclosed accounts of the Quarter Master General's Department in Virginia[19] before Lord Cornwallis. As those expences were incurred previous to his Lordship's taking the command of this army, he declines interfering with them.

I have the honour to be, sir,
Your most obedient and most humble servant

H HALDANE

Haldane to Vallancey, 18th September 1781

89(39): C

Head Quarters
18th September 1781

Captain Vallancey
Acting as Deputy Paymaster General

Sir

Lord Cornwallis has directed me to acquaint you that he desires you will take whatever cash the merchants offer, provided they are willing to take your orders at parr on New York to receive there bills of exchange on England.

I have the honour to be etc

H HALDANE

---

[19] *the inclosed accounts..*: no copies.

York
September 25th 1781

Lt Colonel de Fuchs commanding at Glocester

Sir

Upon my making the signal of lowering the colours on the flag staff three times, you will please to put the Regiment of Hereditary Prince into the boats and come over with them with all possible expedition, leaving fifty men at Glocester. You will order your field pieces to follow as fast as possible. I do not mean that this order should interfere with the common duty at Glocester or with foraging or any other parties that you may think proper to send out. Such detachments will be ordered to follow you on their return.

If Lt Colonel Simcoe cannot procure any old corn, perhaps it may not be imprudent to lay in some new, for altho' it is unwholesome and bad forage, it may be found better than a total want. I do not mean to propose this to Lt Colonel Simcoe in preference to barley or any other forage, but only to say that it may be of some use if nothing else can be procured.

I am, sir,
Your most obedient humble servant

CORNWALLIS

§ - §

CHAPTER 60

Letters to, from or concerning British officers in the Carolinas[1]

1 - To, from or concerning Rawdon

Cornwallis to Rawdon, 23rd July 1781[2]   *88(46): C*

Portsmouth
Virginia
23rd July 1781

Rt Hon Lord Rawdon

My dear Lord

It gave me the greatest pleasure to hear that you had succeeded in the relief of 96. The officer who came with the flag of truce to James Town assured me that you was perfectly well, but as he had not seen you, I dare not be so sanguine as to hope that you can or ought to stay in Carolina. I have not time to explain to you my situation. Suffice it to say that the C[3] is determined to throw all blame on me and to disapprove of all I have done, and that

---

[1] It is uncertain whether the letters written in the Carolinas were received by Cornwallis before his capitulation and return to New York. They are included here for ease of reference.

[2] An extract is published in Ross ed, *Cornwallis Correspondence*, i, 106. It contains no differences other than the omission of Gould's name.

[3] *C*: Commander in Chief.

nothing but the consciousness that my going home in apparent disgust would essentially hurt our affairs in this country could possibly induce me to remain. I offered to return to Carolina but it was not approved of, and it became absolutely necessary to send Leslie lest the command should have devolved on Gould. In all my mortifications it gives me the most heartfelt satisfaction to reflect on the reputation which you have acquired. That you may recover your health amongst your friends and enjoy every honour and happiness is the sincere wish of

Your most faithfull and affectionate friend

CORNWALLIS

Rawdon to Cornwallis, 2nd August 1781

6(347): ALS

Charlestown
August 2nd 1781

Lt General Earl Cornwallis etc etc etc

My Lord

In my letter of the 5th of June[4] I had the honor to inform your Lordship that Colonel Gould had consented to reinforce me with the flank companies of the three regiments then just arrived from Ireland, and that I was in consequence about to proceed for the relief of Ninety Six with somewhat more than 1,700 foot, and 150 horse.

I marched from Charlestown on the 7th of June, and Lt Colonel Doyle having joined me at Four Holes Bridge on the 10th with the troops which I had left at Monk's Corner, I pressed my march as rapidly as the excessive heat would admit. On many accounts I decided to take the road which crosses the Little Saluda a short distance above its entrance into the greater river of that name. This route enabled a Colonel Middleton[5] to fall into my rear from Congarees with a corps of about 300 men, part cavalry and part mounted militia. His object was to harrass our rear guard and to impede us in collecting cattle for our support. On the 18th, having been tempted within reach by a prospect of cutting off our foragers, our cavalry under Major Coffin attacked him so vigorously that his corps was totally dispersed and never afterwards approached us. The enemy left four officers and from twenty to thirty men on the field, but the number of those who were wounded and notwithstanding escaped was very considerable. We had but seven privates killed or wounded in this spirited charge.

We crossed the Little Saluda without opposition, altho' the enemy's light troops hovered in our front and made a parade of disputing the passage of the ford. At Orangeburgh I had

---

[4]   *my letter..*: see vol V, p 290.

[5]   Charles Starke Myddelton was a colonel in the South Carolina revolutionary militia. He would be wounded at the Battle of Eutaw Springs. (Moss, *SC Patriots*, 715)

been informed that Augusta had surrendered and that the troops which had been employed against that post were collected to Ninety Six. I therefore could not but suppose that General Greene would give me battle. I understand that he had proclaimed such intention. Upon our approach, however, he raised the siege and retired across the Saluda, having sent off his heavy baggage by the same route three or four days before. Great credit is due to Lt Colonel Cruger and to his garrison for the firmness of their defence. Major Greene[6], who commanded in the redoubt against which the enemy bent their principal efforts, and Lieutenant Barrette of the 23rd Regiment (acting engineer) distinguished themselves highly by their zeal and activity. The enemy had pushed their sap within a few yards of the principal redoubt and had nearly completed a subterraneous passage into the ditch. Our approach induced them to risque a premature assault, in which they were repulsed without much difficulty. The enemy's loss in this siege cannot have been less than three hundred men; that of the garrison falls short of forty. It is unnecessary for me to sollicit your Lordship's notice in favor of Lt Colonel Cruger and the officers acting under him.

It was on the 21st of June that I arrived at Ninety Six. General Greene had then so much the start of me that had he continued his march, a pursuit with my fatigued troops would have been hopeless; but hearing that he had halted within sixteen miles of Ninety Six in a strong position behind Bush River, and learning that he had still some waggons with him, I resolved to try once more to bring him to action. I therefore crossed the Saluda on the night of the 22nd, leaving every kind of baggage, even the packs of the men, at Ninety Six. Greene was upon the watch and moved very quickly after our passing the Saluda. We pursued rapidly and came up to the fords of the Ennoree (forty miles from Ninety Six) not two hours after his army had passed it. Our troops were by that time so overcome with fatigue that I was obliged to halt. Greene, continuing his march across the Tyger and Broad Rivers, left me no further prospect of getting up with him. I learn from the country people that he was obliged to burn several of his waggons before he crossed Broad River.

I returned immediately to Ninety Six. The post was almost entirely destitute of stores and provisions. Under the present circumstances of the country, and at this season, I conceived it impossible to furnish it with the necessary supplies. I therefore resolved to withdraw the garrison, but that no proof of attention to our friends might be omitted I ordered the principal inhabitants to be convened and desired that they should state their wishes. I proposed that, in case the loyalists would keep together and would undertake the defence of the district against the disaffected inhabitants of their own neighborhood, a small party should be left to keep them in countenance and detachments should be occasionally sent from the army on the Congaree in proportion to the force that Greene might at any time send into that quarter. That sufficient time might be allowed to take the sense of our friends upon this article, and to provide for the removal of such families as should prefer being fixed upon the abandoned plantations within the circle which I meant to hold, I left the more active part of my force with Lt Colonel Cruger and marched with 800 foot and 60 horse to Congarees.

---

[6]   Joseph Green (1747-?) was an Irishman who, after fourteen years' service in the British Army, transferred to the Provincial establishment in 1776, becoming major in the 1st Battalion, De Lancey's Brigade, on 6th September of that year. At the close of the war he was placed on the Provincial half-pay list and settled at Parrtown, New Brunswick. (Treasury 64/23(9), WO 65/164(33), and WO 65/165(7) (National Archives, Kew): W O Raymond, 'The Loyalists and Their First New Brunswick Winter', *A Raymond Scrapbook* (Fort Havoc Archives CD), i, 41)

I had written to Lt Colonel Balfour in my way to Ninety Six, stating the expediency of sending a strong corps to Orangeburgh as a provision against any sinister event. Lt Colonel Balfour in consequence of that letter applied to Colonel Gould, who readily granted from the reinforcement under his command a battalion for the purpose which I reccommended. Upon my return from the Ennoree to Ninety Six a letter from Lt Colonel Balfour informed me that the Third Regiment of Foot was to be at Orangeburgh by a certain day, there to await my further directions; and another letter from Lt Colonel Stewart commanding that regiment informed me that he was considerably advanced on his way. It was in consequence of this intimation that I had formed my plan of leaving a strong corps with Lt Colonel Cruger and of moving with a small force to Congarees, at which point I (by many messengers) directed Lt Colonel Stewart to meet me on the 3rd of July. My intention in this movement was not so much to oppose myself to any further effort of the enemy (which I did not much expect) as to try whether a feint of moving against his stores would not decide Greene to fall back as far as Charlotteburg and leave me at liberty to send the reinforcement to your Lordship as soon as the convoy should arrive. Thro' some misapprehension Lt Colonel Stewart was stopped in his march by orders from Charlestown and recalled to Dorchester. Greene had had early information of the force with which I marched and of the route which I followed. I have likewise much reason to believe that Lt Colonel Stewart's answer to me, signifying the change which had been made in his instructions and the consequent impossibility of his joining me at the time appointed, fell into the enemy's hands and invited them to attempt surrounding me in the post where they imagined I should wait in vain expectation of reinforcement. I arrived at Congarees on the 1st of July, having made forced marches in hopes of surprizing a corps of militia at that place. I soon learned that the enemy's light troops were in our neighborhood. On the 3rd, our cavalry having contrary to express order gone out by themselves to forage, they found themselves suddenly surrounded by Lt Colonel Lee's Legion. Two officers and forty dragoons with their horses and appointments fell into the hands of the enemy without any loss on their part. Altho' this accident enabled the enemy to watch very closely all the avenues to our camp, I notwithstanding found means to obtain intelligence, by which I clearly saw the enemy's design. I therefore resolved to march immediately and meet Lt Colonel Stewart at Orangeburgh or wheresoever he might be advanced. Our route lay across Congaree Creek (about two miles from our position), which is broad, in most parts deep, and the banks difficult. To prevent our attempting that passage Lt Colonel Lee had posted himself behind the creek with a considerable body of cavalry and some infantry, had destroyed the bridge, and had felled trees to render the fords impracticable. Coming, however, at noon to the fords, when from the violent heat our approach was unexpected, after the exchange of only a few ineffectual shots, we threw over a body of infantry, before which the enemy immediately dispersed and left us at liberty to clear the fords without interruption. Upon my arrival at Orangeburgh I sent orders to Lt Colonel Cruger to join me as expeditiously as he could by the route which lies between the Forks of Edisto. Lt Colonel Stewart joined me the day after my arrival at Orangeburgh, and intelligence at the same time reached me that Greene had passed the Congaree and was advancing against us. He had collected all the force which he could assemble in the country, and having on the 10th brought his army within four miles of us, he recconnoitred our position that evening at the head of his cavalry. We flattered ourselves that the superiority of his numbers would have tempted him to attack us the next morning, as our situation had nothing of strength further than that by throwing back both our flanks upon the river we remedied in some measure out total want of cavalry and reduced the enemy to a direct attack. During the night, however, Greene retired so rapidly that under cover of his light troops he had secured his passage back across the Congaree before I was apprised of his retreat. Lt Colonel Cruger arrived at Orangeburgh the next evening. The loyalists of the Ninety Six District had decided to accompany him with their families that they might put them into a situation where they would be secure against the savage cruelty of the rebel militia, after which the men proposed to embody and make incursions into the disaffected settlements. The retreat of Greene closed the campaign. Sumter, Lee and Marion made an attempt on the 19th Regiment, which Colonel Gould and Lt Colonel Balfour had stationed at Monk's Corner. They then crossed the Santee and joined Greene on the High Hills, where the enemy's army still continues. I conceive they must have hopes of cooperation from some foreign force, for they are not at present in a state to undertake much of themselves. I left Lt Colonel Stewart to command on the frontier, making the Congaree and Santee our boundaries during the continuance of the heat, and the total failure of my health obliges me now with great regret to make use of the leave of absence which the Commander in Chief had the goodness to grant me at the beginning of the year. I cannot close this letter without mentioning to your Lordship the remarkable chearfulness with which the troops bore the excessive fatigue of continual forced marches in such an intemperate season and the distress for provisions to which the circumstances of the country and the nature of our service very often reduced us. No corps was more distinguished by this manly conduct than a detachment of Hessians which Lt General de Bose[7] had been good enough to lend me. I must beg permission upon this occasion to express the obligations which jointly with Lt Colonel Balfour I owe to His Excellency Lt General de Bose, who has given the most ready assent to every plan that promised public utility and the most chearful aid in every enterprize that could forward His Majesty's Service.

As I have not entered into any detail respecting the siege of Augusta, I should inform your Lordship that the post (in itself a very bad one) was gallantly defended by Lt Colonel Browne and not surrendered but in the last extremity.

I have the honor to be, my Lord, with great respect
Your Lordship's most obedient and affectionate servant

RAWDON

Cornwallis to de Grasse, 5th September 1781[8]   92(36): ADf

Monsieur

Ayant appris que mon ami my Lord Rawdon est prisonnier sur la flotte commandée par votre Excellence, et étant extremement interessé de recevoir des nouvelles certaines de l'etat de sa santé, j'ai pris la liberté de m'addresser a votre Excellence pour la permission de recevoir une reponse a la lettre ci joint.

---

7   Carl von Bose had been promoted to lt general in the Hessian service on 8th March 1781. He was the nominal commander of the Regiment von Bose, which was named after him. (WO 65/164(23) (National Archives, Kew))

8   Published with one inconsequential difference in Ross ed, op cit, i, 117.

Un enseigne de vaisseau, un volontaire et caporal de vos troupes ayant tombé entre les mains de nos patrouilles, je les ai renvoyés, vous priant d'avoir la bonté de me rendre trois prisonniers anglais de rangs egaux.

J'ai l'honneur d'etre etc

[CORNWALLIS]

TRANSLATION

Sir

Having learnt that my friend Lord Rawdon is a prisoner with the fleet commanded by your Excellency, and being extremely interested in receiving definite news of the state of his health, I take the liberty of applying to your Excellency for permission to receive a reply to the enclosed letter[9].

A naval ensign, a volunteer and a corporal of your troops having fallen into the hands of our patrols, I send them to you, begging you will be so kind as to return to me three British prisoners of equal ranks.

I have the honour to be etc

[CORNWALLIS]

De Grasse to Cornwallis, 15th September 1781[10]   *92(53): LS*

A bord du vaisseau *la Ville de Paris*
le 15 7bre 1781

A son Excellence Milord Cornwallis

Monsieur

J'ai recû la lettre que votre Excellence a eû la bonté de m'écrire ou etoit jointe celle du Lord Rauden. Je la lui ferai remettre du moment qu'il sera en mon pouvoir, et j'enverray tout de suitte tranquiliser votre Excellence sur la santé de cet ami. Le bâtiment sur lequel est le Lord n'est pas actuellement sous mon pavillon, mais sous peu de jours il sera rejoint. Si votre Excellence veut ajouter quelque foy à ce que j'ai l'honneur de lui mander, je l'assurerai que le Lord est en bonne santé, ainsi que tout ce qui l'accompagne, et qu'il ne se trouve pas mal d'être avec nous, malgré le desir qu'il a de retourner dans sa patrie pour retablir sa santé qu'il dit avoir besoin de repos, quoique sa phisionomie trompeuse le dement.

---

9   *the enclosed letter*: to Rawdon. There is no copy.

10   The first paragraph is published with an inconsequential difference in Ross ed, op cit, i, 118.

J'étois inquiet sur le compte de Monsieur d'Ars, enseigne de vaisseau, et je vous suis obligé d'avoir eû la complaisance de me le renvoyer. Je renvoye en sa place et en échange Monsieur David Conway, lieutenant de vaisseau de Sa Majesté Britannique, qui est le plus ancien des prisonniers que j'ai à mon bord. Le même bâtiment porte aussi un caporal et un matelôt en place du caporal et du volontaire.

J'ai l'honneur d'être, monsieur,
Votre très humble et très obeissant serviteur

LE COMTE DE GRASSE

TRANSLATION

On board *la Ville de Paris*
15th September 1781

His Excellency Lord Cornwallis

Sir

I have received the letter your Excellency so kindly wrote to me, together with one enclosed to Lord Rawdon. I shall transmit it to him as soon as it is within my power to do so, and I at once send word to your Excellency to reassure you about the health of your friend. The vessel conveying his Lordship is not presently under my immediate command, but within a few days it will rejoin. If your Excellency is prepared to lend credence to what I have the honour to report, I assure you that his Lordship is in good health, as are all who accompany him, and that he does not fare badly from being with us, notwithstanding his wish to return to his homeland to recover his health since he says he has need of rest, although his misleading appearance belies it.

I was anxious about Monsieur d'Ars, the naval ensign, and I am obliged to you for your kindness in returning him to me. I send in his place and by way of exchange Mr David Conway, a naval lieutenant of His Britannic Majesty, who is the most senior of the prisoners I have on board. The same vessel also carries a corporal and a seaman in place of the corporal and volunteer.

I have the honour to be, sir,
Your very humble and very obedient servant

LE COMTE DE GRASSE[11]

---

[11] Promoted to rear admiral in the French navy on 22nd March 1781, François Joseph Paul, Comte de Grasse (1722-1788) sailed from Brest on the same day with a fleet of twenty ships of the line, three frigates, and a convoy of 150 ships for the West Indies. Reaching Martinique on 28th April, he picked up four French ships which had been blockaded by Hood off Fort Royal and engaged in some relatively minor operations before putting into Cape François on 26th July. There he found the *Concorde* waiting with dispatches which sought his support in operations against New York City or in the Chesapeake. Sending word back by the *Concorde* that he was coming

2 - Craig to Balfour

Craig to Balfour, 30th July 1781   *6(338): ALS*

Willmington
30th July 1781

Dear Sir

A particular opportunity offers, which I think promises fair to arrive safe, but it is so sudden and myself in such a predicament that I shall not have time to write so fully as I could wish.

The fleet sail'd last Tuesday, but the wind shifting immediately has been so perverse ever since that I much doubt whether they are not at this moment to the northward of this. Circumstances prevented my writing during the last days of their stay, so that my letters will be of a very old date indeed when you get them. However, nothing extraordinary had happen'd. Since then some events have taken place which I am glad to communicate. I have at this moment about *six or seven hundred Tories under arms*, who are employed in *disarming every man they can lay hold of*. There are all the *Highlanders* and *Bladen people*. Could I venture to *go among them as high as Cross Creek*, I should certainly get *near a thousand* of the former and a great number of the country people, but the consideration of *Lord Cornwallis's men* prevents me. But of all things I feel the want of *bayonets for the Highlanders* in particular, *who are raving* for them. I have not one. On the other side of me about 400 men are assembled and have taken a pretty strong post about 40 miles off. Luckily the bridge and post is just finish'd. I march this evening and on Thursday morning shall be at the back of them. However, it is possible they may escape. If they don't, it will be the means of all the *Tories on* the *Nuse, who are in great numbers, rising*. I have not yet determin'd whether to *make them join me* or no. The latter is most convenient, and the principal inducement to the former would be *a move towards Green*, which from the circumstance of *Lord Cornwallis's men* is for the present at an end. However, *I have made bustle enough to prevent his getting men from this part*.

General Grene has got few reinforcements from this province. What he has has been from Rowan and Mecklenburgh Counties chiefly and I am well inform'd does not exceed 800 men, for which to my knowledge the province could not furnish a firelock. The taxes laid on by this Assembly have been higher than ever and have rais'd a universal ferment in the country. Their levies go on very slow and they have not a grain of ammunition. The only thing that distresses me now is lest *you should not be able to send me any men* when Lord Cornwallis's

---

to the Chesapeake, he was under way on 13th August with thirty-four ships of war and 3,000 troops and arrived off the Capes of Virginia two weeks later. The rest is history. After Yorktown he returned to the West Indies, where he was captured with his flagship, the 110-gun *Ville de Paris*, in an engagement off Saints Passage on 12th April. A prisoner on parole, he went on to serve as a useful intermediary between Shelburne and the French Government during the important preliminary phase of the peace negotiations. He died at his town house in Paris. (Boatner, *Encyclopedia*, 444-5, 1237)

men go or lest any arrangement should occasion us *to leave this. In either case the cry* against us *will be terrible* and the *consequences bad.*

A very *particular friend* of mine writes me that the French embassador has wrote to the new Governor that by the time he receiv'd that letter he might expect the French fleet on the coasts of the southern colonies, but he does not mention the authority. I have already given you my opinion how far a judgement may be form'd on this subject from Grene's movements. I am not in much fear of their coming here. I have already wrote to you on that head.

One of my Tory parties under a Colonel Fanning[12], who is exceedingly active, surpriz'd a few days ago the whole heads of Chatham County to the number of 36, who were assembled in the court house to draft men. He parol'd 24 but brought down 12 of the worst here, one of whom observ'd he had *beheaded the county.* A few such strokes would be of great service.

It will be necessary to send us *provisions soon. We have about ten weeks'.*

I am with great truth, dear sir,
Your most obedient and very humble servant

J H CRAIG

§ - §

---

[12] David Fanning (*c.* 1755-1825) had been living in the Back Country of South Carolina when the revolutionary war began. A serjeant in a militia company, he remained loyal to the Crown and for the next five years was in and out of jail for his loyalism. By 1781 he had moved to North Carolina, where on 5th July he was commissioned by Craig as colonel of the loyalist militia in Randolph and Chatham Counties. He now embarked on a remarkable ten months' campaign which began with the surprise of the court at Petersborough (which Craig now relates) and involved in September the capture of Governor Burke and many others at Hillsborough. One-sidedly accused by revolutionaries of cruelty and murder, whose views were tamely followed by historians for many years, he has come to receive a more balanced assessment as the years have passed by. DeMond, for example, makes the point that his killings were, in the savage internecine war then being waged, no more than retaliation for like offences committed by the revolutionaries, whereas A W Savary, in his introduction to Fanning's *Narrative,* concluded that 'Fanning had been grievously maligned by American writers who have been unable to view his career with other than the jaundiced eyes of the partisan. If he had done just what he had done in the American cause instead of the loyal cause, he would have been acclaimed as one of the bravest and best of their leaders.' In June 1782 Fanning fled to Charlestown, from where he migrated by way of East Florida to Canada. From 1791 to 1801 he served in the New Brunswick legislative assembly but was expelled for some unknown offence for which he was sentenced to death and pardoned. Moving on to Digby, Nova Scotia, he became a colonel of militia. (DeMond, *Loyalists in NC,* 140-152; David Fanning, *Colonel Fanning's Narrative of His Exploits* (Toronto, 1906); *DAB*)

3 - Cornwallis to Balfour or Leslie

Haldane to Balfour, 14th August 1781   **_89(19): C_**

York in Virginia
14th August 1781

Lt Colonel Balfour
Commandant of Charlestown

Sir

Lord Cornwallis has directed me to acquaint you that Portsmouth is evacuated and that he has taken possession of this harbour, that you may be pleased to order all vessels coming from Charlestown to the Chesapeake to put into York River.

I have etc

H HALDANE

Cornwallis to Leslie, 27th August 1781[13]   **_89(31): ADfS_**

York in Virginia
August 27th 1781

Hon Major General Leslie etc etc etc

Dear Leslie

It is long since I have had any news from Carolina. There was a report of an action at Monk's Corner not much to our advantage, but as I have seen no rebel account from authority of it, I hope it was not of much consequence.

A vessel from Bermuda informed us that you had a very long passage and had lost all your horses, which gave me much concern.

Sir Henry has written to me lately to say that if any part of the troops lately arrived from Europe could be spared from South Carolina, he wished you to send them to New York. I informed him that I should submit it to your opinion and at the same time said that, as my intercourse with South Carolina was very precarious and as there could be no cooperation

---

[13] This letter is partly published in Ross ed, op cit, i, 117. It and later letters of the same date to Charlestown miscarried. They were conveyed in the *Guadeloupe*, which fell in with the French fleet and returned.

between the troops employed there and at this post, I wished him to transmit any commands he might have for Carolina directly to you.

I have prevailed on my friend Symonds to send the *Guadalupe* to Charlestown, but you must make a point of it with Barkley not to detain her except for the purpose of convoying stores, convalescents etc to this place. The regiments here are ruined for want of their paymasters, clothing and necessaries. I trust you will lose no time in sending the convalescents, clothing, stores etc, as it is of the utmost consequence to the troops to receive them before they take the field, which Sir Henry proposes doing the 1st week in October.

I should wish that those men belonging to the regiments here who are unfit for service may be invalided at Charlestown and as few as possible of those men who have fought so gallantly sent to the Garrison Battalion.

I fear Craig must have destroyed the men left at Wilmington, as that place has been always represented as being remarkably unhealthy. You must certainly be able to form a better judgement at Charlestown than I can do here, but I cannot conceive that he can have rendered any essential service in the country about Newberne, where I understand he has been, nor by any diversion in North Carolina unless he had been strong enough to have gone between the NW Branch of Cape Fear and the Pedee. I believe I desired you, if you thought it right to recall him and felt any delicacy about doing it, to make use of my name.

We are busily employed in fortifying this post, which will be a work of great time and labour and after all, I fear, not be very strong. I shall be happy to hear from you by every opportunity. Perhaps sometimes you might send a line in cypher by land written in the sort of way not to expose the bearer to a possibility of detection, either on the back of a Congress note or any ordinary piece of paper.

I shall write to Balfour and to save you trouble shall inclose to him all the applications which I have received relative to civil matters.

Our troops are remarkably healthy for the season.

My friend Sir A Hammond has recommended to me in the strongest manner Lieutenant Masterson of the 19th. I shall be much obliged to you for any civilities which you may have an opportunity of shewing him. In consequence of Lord Shelburne's recommendation I should wish you to take some notice of Dr Turnbull unless you should think him undeserving of it.

Most sincerely wishing you all possible success, honour and happiness, I am, dear Leslie, with great truth
Your most obedient and faithfull servant

CORNWALLIS

York in Virginia
August 27th 1781

Hon Lt General Leslie etc etc etc

Dear Leslie

As the application of officers for leave to go to New York is attended with great delay by coming thro' me, I beg that (untill the Commander in Chief signifies his pleasure that your command should be totally independent of mine, which will, I hope, soon be the case) you will consider yourself as entirely invested with my powers and exercise them as you may think fit. I shall be much obliged to you if you will send Mr Gale, the Deputy Paymaster, by the first convenient opportunity.

Yours etc

[CORNWALLIS]

Cornwallis to Balfour, 27th August 1781   *89(25): ADfS*

York in Virginia
August 27th 1781

Lt Colonel Balfour etc

Dear Balfour

It is long since I have had the satisfaction of hearing any thing of my friends in South Carolina. A vague report was propagated here that Lord Rawdon was very ill at Charlestown and that the 19th Regiment had received a severe check at Monk's Corner. Both these tales I hope are either totally false or greatly exaggerated. I inclose to you all the applications which I have received relative to South Carolina business. I was likewise desired by a near relation of mine to inquire whether Mr Hobson Pinckney[14] was alive. The *name* is not a good one.

Ross writes fully to you. I therefore refer you to him for my situation in every particular.

The enemy pretend to have sent in a great many prisoners to Charlestown and consequently to owe us very few. I shall be obliged to you for a clear state of all that business.

You must not keep the *Guadalupe* on any account except for a convoy for our clothing, stores, convalescents etc, as it is a great favour that I obtained from my friend Symonds to let her go.

---

[14] As Cornwallis suspected, Hopson Pinckney was not a loyalist. Under the revolutionary constitution of South Carolina he served as Sheriff of Charlestown District. (Moss, *SC Patriots*, 774)

Tarleton applied to me about the stoppage of the sixpences for forage. I do not by any means think that they ought to be paid to the Legion, nor do I think that the commissary ought to pocket them. Suppose a day was fixed for the receipts to be brought in and, after they are paid, that the balance should be placed in the hands of the Paymaster General to be disposed of by the Commander in Chief.

I have promised a permission for 400 hogsheads of tobacco for the payment of the debts of the prisoners of the Virginia regiment at Charlestown.[15] I should be very unwilling to grant any more permissions of that sort and hope you will take care that the quantity allowed is disposed of for the purposes only for which it was requested.

Do all in your power to forward the dispatching as soon as possible our convalescents, clothing, stores etc.

I beg you will accept of my very sincere good wishes, and believe me to be with the greatest regard

Most faithfully yours

CORNWALLIS

Haldane to Balfour, 1st September 1781[16]   *89(37): ALS*

York Town in Virginia
1st September 1781

Lt Colonel Balfour
Commandant of Charlestown

Sir

I am directed by Earl Cornwallis to acquaint you that there are between thirty and forty sail of enemy's ships, mostly large ships of war, within the Capes of the Chesapeake Bay, and that his Lordship desires that no vessels may be sent to this port untill you receive further orders from him.

I have the honour to be
Your most obedient and most humble servant

HENRY HALDANE
Aide de camp

§ - §

---

[15]   See Cornwallis to Lafayette, 28th June, vol V, p 237.

[16]   Annotated: 'Miscarried and returned'.

4 - Stewart to Cornwallis

Stewart to Cornwallis, 15th August 1781   *70(24): ALS*

Buckhead
15th August 1781

Lord Cornwallis

My Lord

Your Lordship no doubt has been informed by Lord Rawdon and Colonel Balfour [of] the situation of this country. They would likewise inform you that Lord Rawdon's health would not permit him to remain any longer with the army on the frontier in this province. He therefore gave up the command of it to me at Orangeburgh the 16th of last month and went down to Charles Town. When he left me, a large detachment of the army was down at Dorchester for provisions. I was obliged to make a move towards [Serj¹?] Campbell's on the Santee in order to cover the march of the convoy. As soon as they joined me, I moved to this place and arrived here the 3rd of this month, where I have been very well supplyed with provisions, which was by no means to be got at Orangeburgh before I left it. We were obliged to send seventeen miles for indian corn and then had no mills to grind it in, the rebells having destroyed them two days after Lord Rawdon arrived there. General Green is at present (and has been ever since I came here) at the Widow James's plantation on the High Hills of Santee about twenty miles below Cambden. I'm informed he has been lately reinforced by a General Sumner with five hundred men drafted or inlisted from the North Carolina militia for ten months. What he will do now I know not, but I should think he would hardly come over the river to attack me. If he does, I have very little doubt but I shall beat him. I shall endeavor in the mean time to cover the country as well as I can, but from the great superiority of the enemy in light troops it will be difficult, and they never will allow my infantry to get near them. I shall move from time to time in order to preserve the health of the army. Our rains are set in. We have had four days' constant rain, which has raised the rivers. Your Lordship may be assured that nothing shall be wanting in my power for the good of His Majesty's Service and the preservation of the province, and it will be highly pleasing to me if my conduct can meet with your approbation during the time I command.

I have the honor to be with respect and regard, my Lord,
Your Lordship's most obedient and most humble servant

ALEXᴿ STEWART
Lt Colonel commanding the army on the frontier, South Carolina

§ - §

5 - Cornwallis to Barkley

Cornwallis to Barkley, 27th August 1781   *89(27): ADfS*

York in Virginia
August 27th 1781

Andrew Barkeley Esq commanding His Majesty's ships
   on the Southern Station

Dear Sir

I did myself the honour of writing to you in the month of June[17] to thank you for your kind attention to my request of sending my aide de camp Captain Broderick to England in a ship of war. I have since heard that the vessel which carried that letter was taken. I must therefore take this opportunity of repeating my acknowledgements to you.

I prevailed on my friend Captain Symonds to send the *Guadalupe* to Charlestown not only to carry dispatches of consequence to Major General Leslie but to assist, in case she was wanted, in convoying the clothing, stores and necessaries, of which the troops under my command are in the greatest want, to this place. Without their speedy arrival the army cannot take the field at the time that Sir Henry Clinton expects them to be ready. If the clothing etc should have left Charlestown before the arrival of the *Guadalupe*, I have no doubt of your permitting her to return immediately with Major General Leslie's answers to my dispatches.

I have the honour to be with great esteem, dear sir,
Your most obedient and most humble servant

CORNWALLIS

§ - §

---

[17] No letter thanking Barkley is extant.

CHAPTER 61

Letters to or from the enemy

---

1 - Between Cornwallis and Greene or Lafayette

Lafayette to Cornwallis, 11th September 1781   **_92(37): LS_**

Head Quarters
11th September 1781

Lt General Earl Cornwallis

My Lord

This will be accompanied by a letter from Major General Greene which it was requested should be forwarded immediately to your Lordship.

I have the honor to be
Your Lordship's most obedient servant

LAFAYETTE

Head Quarters
South Carolina
August 26th 1781

Lt General Earl Cornwallis

My Lord

I am sorry to inform you that the exchange of prisoners agreable to the late cartel settled between us is interrupted by the execution of Colonel Haynes[2], one of our militia colonels, and by other discriminations among the prisoners contrary not only to the spirit but the letter of the cartel, all which I flatter myself are contrary to your Lordship's intentions; and it is for this purpose that I address myself to you upon this occasion that you may signify your disapprobation and remove the farther obstacles to future exchanges agreable to the principles of the cartel.

I flatter myself your Lordship is too well acquainted with the feelings of human nature from the history of mankind to suppose that any national advantage can result from those cruel distinctions which can only serve to encrease the miseries of individuals, nor can I suppose your Lordship can have a single doubt that a people who have gone thus far in support of their liberties will hisitate a moment to retaliate for every violence offered to their adherents.

Persuaded that your Lordship considered the present war upon national principles, and that cruelties exercised upon individuals only served to confirm opposition, and that the opinion and influence of the inhabitants in all disputes of this nature would be directed by their feelings, I was happy to have the cartel established upon so broad a basis as to consider all as prisoners of war taken in the service of either side, especially as a contrary conduct could only encrease the miseries of war without gaining any national advantage.

I do myself the honor to inclose your Lordship copies of my letters upon the subject that you may give such orders upon the occasion as you may think the honor of your King and the service of your country require.

---

[1]   Published with no differences in *The Greene Papers*, ix, 253.

[2]   A planter, horse breeder, and officer of the Colleton County revolutionary militia, Isaac Hayne (1745-1781) had been taken prisoner in the capitulation of Charlestown. He did not enter into a parole but proceeded to take protection and become a British subject, swearing an oath of allegiance to the Crown. In the summer of 1781, as revolutionary forces continued to overrun South Carolina, he violated his oath and took up arms on the revolutionary side as a colonel of militia. In early July he captured Andrew Williamson near Charlestown but was surprised by Thomas Fraser and taken prisoner. Williamson was released. A court of inquiry into his status determined that he had violated his oath by taking up arms and he was condemned to death. On 4th August he was hanged. The circumstances of his case were clouded by controversy, reflecting the political divide — a controversy which has continued to this day. (Walter B Edgar, N Louise Bailey, et al, *Biographical Directory of the South Carolina House of Representatives*(University of South Carolina Press, 1977-81), ii, 310-11; David K Bowden, *The Execution of Isaac Hayne* (The Sandlapper Store, 1977); Moira (Rawdon) to Lee, 24th June 1813, in Lee, *Memoirs*, 613-620)

I have the honor to be, my Lord, with great respect
Your Lordship's most obedient and most humble servant

NATH GREENE

Enclosure (1)
Greene to Balfour, 2nd August 1781[3]   *92(39): C*

August 2nd '81

Colonel Balfour etc etc etc

Sir

Major Hyrne[4], the Deputy Commissary General of Prisoners for the American Army of the Southern Department, has represented to me that several of our people, and among others Messrs Wm Starke, Wm Moore, Jno Postel, James Smith and Ch^s Skirving, were refused their exchange agreeable to the principles of the cartel settled between Earl Cornwallis and myself for the relief of the captives belonging to both armies. It has ever been my wish, and it was the first object of my attention when I came to this department, to render the condition of the prisoners on both sides as eligible as possible, and for this purpose I proposed to his Lordship an early exchange upon the most just and equal footing. The subject was long canvased and the relief of the prisoners protracted, but finally it was agreed to upon the extensive scale upon which it now stands; and as his Lordship made no reserve, and as he must have been sensible I should never have agreed to any, I cannot persuade myself that this measure will meet his approbation, especially as he must be convinced no further exchanges will take place untill these men are released. For the honor of humanity as well as the reputation of the American Army I have ever been careful not to invade the rights of one or stain the glory of the other by acts of severity to those whom the fortune of war put into my power, and I appeal to your officers whether they have not been treated with every attention and indulgence that our situation could afford. Should they meet with a contrary conduct in future, they must blame you not me, for tho' I abhor cruelty, yet justice to our own people will oblige me to retaliate for every injury offered them.

---

[3] Published with inconsequential differences, together with a summary of Balfour's reply, in *The Greene Papers*, ix, 124 and 202.

[4] Edmund Massingberd Hyrne (1748-1783) was commissioned a captain in June 1775 in a regiment being raised by the South Carolina Provincial Congress and was transferred with it to the Continental line in September 1776. In 1778 he was appointed Deputy Adjutant General in the Southern Department, an office he would hold till the close of the war. Promoted in 1779 to major, he was wounded early in the siege of Charlestown and escaped capture. He went on to serve as an aide-de-camp to Greene besides acting as his commissary of prisoners and as his liaison officer with Sumter. Soon he would be commended by Congress for his part in the Battle of Eutaw Springs. Shortly afterwards he was elected to the South Carolina revolutionary assembly which met at Jacksonborough in January 1782. He died in December 1783 at his plantation, 'Ormsby', in St Bartholomew's Parish, South Carolina. (*DAB*; Heitman, *Historical Register*, 313)

As I am sensible no threats will influence your conduct, so I beg you to be persuaded that nothing but the release of those gentlemen will afford to the prisoners on both sides those extensive advantages which was the object of the cartel. The reasons offered for the detention of these gentlemen have so little force, and the measure is so opposite to the spirit of the cartel, that on further reflection I am confident you will be no less convinced of the injustice and impolicy of this measure than that you have been of the cruelty of confining and devoting our prisoners in retaliation for enormities that might happen between the Whigs and the Tories from the present animosities subsisting between them.

Another thing I have to complain of is your admitting into service prisoners on parole at an earlier period than the conditions of capitulation or exchange will authorize. I mean Captain Fenwick's corps. Public faith is so essential, and the honor of the nation so deeply concerned, that I am persuaded the circumstances must be unknown to you, for I cannot believe that for the sake of the little advantage that would result from the service of a few men you would authorize a measure no less dishonorable to yourself than to the nation with whom you are connected.

I am, sir,
Your most obedient humble servant

NATH GREENE

Enclosure (2)
Greene to Balfour, 26th August 1781[5]   *92(45): C*

August 26th '81

Colonel Balfour etc etc etc

Sir

I wrote you the 2nd of this instant respecting a number of prisoners detained contrary to the express conditions of the late cartel settled for the exchange of prisoners in the Southern Department.

Since I wrote you, I am informed of a more flagrant violation than the former in the cruel and unjust execution of Colonel Haynes, for which I mean an immediate retaliation unless you can offer something more to justify the measure than I am informed of or is mentioned in the Charles Town paper.

For the honor of humanity, from an abhorrence of every thing that bears the marks of cruelty, and with a desire to give every man an opportunity to act agreable to his own sentiments and inclinations, it was my wish to have all considered as prisoners of war who

---

[5] Published with inconsequential differences, together with Balfour's reply and a summary of the address, in *The Greene Papers*, ix, 217, 249 and 283.

should be found in arms and made captives on either side; and I am fully persuaded that it was no less consonant to Lord Cornwallis's intentions that they should be exchanged as such than it was correspondent with my own wishes. And I shall take the earliest opportunity of informing his Lordship of the violence done to the business of exchange and the disagreable necessity I am laid under to retaliate, and of its being my determination not only in this instance but to repeat it as often as any violence is done to the good people who adhere to our cause. I shall publish to the world my intentions, the principles upon which I proceed, and the objects I mean to retaliate upon, who are British officers and not Tory militia; and this is not only my own sentiments but the measure is supported by the opinion and wish of the whole army, as you may see by the inclosed address.

Should there be a balance of private soldiers due from us to you so soon as the commissaries can adjust it, they shall be immediately sent in. All other exchanges will be discontinued in future untill the present obstacles which interrupt its operations are fully removed.

I am, sir,
Your most humble servant

NATH GREENE

Cornwallis to Lafayette, 15th September 1781   *92(55): Df*

15th September

Major General Marquis de la Fayette etc etc etc

Sir

I was honoured with your letter of the [11th] instant accompanied with one from General Greene, to which I now trouble you with my answer and request that you will be pleased to forward it with all convenient dispatch. I find that on account of some late transactions in South Carolina General Greene has thought proper to interrupt the general operation of the cartel settled between us, but I have no doubt of your giving orders that such of the prisoners delivered to you as are not regularly exchanged shall remain unemployed, and I shall always be ready to agree to any reasonable exchanges of officers that you may have occasion to propose.

I have constantly given directions that your prisoners in our possession should be treated with as much indulgence and attention as circumstances will permit, but our present situation obliged me to decline receiving your commissary of prisoners to visit them.

Last night some English sailors who had escaped informed me that the *Wortley* brig, one of our cartel vessels coming round from James Town to York, had been seized by the French fleet and the sailors made prisoners as well as the soldiers that had been released by you, and the master and crew plundered. I must request that you will be pleased to enquire into this matter, and if my information is well founded, I shall depend upon you to procure ample satisfaction and restitution from the Count de Grasse.

I have the honour to be, sir, etc

[CORNWALLIS]

Enclosure
Cornwallis to Greene, 15th September 1781[6]

92(57): ADf

15th September

Sir

I have received your letter of the 26th of August inclosing copies of two letters written by you to Lt Colonel Balfour.

I am exceedingly concerned to find that an interruption to the cartel is likely to take place. From motives of humanity to both sides I was anxious to carry it into execution.

My good opinion of Lt Colonel Balfour will not suffer me easily to believe that he can be guilty of an act of cruelty or injustice. I have had no accounts from him of the transactions you complain of and I am convinced that you must be too candid to expect that I should condemn him unheard. I shall write to him by the first opportunity and shall be happy if his answer should put it in my power to remove every obstacle to the continuation of the cartel consistent with my duty and the protection which I owe to the loyalists of this Continent.

I trust that you will take time to investigate this business with coolness and temper before you proceed to retaliation, as the consequences of it may be very fatal to many innocent individuals on both sides.

If you should think it necessary at present to stop the operation of the cartel, I have no doubt of your ordering the officers who have returned home on parole to proceed immediately to Charlestown and a number of our prisoners to be sent to us equal to those of your army who have been released.

I have the honour to be etc

[CORNWALLIS]

---

[6]   Published with one inconsequential difference in *The Greene Papers*, ix, 348.

Lafayette to Cornwallis, 25th September 1781   92(58): LS

Williamsburg
25th September 1781

Lt General Earl Cornwallis etc etc

My Lord

I have been honored with a letter from you enclosing one for General Greene, which I shall forward as soon as possible. Your Lordship is certainly convinced that nothing can affect my former promises. As to future arrangements, I shall receive orders from his Excellency General Washington, who has taken the immediate command of the combined armies in this quarter.

Our commissary reports that more prisoners have been deliver'd on our side than received from yours. I shall enquire particularly into this matter.

Before your letter came to hand I had wrote to the French admiral respecting the cartel vessels. It appears that their papers were not regular, and some other matters have been mention'd which render their case doubtful. However, I will make that business my own and will satisfy your Lordship that proper regard has been paid to their situation and your recommendation.

I have the honor to be
Your Lordship's most obedient humble servant

LAFAYETTE

Lafayette to Cornwallis, 3rd October 1781   92(60): A(in part) LS

Camp
3rd October 1781

Lt General Earl Cornwallis

My Lord

Inclosed I have the honor to send you the answer to a letter to Count de Grasse respecting the vessel mentioned by your Lordship. I have requested the Count that vessels in his possession under the description of flags on the business of exchanges, without considering irregularities either in their lading or papers, be treated as flag ships until the matter may be fully explained with your Lordship.

I am requested by Lord Rawdon to pay his affectionate respects to your Lordship and let you know that his health is much better than when he left Carolina.

I have the honor to be
Your Lordship's obedient servant

LA FAYETTE

Enclosure
De Vaugirauld to Lafayette, 25th September 1781   270(5): ALS

Abord de *la Ville de Paris*
le 25 7bre 1781

Monsieur

La requete qui vous a été presentée par le capitaine du brik nomé le *Yorc* pour être reintegré dans le commandement de son batiment n'a sans doute d'autre objet que celuy d'intéresser votre sensibilité et obtenir de votre generosité ce qu'il ne peut espérer par les loix qui preservent les batiments qui sont de bonne prise.

J'ay l'honneur de vous assurer que les papiers de ce batiment n'etois nullement conforme a ceux que doivent avoir les parlementaires ainsy qu'il l'a voulu persuader. Son équipage est même convenu d'une voix unanime qu'il les avait écrit luy même au moment de notre premiere apparition au mouillage du Cap Henry, et ont pareillement deposér que le batiment etoit un hopital. Rien ne le mieux prouve que la quantité de malades qui se sont trouvé a son bord et que la disposition de l'amenagement, semblable a ceux des hopiteaux. Il s'est trouvé de plus une tres grande quantité de boulêts dans la cale.

Il est d'ailleurs bien constaté qu'il est convenu qu'il avait été loyalement pris.

Monsieur le Comte de Grasse me charge de vous connoitre tous les détails. Je le fait avec d'autant plus de plaisir que cela me procure l'avantage de vous offrir l'hommage du au merite distingué, auquel je joint les sentiments respectueux avec lesquels j'ay l'honneur d'être, Monsieur le Marquis,

Votre tres humble et tres obeissant serviteur

DE VAUGIRAULD
Major genéral de l'armee navale
Aux voix de Monsieur le Comte de Grasse

TRANSLATION

On board *la Ville de Paris*
25th September 1781

Sir

The request presented to you by the captain of the brig *York* to be reinstated in the command of his vessel has, I suppose, no other purpose than to excite your compassion and obtain by your generosity what he cannot hope to do by the laws which retain vessels which are lawful prizes.

I have the honour to assure you that the papers of this vessel in no way conformed to those which, as he has sought to demonstrate, flag vessels must have. In fact his crew are unanimously agreed that he wrote them himself on our first appearance in the road off Cape Henry, and have likewise affirmed that the vessel was a hospital. There is no better proof than the number of sick on board and the arrangement of the accommodation, which resembles that of hospitals. There are, besides, a very large number of cannonballs in the hold.

Moreover, it is well established that she is agreed to have been properly taken.

The Comte de Grasse bids me notify you of all the details. I do so with all the more pleasure as it affords me the privilege of paying homage due to distinguished merit, and have the honour to be, Monsieur le Marquis, with sentiments of respect

Your very humble and very obedient servant

DE VAUGIRAULD[7]
Major General of the naval troops
At the behest of the Comte de Grasse

§ - §

---

[7] De Vaugirauld has not been identified beyond what he reveals of himself in this letter. Possessing an uncommon name, he may have been related to the de Vaugiraulds of Nantes and the Pays de la Loire.

2 - Between Cornwallis and Thomas Nelson Jr

Nelson to Cornwallis, 23rd July 1781   *90(17): LS*

Richmond
July 23rd 1781

My Lord

The frequent applications that are made to me by the citizens of this Commonwealth to grant flags for the recovery of their Negroes and other property taken by the troops under your command induce me to address your Lordship for information whether restitution will be made at all, what species of property will be restored, and who may expect to be the objects of such an indulgence.

Mr Archer[8] and Mr Royall[9], inhabitants of the County of Amelia, were lately made prisoners by a detachment of your troops commanded by Lt Colonel Tarliton. The former of these is of an age which exempts him from military duty; the latter bears no other character than that of a citizen of the State. As I cannot suppose that your Lordship regards such persons as the objects of hostile treatment, I flatter myself you will on this representation have them immediately restored to their liberty.

I am your Lordship's obedient and very humble servant

THO^S NELSON Jr

Cornwallis to Nelson, 6th August 1781   *90(19): Df*

York
August 6th 1781

Sir

I have received your letter of the 23rd July.

---

8   William Archer (*c*. 1710-1781) had over the years amassed a land holding of some 1,500 acres on the Appomattox River in Amelia County. He had served several terms as a Justice of the Peace, two as a vestryman of Raleigh Parish, and one as sheriff of the county. He had also been commissioned colonel of the county's revolutionary militia, an appointment which almost certainly was honorary in nature in view of his advanced years. Cornwallis would soon agree to his release on parole, but it was too late, as he had died of smallpox on a prison ship. (John W Pritchett, 'Virginians: The Family History of George Archer I (?-1675)' (Internet, 21st June 2006); *Va Military Records*, 4, 765)

9   John Royall owned land on Appomattox River adjoining that of William Archer, who was an uncle of John's wife, Elizabeth. John, who would soon be released on parole, never held any revolutionary office during the war, either civil or military, but his son John Jr served as an officer in the Amelia County revolutionary militia. (John W Pritchett, op cit)

No Negroes have been taken by the British troops by my orders nor to my knowledge, but great numbers have come to us from different parts of the country[10]. Being desirous to grant every indulgence to individuals that they can reasonably claim or that I think consistent with my public duty, any proprietor not in arms against us or holding an office of trust under the authority of Congress and willing to give his parole that he will not in future act against His Majesty's interest will be indulged with permission to search the camp for his Negroes and to take them if they are willing to go with him, and if horses have been taken from persons of that description they will be restored or paid for.

Having given orders some time ago to release such persons as you describe Messrs Archer and Ryall to be, I hope they are before now at their own homes.

I have the honour to be etc

[CORNWALLIS]

Nelson to Cornwallis, 3rd September 1781   90(21): LS

Richmond
September 3rd 1781

My Lord

From the assurance given me in a letter I received from your Lordship of August 6th that all such persons as I described Messrs Archer and Ryall to be were ordered to be released, I rested satisfied that those gentlemen had obtained their liberty. But I am just informed that they are still confined on board of one of your prison ships, which from your letter I must suppose to be a circumstance with which you are not acquainted. I am therefore again to desire your attention to these gentlemen and assure myself that you will order them to be released.

I have the honour to be
Your Lordship's most obedient and most humble servant

THO^S NELSON Jr

Cornwallis to Nelson, 8th September 1781   90(23): Df

Head Quarters
8th September 1781

Governor Nelson etc etc etc

Sir

When I left Portsmouth I gave directions to release all prisoners who had not been taken in arms or who were not remarkable for persecuting their countrymen of different political

---

[10]   After 'country' the following words are deleted: 'and in general are more burdensome than usefull.'

opinions, and when I answered your former letter I thought it probable that Messrs Ryall and Archer had been released as not coming under either of those descriptions. But it having appeared to the commanding officer of Portsmouth[11] that those gentlemen were made prisoners not only for refusing to give their own paroles but because they had threatened to force their neighbours to break theirs, he thought proper to detain them; and for the same reasons I find myself under the necessity of continuing them in confinement.

I have the honour to be, sir,
Your most obedient and most humble servant

[CORNWALLIS]

Cornwallis to Nelson, 15th September 1781   92(56): C

Head Quarters
15th September 1781

Governor Nelson etc etc etc

Sir

Although the political reasons for the confinement of Messrs Archer and Royall still subsist, I have on account of their infirmities and the age of the former given directions to release them on parole.

I have the honour to be, sir, etc

[CORNWALLIS]

Nelson to Cornwallis, 18th September 1781   90(25): LS

Williamsburg
September 18th 1781

Lt General Earl Cornwallis etc etc etc

By flag of truce

My Lord

The officers of the Virginia line who contracted the debts in Charlestown for the payment of which we are now sending tobacco[12] are desirous that Lt Colonel Wallace[13], one of their

---

[11] The words from 'But' to 'Portsmouth' are substituted for: 'But having since that time been informed by Lt Colonel Tarleton'.

[12] *debts... tobacco*: for further papers, see pp 93-4.

number and still a prisoner on parole, be permitted to go in the flag, his knowledge of their contracts qualifying him better than any person who is a stranger to them to settle them in a just and satisfactory manner. If your Lordship thinks proper to grant this permission, you will be pleased to enclose to me a passport for him.

I am informed that Major Arthur Dickinson[14] of the York County militia is under close confinement in your provost. Your Lordship will oblige me by acquainting me with the reason of his being treated in this rigorous manner.

I am your Lordship's most obedient and very humble servant

THO^S NELSON Jr

Cornwallis to Nelson, 20th September 1781   90(27): Df

Head Quarters
20th September 1781

Governor Nelson etc etc etc

Sir

Inclosed is a pass for Lt Colonel Wallace to go to Charlestown to assist in applying the produce of the sales of the tobacco for discharging the debts contracted by the prisoners of war.

Major Dickenson of the York County militia, having come into this post without permission and without discovering his rank, was taken when known and he was confined in consequence of the opinion of a court of enquiry that there were strong reasons to suspect him of being a spy.

I have the honour to be, sir,
Your most obedient and most humble servant

[CORNWALLIS]

---

[13] Born in Stafford County, Virginia, Gustavus Brown Wallace (1751-1802) had been Lt Colonel of the 11th Virginia Continental Regiment when he was taken prisoner in the capitulation of Charlestown. He would remain on parole for the rest of his service. After the war he was awarded 7,960 acres. His remains lie in the Masonic Cemetery, Fredericksburg. (Reverend Horace Edwin Hayden, *Virginia Genealogies*...(Genealogical Publishing Co, 1983); *Va Military Records*, 822, 843; Gwathmey, *Historical Register*, 802; Heitman, *Historical Register*, 566)

[14] Arthur Dickinson, who had been serving as major in the York County revolutionary militia for at least four years, was confined for the reasons stated in Cornwallis's reply. If he survived the bombardment, then the siege and capitulation of Yorktown may have saved him from execution, as he was apparently still alive in mid October. (*Va Military Records*, 462; Gwathmey, op cit, 223; *The Cornwallis Papers*)

Enclosure
Passport for Wallace, 20th September 1781   *90(29): C*

By Charles Earl Cornwallis
Lt General of His Majesty's forces etc etc etc

Permission is hereby granted to Lt Colonel Wallace of the Virginia line at present prisoner on parole to pass to Charlestown, in any of the flag of truce vessels that he thinks proper, for the purpose of applying the produce of the sales of the tobacco, permitted to be carried to that port, for discharging the debts contracted by the prisoners of war, Lt Colonel Wallace reporting his conduct and receiving directions in this business from the Commandant of Charlestown.

Given under my hand at York Town in Virginia
this 20th day of September 1781

[CORNWALLIS]

Nelson to Cornwallis, 25th September 1781   *6(385): ALS*

Williamsburg
September 25th 1781

Lord Cornwallis

By a flag of truce

My Lord

Many of the former inhabitants of York having applied to me for a flag to bring out their effects, your Lordship will do me the favor to inform me whether it will be agreeable to you to allow them this liberty and, if it is, at what time it will be most proper for their waggons etc to attend for this purpose.

If your Lordship will permit such of the inhabitants as are now in York to come out with their effects, waggons will be sent at the same time for their use.

I must request that your Lordship will inform me of the reason of Doctor Griffin's[15] confinement on board of one of your prison ships.

---

[15]   Dr Corbin Griffin (?-1813) of Yorktown had read medicine at the University of Edinburgh in 1769 before returning to Virginia to become a member of the York County committee of safety in 1775-6. He had also been serving as a surgeon to the Virginia state troops and the Virginia state navy. In 1780 he was elected to the senate of the Virginia revolutionary legislature. (Lyon Gardiner Tyler, 'Education in Colonial Virginia: Part IV, The Higher Education', *William and Mary College Quarterly Historical Magazine*, vi, N° 3 (January 1898), 176; Tyler, *Encyclopedia*, i, 248-9; *Va Military Records*, 641, 781)

I have the honor to be
Your Lordship's most obedient and very humble servant

THO^S NELSON Jr

Cornwallis to Nelson, 26th September 1781

90(31): C

Head Quarters
26th September 1781

Governor Nelson etc etc etc

Sir

I have not the least objection to any of the inhabitants at present in this place going out with their families and effects nor to those who formerly resided here sending for their wives and families, who will likewise be permitted to take their effects with them, and any waggons that you think proper to send to assist them will be received at our out post on the Hampton road.

Information having been given to me that Doctor Griffin had been particularly attentive to our works with a design to give intelligence to our enemies, he was put on board a frigate, where I have reason to believe that he was well used, and as the suspicions against him do not appear to me to be well founded, he is now set at liberty.

I have the honour to be, sir,
Your most obedient and most humble servant

[CORNWALLIS]

Nelson to Cornwallis, 14th October 1781

90(33): ALS

October 14th 1781

My Lord

I have received information that there are at this time many citizens of the State confined on board your prison ships, where they are suffering extreme distress. Several of them have families, which, deprived of their assistance, are also involved in ruin. As I have not heard that the persons alluded to have done anything which ought to make them particularly obnoxious, I am at a loss to account for the severity of their treatment. Your Lordship will, I hope, consider that proceedings of this nature can answer no other purpose than unnecessarily to augment the horrors of war, inevitably too great. And I am willing to believe that your regard for humanity would have prevented my application to have these unfortunate men released had their situation or the wretchedness of it occurred to you before.

Major Dickinson of the York militia I understand is still untried and confined. If his conduct while within your lines gave you reason to regard him as a spy, your Lordship is not to be informed that the usage of war prescribes that he be tried and, if found guilty, punished, but, if not, discharged.

I have enclosed the names of such of these sufferers as have been mentioned to me.

I am your Lordship's most obedient and very humble servant

THO^S NELSON Jr

Enclosure

A list of prisoners confined on board the British prison ships

Anthony Lawson	Princess Anne County
—— Gurland	Norfolk County
Robert Barron	Ditto
Thomas Nash	Ditto
Edward Wonycott	Ditto
Richard E Lee	Elizabeth City County
Moss Armistead	Ditto

§ - §

3 - Concerning the discharge of prisoners' debts at Charlestown

Maury to Ross, 31st August 1781   *6(381): ALS*

Outposts
31st August 1781

Major Ross

Sir

Here are the particulars of three vessells now ready. Burden 212 hogsheads. Two other vessells now taking in the 188 remaining hogsheads will be so in the space of a few days, but as you object to granting passports under this latter description, I do not give you their other particulars. As we wish the whole five to sail together, I beg the 3 now ready may be permitted to wait for the others at their present moorings in Rappahannock or at any other place within the bay that shall be more agreeable. Mr Potty goes with the intention of returning to Scotland and is well known to Captain Magill of the Queen's Rangers, Mr James Robertson, merchant, and many other gentlemen in your lines who formerly lived in Virginia. If it be found inconvenient to admit me within your posts, I would deem it a particular favor of you to have these notes[16] contrived to the gentlemen to whom addressed.

I have the honor to be with much respect, sir,
Your most obedient servant

JAMES MAURY

Enclosure
Particulars of three vessels   *6(380): D*

The brigantine *Judith and Maria*, Mark Towel master, cargo 108 hogsheads tobacco, navigated by master, mate, ten mariners and two cabbin boys, George Potty, his wife, child and servant passengers. Bill of stores: 22 barrels flower, bread and pork.

Sloop *Sally*. John Surtie master, cargo 80 hogsheads tobacco, navigated by master and 6 mariners. 15 barrels flower, bread and pork.

Sloop *Rambler*. John Currie master, cargo 24 hogsheads tobacco, navigated by master, 4 mariners and a boy. Ten barrels flower, bread, and salt provisions.

---

[16] *these notes..*: no copies.

Passport for the brigantine *Judith and Maria,* 31st August 1781

6(377): Df

A Flag of Truce

By Charles Earl Cornwallis,
Lt General of His Majesty's forces etc etc etc,
and Thomas Symonds Esq,
commanding His Majesty's ships in Chesapeak Bay

WHEREAS by the consent of Lt Colonel Balfour it was agreed that a certain quantity of tobacco should be sent from Virginia to Charlestown for the sole purpose of discharging the debts contracted by the prisoners of war at that place, we therefore do hereby give permission to the brigantine *Judith and Maria,* Mark Towel master, navigated by the master, a mate and ten other mariners and two cabin boys, with George Potty, his wife, child and servant as passengers, to proceed unmolested from the River[17] to Charlestown under the sanction of this flag of truce, she sailing as soon after the date of this passport as wind and weather will permit and steering as direct a course as possible for Charlestown, having on board one hundred and eight hogsheads of tobacco for the purposes above mentioned with twenty two barrells of flour, bread and pork as provisions for the crew, upon their arrival there to be immediately reported to the commanding officer of His Majesty's navy and to the Commandant of Charlestown, having no intercourse with the enemies of Great Britain nor carrying any letters, trade or articles not licensed by this passport, but observing in every respect the spirit of a flag of truce untill regularly dismissed by the Commandant of Charlestown, who will in conjunction with the naval commander grant a passport to return to the port from whence the vessel sailed.

> Given under our hands at York Town in Virginia
> this 31st day of August 1781
>
> [CORNWALLIS
> THO^S SYMONDS]

Particulars of two vessels, undated

6(379): D

The brigantine *Potomack* in the port of Alexandria on Potomack River, navigated by Edward Ross master and ten other mariners, William Du Vall, his wife, Peter Hay and two servants as passengers, having on board eighty five hogsheads of tobacco and twenty six barrels of bread, flour and salt provisions.

The brigantine *Marquis de la Fayette* in the port of Port Royal on Rappahannock River, navigated by Elijah Luce master and twelve other mariners, having on board one hundred and three hogsheads of tobacco and twenty five barrels of bread, flour and salt provisions.

---

[17] Before 'River' is deleted 'Rhappahannock'.

4 - About prisoners in Maryland or Virginia

Parker to Cornwallis, 23rd July 1781   **6(337): ALS**

Camp
Isle of Wight
July 23rd 1781

His Excellency Lt General Earl Cornwallis or officer commanding
the British forces at Portsmouth

Flagg

My Lord

I send you twelve naval prisoners, to wit Lieutenant Williams, Prize Master Vallance, Thos Thomas, Jonah Jenkins, John McCulluch, Ja^s Thomas, Nehemiah Kilby, John Cain, John Lawrence, John Morgan, Thos Holt and Ja^s A Wright. I wou'd wish as many of the *Minirva*'s crew might be sent out in exchange, as they were each captured out of privateers. Shou'd allso be glad to be inform'd whether the men proposed for the three first prisoners I sent in are to be sent out or not.

I have the honor to be
Your Lordship's most obedient servant

J PARKER
Colonel Commandant

Tucker to Cornwallis, 14th August 1781   **6(359): ALS**

Williamsburg
August 14th 1781

The Rt Hon Earl Cornwallis

My Lord

I have just now receiv'd information that Mr Evan Lewis, apothecary's mate in the Continental hospital, and three other men employ'd in the service of the said hospital, being on Saturday night last on the road with a cart coming for some of the hospital stores in this town for the use of the sick at Hickery Neck Church about 12 miles distant, fell in with a party of British troops, who put them under guard and sent them to York. I beg leave to inform your Lordship that the sick at Hickery Neck Church are a part of those who came lately from Charlestown and that they were, on the arrival of your army at York, remov'd from hence before I cou'd get sufficient assurance that our hospital was to be consider'd as under the sanction of a flag. But upon being certified by Major General the Marquis de la Fayette that it was to remain sacred, and seeing the same assented to in a letter from Captain Cooke[18] written by your Lordship's authority, I thought it unnecessary either to remove the remainder of our sick from Williamsburg or to have those at the church convey'd farther into the country. In this situation it was impossible for our officers to do their duty to the sick at both places without being at liberty to go and return at pleasure, which I conceive to be fully authorized by your Lordship's consent.

I presume that this explanation will be thoroughly satisfactory to your Lordship, and as I do not apprehend that Mr Lewis can in any instance be charged with the smallest violation of his parole, I request that you will order him and the men that were with him to be released and the cart restored that they may return immediately to their duty.

I have the honor to be
Your Lordship's most obedient servant

THO^S TUD TUCKER
Physician in Continental hospital

The Governor and Council of Maryland to the British army or naval commander at Portsmouth, 15th August 1781   6(361): LS

Maryland
In Council
Anapolis
15th August 1781

The commanding officer of the British Navy or land forces
      at or near Portsmouth

Sir

A boat, the *Dolphin*, belonging to this State, commanded by Mr William Middleton, was in the month of March last taken by one of the British squadron then in Chesapeak.

Soon afterwards the captain of a French armed vessel brought in here Captain Penny and part of the company of a British vessel, the *Endeavour*, which he had taken on his passage.

Captain Penny represented himself to be related to gentlemen of rank in the British Navy and requested that his parole might be taken to return Middleton in his stead. A copy of his parole we have the honor to enclose, but we have not heard since from Captain Penny, neither has Middleton been released.

---

[18] Captain Robert Cooke, a British commissary of prisoners.

We request, sir, that enquiry may be made and that Middleton may be released or Penny returned according to the terms of the parole.

We have also to inform you that about the first of July past one of the British barges captured in the mouth of Patuxent a small bay schooner laden with tobacco, on board of which was a young gentleman, Mr James Thomas[19], owner of the vessel and tobacco. His parents, who are people of credit, have heard that he is ill in jail at Portsmouth, and since he was a prisoner badly wounded, and that he suffers for want of the conveniencies of life.

Under these circumstances common humanity induces us to comply with the request of the parents and relations of Mr Thomas in giving the bearer hereof, Lt Colonel John Thomas of the St Mary's militia, permission to go with a flag to endeavour to obtain the release of his brother either on parole or on exchange, at the same time to carry him some money and necessaries for his support and recovery. He will be attended by Doctor Mudd and four hands to navigate the boat.

There are in Maryland several persons who have been taken by the inhabitants, plundering on the shores.

If you think proper to release Mr Thomas, we will immediately release in his stead any British citizen who is a prisoner here in like circumstances.

As we have truly stated the only motives for this address, we have to request that the bearer, who will comply with the formalities required, may be received with the indulgence and respect shewn to flags of truce.

We are, sir,
Your most humble servants

THO S LEE[20]

Enclosure (1)
Penny's parole, 2nd May 1781
6(363): C

I, John Penny, mariner, late commander of the brigantine *Endeavour*, do acknowledge myself a prisoner of war to the State of Maryland and do solemnly promise and engage upon my honor that I will not directly or indirectly say or do any thing that may prejudice or tend to the prejudice of the United States of America or either of them, and I do further promise and engage in the most solemn manner that I will upon my arrival in New York use every endeavour to effect an exchange of William Middleton, late commander of the boat *Dolphin* that belonged to the State of Maryland, in my place and stead, and in case such exchange

---

[19] No information about the Thomases has come to light other than their being an extended family of some importance in St Mary's County, Maryland.

[20] Thomas Sim Lee (1745-1819) was the revolutionary Governor of Maryland, having been elected in 1779.

cannot be accomplished I will immediately return to Anapolis in the said State of Maryland and deliver myself up as a prisoner of war.

Given in Council at Anapolis in the State of Maryland
this second day of May 1781

Signed and sealed in presence of

JOHN PENNY ◯

W^M HYDE
T JOHNSON Jr[21]

Enclosure (2)
Thomas's passport, 14th August 1781   *6(365): DS*

Flag of truce

The commanding officer of the British Navy or land forces
   at or near Portsmouth

The bearer, Lt Colonel John Thomas of militia, is permitted to pass with a flag of truce to Hampton Road or the nearest station of the British Navy between this place and Portsmouth to get permission of the commanding officer (if found consistent) to visit, if not to send in some money and cloathing to, his brother James Thomas, a prisoner in Virginia, and to obtain his exchange or parole upon the proposals he carries from the Governor and Council of this State should the same be accepted.

There are going with him in a boat Doctor Joseph Mudd and four hands, who are included in the sanction of the flag.

GIVEN at the camp near Anapolis
the 14th day of August 1781

W SMALLWOOD
Major General

---

[21] Thomas Johnson Jr (1732-1819) had been appointed Secretary of the Council of Maryland in 1780, and William Hyde served in a similar capacity. Johnson had been a delegate to the Continental Congress in 1774-6, a member of the Maryland revolutionary convention in 1776, and the revolutionary Governor of Maryland in 1777-9. For several years after the war he would hold legislative, judicial, and executive offices. (Charles Thomson to Thomas Johnson Jr, 20th January 1781, in Paul Hubert Smith et al, eds, *Letters of Delegates to Congress, 1774-1789*, xvi (Library of Congress, 1989); (Joel D Treese and Dorthy J Countryman, *Biographical Directory of the United States Congress 1774-1996* (Cq Pr, 1996))

Cooke to Ewell, 2nd September 1781 $\qquad$ *92(47): ALS*

York brig
James River
2nd September 1781

Captain Ewell
Commissary, American prisoners

Sir

You have Lord Cornwallises permition to goe to York Town as soon as you think propper to vissit the prisoners and also any exchange you may have to mack you can doe it at that time with Mr McCallister.

I am, sir,
Your most obedient humble servant

ROB^T COOKE
Commissary, prisoners

McHenry to Ross, undated $\qquad$ *270(159): AL*

Wednesday

Major Ross
Aide de camp to Lt General Earl Cornwallis etc etc etc

Major McHenry's[22] compliments to Major Ross. There is a Mr Freneau[23] on board the prison ship *Favorite*, who was taken some weeks since in the bay in a small trading vessel. He has refered his situation to me and I have ventured to place it in better hands. As Freneau is a citizen only, I should consider myself obliged to Major Ross if he could be set at liberty. If at any time it is in my power to procure a like indulgence for a British subject, it will give me infinite pleasure.

§ - §

---

[22] Born in Ballymena, Ireland, James McHenry (1753-1816) received a classical education in Dublin before migrating to the American colonies in 1771. He went on to study medicine in Philadelphia, and when the revolutionary war began, he was appointed a surgeon in the Continental medical service. Captured at the fall of Fort Washington, he was exchanged in March 1778 and became a secretary to Washington two months later. Having won the confidence of Washington for his ability and prudence, he transferred to the staff of Lafayette in August 1780. Commissioned a major in May 1781, he was Lafayette's principal aide-de-camp. After the capitulation of Yorktown he would play a prominent part in public affairs, serving, *inter alia*, as Secretary of War between January 1796 and May 1800. From the close of 1802 till his death he lived in retirement on his pleasant estate at Fayetteville near Baltimore. (*DAB*)

[23] Freneau has not been positively identified. He may, for example, have been Peter Freneau (1757-1813), a younger brother of Philip, the American journalist and poet. See Terry W Lipscomb ed, *The Letters of Pierce Butler 1790-1794* (The University of South Carolina Press, 2007), 213n.

CHAPTER 62

Miscellaneous papers

---

1 - Reports of the French fleet

Report from HMS Guadeloupe, 29th August 1781   *6(371): DS*

Remarks on board His Majesty's Ship Guadaloupe

August 29th 1781

Winds   At ½ past 5 pm saw a strange fleet standing in from the southward, to which I made the private signal of Admiral Arbuthnot and at 6 hauled it down and made Sir George Bridges Rodney's, which they did not answer. Ditto[1]. Observed them to

SSE   stand off to the northward – Cape Henry bearing SSE distance about 4 miles at ½ past 6 lost sight of them – At 4 am observed the same fleet standing in. At 5 weigh'd and came to sail. At ½ past made Admiral Arbuthnot's private signal. ¾ past haul'd down Admiral Arbuthnot's and made Sir G B Rodney's. Fired 2 guns, which they did not answer. At 7 observed one of the ships in chace of us to have several signals at

S   her mizen peek. Saw 2 of the fleet lying too with their heads to the northward. At 8 am the fleet still in chace of us. At ½ past only 4 ships in chace, Cape Henry SE, distance 4 leagues. Ditto heard 2 guns fired in the strange fleet and a sloop with a flag at her mast. ¼ before 9 made Admiral Rodney's private signal again. At 9 observ'd the sloop to haul the flag down, and at 20 minutes after, as we did not observe them to answer the signal, hauled it down, the ships still chacing us, the *Loyalist* astern distance about 2 miles – we standing from them. At ¼ before 12 the

---

[1]   *Ditto*: Rodney's signal was also hauled down.

Loyalist close in with the ships in chace. Ditto she fired a gun at the ships chacing her, which they returned. The largest of the ships fired 2 guns, 1 to leeward, the other to windward. At 12 the *Bonetta* ahead firing guns with her top gallant sheets flying. At ¼ past 12 the strange ships hoisted French colours and firing at the *Loyalist*, which she returned. 23 minutes after 12 the firing ceas'd. The French frigate bore away. Ditto ½ past the firing began again. Ditto they shott away the *Loyalist*'s main topmast. At ½ past 12 the *Loyalist* struck — one of the enemy firing at us. 35 minutes past 12 three of the enemy chacing us and 2 lying by the *Loyalist*. 45 minutes past 12 the enemy's ships left off the chace, their force being one 2 decker, 2 frigates and a sloop. The fleet, when first seen, suppos'd to be 25 sail of large ships etc. When last seen this morning, some laying with their heads to the northward and some to the southward.

H ROBINSON[2]

St George to Ross, 7th September 1781   6(382): ALS

September 7th 1781

Major Ross

Dear Major

I beg leave to inform you that I was at Buckroe a little before sundown this evening, accompanied by Mr Tuck[3] of the British Legion, from whence we had a view of James River mouth, all Hampton Rode, the Capes and Horse Shoe.

The ships in sight were two in Hampton Rode, two as low as the Capes, two and a brig, one of which under sail working down, one and the brig at anchor, in the swash[4] of the Horse Shoe, two small vessels near them, and two boats near Willoby's Point.

The inclosed is hardly worth reading.

---

[2]   Commissioned a lieutenant in the Royal Navy on 5th August 1761, Hugh Robinson had been promoted to commander on 10th January 1771 and to post-captain some six years later. The *Guadeloupe*, which he now commanded, was a 28-gun frigate launched at Plymouth in 1763. Bottled up at Yorktown, she would be sunk by fire from the enemy's batteries on the night of 10th to 11th October but would be salvaged by the French. Robinson survived and died a superannuated rear admiral. (Syrett and DiNardo eds, *The Commissioned Sea Officers*, 382; Michael Phillips, 'Ships of the Old Navy 2' (Internet, 24th July 2006))

[3]   John Tuck was fortunate to be still the quartermaster of the British Legion, having been acquitted by court martial in June 1780 of the murder of Samuel Wyley near Camden. While commanding a party sent out to secure stores in the neighbourhood, he was approached out of a wood by Wyley, who attempted to shoot him but whose pistol misfired. After Wyley was taken prisoner, Tuck proceeded to cut him down in questionable circumstances. In 1782 or 1783 he took passage for England. (WO 71/92(111) and WO 12/110(99) (National Archives, Kew))

[4]   *swash*: a passage or channel of water lying between sandbanks or between a sandbank and the shore.

Be pleased to send me a pas for a certain bearer who has been stoped for want of one.

I have the honour to be with the most profound respect
Your unchangable servant

H U St GEORGE

PS

The night of the 4th, morning of the 5th, night of the 5th and morning of the 6th a firing was certainly heard far off outsid the Capes.

St G

Enclosure
Selden to Lowry, undated

6(384): ALS

John Lowry Esq
Back River

Dear Sir

I got home just at day break. Now news here. The French ships have left their station after some fleet or other. Some says it's a fleet from the southward; others say it's possiable to be a fleet from New York. No sertainty of either. I hope if you go or send to York you'll not forget my son Miles to get him to me. I understand he belongs to a white bottom schooner in the harbour. It runs in my head that he is not in the light of a prisoner. The French flat boats are come done the river and are gone to York. It's said three thousand French troops will be landed in Gloster or in its neighbourhood.

I remain, dear sir,
Your very much obliged humble servant

R SELDEN

[*Subscribed*:]

Can you spair me any bay[5]? How much? Send word by Crook.

---

[5]   *bay*: baize, originally a fabric of finer, lighter texture than now, used in warmer countries for articles of clothing, shirts, petticoats etc.

1st Division

Neptune	)	Fregate
Provence	)	
	)	Astrée
Auguste	)	
Magnanime	)	

2nd Division

Romulus	)	
	)	
Duc de Bourgogne	)	
	)	Andromaque
Conquerant	)	
	)	
Northumberland	)	

3rd Division

Saggittaire	)
	)
Hector	)
	)
Sceptre	)
	)
Hercule	)

4th Division

L'Eveillé	)	
	)	
Glorieuz	)	
	)	Gentille
L'Esprit	)	
	)	
Solitaire	)	

5th Division

Marseillois	)	
	)	
Palmier	)	
	)	Railleuse
Ville de Paris	)	
	)	
Souverain	)	

6th Division

Caton	)	
	)	
Zelé	)	
	)	L'Aigrette
Destin	)	
	)	
Ardent	)	

7th Division

Le Jason	)	
	)	
Le Bourgogne	)	
	)	Diligente
Le Cæsar	)	
	)	
Le Vaillant	)	

1.	110
4.	80
20.	74
9.	64
1.	60

		1.	50
8th Division		1.	44

Le Citoyen)
)
Le Reflechi)
)
Le Languedoc)   Concorde
)
Le Diademe)
)
L'Experiment)

9th Division

Triton)
)
La Victoire)
)   Surveillante
Le Scipion)
)
Pluton)

Action[6]			*Guns*	
1.	110	E.[7]	1344
3.	80	F.[8]	1806
1.	64		
1.	60		
18.	74		

§ - §

---

[6] *Action*: off the Capes of Virginia, 5th September, between de Grasse and Graves.

[7] *E*: English.

[8] *F*: French.

2 - The death of Daniel McDowall (McDougall)

Weeks to the commanding officer of Gloucester,   *93(22): ALS*
30th August 1781

Botetourt
30th of [August] 81

To the commanding officer of the British Army
Gloucester Town

Flag

Sir

The lenity with which the British have for some time treated those unfortunate men whom the fortune of warr put into their power lead me to beleive they no longer retain'd that inveteted hatred which at the begining of this unhappy dispute excited them to many acts of cruelty, and that the unparell'd good usage with which the Americans have ever treated their prisoners have convinc'd them that they were at warr with a nation who endevour'd by humanity and affection to the unfortunate in some measure to aleviat its horrors, but what construction can be put on the most horrid barbarity exercised on the body of Daniel McDowall, a citazen of this State, by a party of British troops on Wednesday morning? The said McDowall was taken soon after the Britis troops landed in this county and parol'd. He was employing himself in his daily labour for the suport of his family when the Britis troops was fir'd on by a party of Americans. They immediately accus'd McDowall of giving inteligence, which I do declare on the word of a gentleman and on which I still hold dearer, the faith of a Christian, to be false, nor do I know of his ever in any manner breaking his parole. The prayers and tears of two small children and a pregnant wife cou'd not move to compassion the hearts of these barbarous wretches, who shot him, on whom those three unfortunate creatures depended for their daily bread, four times and then to compleat their work stab'd him with their bayonets. It is the officer commanding this party or the men who commited the deed that I in the name of the United States do demand that they may suffer the punishment due for such a crime and to prevent the sheding of innocent blood which retaliation demands, and which shall be executed in case of a refusal on some prisoner now in our hands, whose life you have in your power to save. If the men who comitted this act of cruelty should belong to the navy, as I expect they do by their coming in boats, please to shew this to the Comodore or the captain of the shipp to which they belong. Should be glad of an answear by the bearer of this.

I am your humble servant

A WEEKS
Major commanding light infantry[9]

---

[9] By now a field officer, Amos Weeks had been serving in mid 1778 as a captain in the revolutionary militia of Princess Anne County. (*Va Military Records*, 526; Gwathmey, *Historical Register*, 814)

The Rt Hon Lt General Earl Cornwallis
Commanding Virginia

My Lord

In consequence of your Lordship's commands I have made every enquiry into the unfortunate business of the 29th instant in which Daniel McDugall, an inhabitant upon parole, lost his life.

By the information of the widow of the deceast, and of Mrs Dunlop at whose house this affair happen'd, it appears that betwixt forty and fifty sailors landed from four boats before day break that morning under Mrs Dunlop's house, that they posted a guard in an orchard behind the house and were employed in getting stock when several shots were fired from the corner of the wood near to the orchard. Neither of the women can say by whom these shots were fired, but imagine it to have been by some of the sailors that had stragled towards the wood.

The consequence of these shots being fired was that the sailors got immediatly into very great confusion, threatn'd and abused the people about the house, and shot and bayoneted the deceast (who was at that time assisting his wife in milking the cows for the sailors), accusing him of his being acquainted that there was a party of the rebels there. The women declare that no party of the rebels were seen about that place either before nor after the affair happen'd.

From the information of Lieutenant Dunlop[10] of the Queen's Rangers it appears that he was detach'd by Lt Colonel Simcoe with four light horsemen to find out what the fireing was. By the time he had got to the house of the Widow Dunlop the sailors had left that place and were gone to their boats, that he found Daniel McDugall upon the ground, bayoneted in two places and shot through the thigh and, tho alive, not able to speak to him. Mr Dunlop immediatly enquir'd who had done this and was inform'd that it was done by a party of British seamen who were shooting hogs and that they had just gone to their boats, upon which he went down to the water side and found them just gone off. He used every endeavour to get the officer in the boat to come and speak to him (by pulling of his hatt, showing him his sash and informing him that he belong'd to the Queen's Rangers), in place of which he order'd the men in the boats to pull up their starboard oars and fired upon him several times. Mr Dunlop likeways says that as the Jagars and greatest part of the Queen's Rangers were

---

[10] Charles Dunlap is said to have been a mere lad of thirteen years when he was commissioned an ensign in the infantry of the Queen's Rangers in January 1777. Promoted to lieutenant in the corps' infantry eight months later, he had recently played a distinguished part in the repulse of the enemy at Spencer's Ordinary on 26th June, a part for which Simcoe would make a flattering mention of him several years later. When the regiment was disbanded at the peace, he was placed on the British half-pay list. During the war he lost three brothers, one of whom was James (see vol I, p 74, note 5), a captain seconded to Ferguson's corps who was later promoted to major in command of his own troop of irregular horse. (David Breakenridge Read, *The Life and Times of Gen. John Graves Simcoe...* (G Virtue Publishing Co, 1890), 103; Raymond, 'British American Corps'; WO 65/164(31) (National Archives, Kew); Simcoe's letter in *The Gentleman's Magazine*, January 1787)

past Mrs Dunlop's house before the fireing began, he believes that the sailors were alarm'd by the flanking party of the Queen's Rangers, which they took for rebels.

I have the honor to be with the greatest respect, my Lord,
Your Lordship's most obedient and very humble servant

THOMAS DUNDAS
Lt Colonel, 80th Regiment

§ - §

3 - Other papers

British prisoners delivered under the cartel, 29th July 1781   6(375): D

Portsmouth
July 29th 81

Return of British prisoners exchanged and who arrived within the lines this day			
Artillery	5	South Carolinians	1
7th Regiment	5	Militia	2
71st ditto	9		Total 51
20th ditto	1	*Officers*	
21st ditto	2	Lieutenant Varnol	Legion
63rd ditto	4	Cornet White	ditto
64th ditto	1	Volunteer Wood	ditto
17th Dragoons	1	Captain Curzon	Skinner's
Legion	2	Ensign Swartz	ditto
King's American Regiment	2	Ensign McKeithan	North Carolinians
Prince of Wales	3	Lieutenant Murphy	South Carolinians
Volunteers of Ireland	1	Quarter Master Emming	D' Lancey
Delancey	1	Ensign Old	ditto
Skinner's	7	Ensign Boyle	ditto
North Carolinians	2	Volunteer Sinclair	
Yagers	1		
Queen's Rangers	1		

Balance of prisoners due under the cartel, undated 91(47): D

Prisoners delivered the Americans		735
Credit received by Doctor Hill at Guilfourd	61	
Received by Mr McCalister at James Town	59	
By Doctor Frazer's receapt at Charlestown	467	
Received at James Town by R Cooke	52	639
Ballance due the British Army		96

Notification to inhabitants in the vicinity of Yorktown, 9th August 1781 101(34): C

Notification

The inhabitants of Elizabeth City, York and Warwick Counties, being in the power of His Majesty's troops, are hereby ordered to repair to Head Quarters at York Town on or before the 20th day of August to deliver up their arms and to give their paroles that they will not in future take any part against His Majesty's interest. And they are likewise directed to bring to market the provisions that they can spare, for which they will be paid reasonable prices in ready money.

AND notice is hereby given that those who fail in complying with this order will be imprisoned when taken and their corn and cattle will be seized for the use of the troops.

GIVEN at Head Quarters at York Town
this 9th day of August 1781

By order of Earl Cornwallis

HENRY HALDANE
Aide-de-camp

Robertson to Cornwallis, 22nd August 1781 6(317): LS

New York
22nd August 1781

Earl Cornwallis

My Lord

It having been represented to me that the privateer schooner *Surprise*, Captain Ross of this port, had brought off from Virginia several articles of plate, household furniture and Negroes the property of Mr Ralph Wormley[11] and other inhabitants of that province, whose loyalty has been certified to me by many respectable characters here, I have with the assistance of the owners of the privateer *Surprise* endeavoured to have all such property collected and have ordered permission to be given to the sloop *Sally*, John Swift master, to proceed with such Negroes etc that have been recovered to York Town in Virginia with orders to deliver this to your Lordship and at same time to lay before you his clearances.

I have ever been of opinion that the distressing and plundering of loyal subjects residing among the rebels should on all occasions be discountenanced and, whenever opportunity offer'd, be redressed.

Having every reason to be convinced that my sentiments on this head coincides with your Lordship's, I have no hesitation in requesting your Lordship to give such orders as you may think necessary to have the Negroes etc forwarded from York Town to their respective owners.

I have the honor to be with the greatest respect, my Lord,
Your Lordship's most obedient and most humble servant

JAMES ROBERTSON

Booth to assistant commissaries of captures 30th September 1781

6(387): CS

Yorktown
the 30th September 1781

To Mr A B

Sir

You are at all times diligently to procure information concerning provisions, spirits, and whatever may be necessary for the subsistence of His Majesty's army.

When you shall receive any such information, you are as soon as possible to view and inspect the same, and to make a moderate estimate of what you shall find, and to give an account thereof forthwith to me or to Head Quarters in case of my absence.

You are at all times to secure the persons of your informants, especially if upon examination you shall observe them to hesitate or prevaricate, for in that case you may be assured they mean to impose upon you. These people may generally be made very useful as

---

[11] The Hon Ralph Wormeley (1744-1806) of 'Rosegill', Middlesex County, was a member of one of the most distinguished and wealthy families in Virginia. Educated in England at Eton and Cambridge, he was on his return appointed a member of HM Council for Virginia in 1771. Of the loyalist persuasion he took no active part in the revolutionary war but suffered much from fines and imprisonment. After the war he continued to reside at 'Rosegill' until his death. (Donald Jackson ed, *Diaries of George Washington* (University Press of Virginia, 1978), iii, 54; The Ralph Wormeley Papers, Virginia Historical Society)

guides, but in order to get themselves released from the service which you shall devote them to they will frequently tell you of others who know the country and roads better than themselves. In such case it will always be best to secure both persons, let their complaints be what they will, and you will generally find this rule to succeed well.

You will always on a march endeavor to be early on the encamping ground, near where you shall find Head Quarters fixed, in order that I may be enabled the more readily to find you to give you special instructions if any extraordinary occurrence shall intervene; and you will with care and industry procure the earliest and best information in your power of all grist mills in that neighborhood. Observe to learn minutely their situation, distance, the nature of the roads to them respectively, and to get good guides. You will generally find Negroes, at the house where Head Quarters will be, to be useful and intelligent in these matters, and here a few fair words and the exercise of a little flattery (if you have any) will sometimes have a very good effect, as well with white as with black people, and your own judgment with a little attention and discernment will soon teach you when to administer it properly.

When you shall go to any mill, never fail to be very vigilant and to use great attention. Observe circumspectly the repairs of such mill. Learn its force, what supply of water can be depended on, what stores are within, how such mill can be supplied with grain or corn, how near and thro' what kind of roads, what quantity she will grind an hour — and here observe well that in all these sort of estimations and reckonings take care to be moderate and never to exceed the real quantity, for it is a very silly and a treachrous maxim to overrate any stores for an army.

In general you will find that an hogshead well paked with meal will hold near 700 lbs weight and that the barrels of flour of this country will seldom average more than 200 lbs weight but generally not more than 190 lbs weight.

You will always find yourself imposed upon by the Quarter Master General's people respecting the goodness of their waggons and teams, but you will always observe that, let them say what they will to the contrary, their waggons never did, nor ever will, carry more than six barrels of flour on an average or otherwise 1,300 lbs weight of any other article. And always take especial care to have good sentrys placed over the provisions, especially the spirits, for, with all your vigilance and care, the waggoners will eternally commit little pilferings on the public stores. They are invincible in these kind of thefts, and what contributes greatly to their security is the wilful blindness of their conductors, who may too justly be compared to receivers of stolen goods.

You will never suffer any cloaths or other baggage, especialy women's, to be carried in the same waggons with provisions, for this conduct only gives the owners a specious pretended right of access to these waggons at all times in the night, whereby they escape the vigilance of the sentrys and continually steal the public stores with impunity.

Whenever you shall be appointed to go on business with any waggons in charge, you must make the waggoners obey your instructions in all cases without any altercation, except what shall regard the conducting of their teams only.

If ever you shall be appointed to issue provisions or spirits to the army, you will be careful to obey the following instruction and never dispense with it on any pretence, viz: be sure always to take a receipt for such provision or spirits signed by the proper officer before you issue the same, and never trust to the fair tales of quarter master serjeants, for, since it will be their intrest, so they will most assuredly never fail to cheat you.

And finally, it is most essentially necessary that at all times you shall be well provided with pen, ink, and a small memorandum book, for these things, properly used, will aid you more in the execution of your duty than, without experience, you can possibly be aware of. Your memory then will never be fettred with doubts, your reports will more safly be relied on, and upon the whole all your ASSISTANCE will be stamped with certainty and precision; but, without a strict observance of this rule, you may rest assured that all your other diligence and industry will neither answer the public nor any other just expectation.

BB

[*Superscribed*:]

The following instructions are indispensably necessary for the observance of an assistant commissary of captures in Mr Booth's line of the departments. They are not the wild branches of whimsical theory but the pure result of sober experience, and they will, if steadily attended to and executed, rarely fail of procuring such supplies as will generally secure the approbation and smiles of the army.

[*Subscribed*:]

Three fair copies of these instructions were made and delivered to my assistants, in expectation of another campaign, at the beginning of the siege of little York.

§ - §

CHAPTER 63

The capitulation of Yorktown and Gloucester

1 - Correspondence between Cornwallis and Washington

Cornwallis to Washington, 17th October 1781[1]   *74(118): C*

York in Virginia
17th October 1781

His Excellency General Washington
Commanding the combined forces of France and America etc etc etc

Sir

I propose a cessation of hostilities for twenty four hours, and that two officers may be appointed by each side to meet at Mr Moore's house to settle terms for the surrender of the posts of York and Gloucester.

I have the honour to be, sir,
Your most obedient and most humble servant

CORNWALLIS

---

[1] Published with no differences in Stevens, *Clinton-Cornwallis Controversy*, ii, 189.

Washington to Cornwallis, 17th October 1781[2]

74(120): LS

Camp before York
17th October 1781

His Excellency Lt General Earl Cornwallis

My Lord

I have had the honor of receiving your Lordship's letter of this date.

An ardent desire to spare the further effusion of blood will readily incline me to listen to such terms for the surrender of your posts and garrisons at York and Gloucester as are admissable.

I wish, previous to the meeting of commissioners, that your Lordship's proposals in writing may be sent to the American lines, for which purpose a suspension of hostilities during two hours from the delivery of this letter will be granted.

I have the honor to be, my Lord,
Your Lordship's most obedient and most humble servant

G^{O} WASHINGTON

Cornwallis to Washington, 17th October 1781[3]

74(122): C

York in Virginia
17th October 1781
½ past 4 pm

His Excellency General Washington
Commanding the combined forces of France and America etc etc etc

Sir

I have this moment been honoured with Your Excellency's letter dated this day.

The time limited for sending my answer will not admit of entering into the detail of articles, but the basis of my proposals will be that the garrisons of York and Gloucester shall be prisoners of war with the customary honours, and, for the convenience of the individuals which I have the honour to command, that the British shall be sent to Britain, and the Germans to Germany, under engagement not to serve against France, America or their allies

---

[2]   Published with no differences in Stevens, op cit, ii, 190.

[3]   Published with one inconsequential difference in Stevens, op cit, ii, 192.

untill released or regularly exchanged, that all arms and publick stores shall be delivered up to you, but that the usual indulgence of side arms to officers and of retaining private property shall be granted to officers and soldiers and that the interests of several individuals in civil capacities and connected with us shall be attended to.

If your Excellency thinks that a continuance of the suspension of hostilities will be necessary to transmit your answer, I shall have no objection to the hour that you may propose.

I have the honour to be, sir,
Your most obedient and most humble servant

CORNWALLIS

Washington to Cornwallis, 18th October 1781[4]

74(124): LS

Camp before York
18th October 1781

His Excellency Lt General Earl Cornwallis

My Lord

To avoid unnecessary discussions and delays I shall at once, in answer to your Lordship's letter of yesterday, declare the general basis upon which a definitive treaty of capitulation may take place.

The garrisons of York and Gloucester, including the seamen, as you propose shall be received prisoners of war. The condition annexed of sending the British and German troops to the parts of Europe to which they respectively belong is inadmissable. Instead of this, they will be marched to such parts of the country as can most conveniently provide for their subsistence, and the benevolent treatment of prisoners which is invariably observed by the Americans will be extended to them. The same honors will be granted to the surrendering army as were granted to the garrison of Charlestown.

The shipping and boats in the two harbors with all their guns, stores, tackling, furniture and apparel shall be delivered in their present state to an officer of the navy appointed to take possession of them.

The artillery, arms, accoutrements, military chest and public stores of every denomination shall be delivered unimpaired to the heads of departments to which they respectively belong.

The officers shall be indulged in retaining their side arms and the officers and soldiers may preserve their baggage and effects – with this reserve, that property taken in the country will be reclaimed.

---

[4] Published with two inconsequential differences in Stevens, op cit, ii, 193.

With regard to the individuals in civil capacities whose interests your Lordship wishes may be attended to, untill they are more particularly described, nothing definitive can be settled.

I have to add that I expect the sick and wounded will be supplied with their own hospital stores and be attended by British surgeons particularly charged with the care of them.

Your Lordship will be pleased to signify your determination either to accept or reject the proposals now offered, in the course of two hours from the delivery of this letter, that commissioners may be appointed to digest the articles of capitulation, or a renewal of hostilities may take place.

I have the honor to be, my Lord,
Your Lordship's most obedient and humble servant

Gᵒ WASHINGTON

Cornwallis to Washington, 18th October 1781[5]   74(126): Df

York in Virginia
18th October 1781

His Excellency General Washington
Commanding the combined forces of France and America etc etc etc

Sir

I agree to open a treaty of capitulation upon the basis of the garrisons of York and Gloucester, including seamen, being prisoners of war, without annexing the condition of their being sent to Europe, but I expect to receive a compensation in arranging the articles of capitulation for the surrender of Gloucester in its present state of defence.

I shall in particular desire that the *Bonetta* sloop of war may be left entirely at my disposal from the hour that the capitulation is signed to receive an aide de camp to carry my dispatches to Sir Henry Clinton and such soldiers as I may think proper to send as passengers in her, to be manned with fifty men of her own crew and to be permitted to sail without examination when my dispatches are ready, engaging on my part that the ship shall be brought back and delivered to you if she escapes the dangers of the sea, that the crew and soldiers shall be accounted for in future exchanges, and that she shall carry off no officer without your consent nor publick property of any kind. And I shall likewise desire that the traders and inhabitants may preserve their property and that no person may be punished or molested for having joined the British troops.

If you chuse to proceed to negociation on these grounds, I shall appoint two field officers of my army to meet two officers from you, at any time and place that you think proper, to digest the articles of capitulation.

---

[5] Published with inconsequential differences in Stevens, op cit, ii, 195.

I have the honour to be, sir,
Your most obedient and most humble servant

CORNWALLIS

§ - §

2 - State of the army in Virginia, 18th October 1781
103(35): D

State of the Army in Virginia under the command of Lt General Earl Cornwallis, October 18th 1781			
	Rank and file present and fit for duty	*Rank and file : sick and wounded present*	*Total*
Garrison of York:			
Royal Artillery	127	40	167
Guards	323	167	490
Light infantry	577	209	786
17th Regiment	74	114	188
23rd Regiment	67	97	164
33rd Regiment	141	37	178
43rd Regiment	94	168	262
71st Regiment	163	65	228
76th Regiment	427	134	561
80th Regiment	171	269	440
Two battalions of Anspach	718	191	909
Prince Hereditaire	232	135	367
Regiment de Bose	159	115	274
Total	3273	1741	4014[6]

---

[6] *4014*: 5014.

Garrison of Gloucester:			
Detachment of the 80th Regiment	84	-	84
Queen's Rangers	268	119	387
British Legion etc	208	24	232
Yagers	42	5	47
23rd & 82nd light companies	44	26	70
North Carolina Volunteers	98	18	116
Total	744	192	936
TOTAL	4017	1933	5950

§ - §

3 - Articles of capitulation, 19th October 1781[7]
74(128): DS

Articles of capitulation settled between his Excellency General Washington, Commander in Chief of the combined forces of America and France, his Excellency the Count de Rochambeau, Lt General of the armies of the King of France, Great Cross of the Royal and Military Order of St Louis, commanding the auxiliary troops of His Most Christian Majesty in America, and his Excellency the Count de Grasse, Lt General of the naval armies of His Most Christian Majesty, Commander of the Order of St Louis, commanding in chief the naval army of France in the Chesapeak, on the one part and the Rt Hon Earl Cornwallis, Lt General of His Britannick Majesty's forces, commanding the garrisons of York and Gloucester, and Thomas Symonds Esq, commanding His Britannick Majesty's naval forces in York River in Virginia, on the other part.

Article 1st   *Article 1st*

The garrisons of York and Gloucester,   Granted.
including the officers and seamen of His

---

[7]   Published in Stevens, op cit, ii, 199. There is a material difference in the general format, together with another in the punctuation of article 8. Other differences are inconsequential.

Britannic Majesty's ships as well as other mariners, to surrender themselves prisoners of war to the combined forces of America and France. The land troops to remain prisoners to the United States. The navy to the naval army of His Most Christian Majesty.

Article 2nd

The artillery, arms, accoutrements, military chest, and public stores of every denomination shall be delivered unimpaired to the heads of departments appointed to receive them.

Article 3rd

At 12 o'clock this day the two redoubts on the left flank of York to be delivered, the one to a detachment of American infantry, the other to a detachment of French grenadiers. The garrison of York will march out to a place to be appointed in front of the posts at 2 o'clock precisely with shouldered arms, colours cased and drums beating a British or German march. They are then to ground their arms and return to their encampment, where they will remain untill they are dispatched to the places of their destination. Two works on the Gloucester side will be delivered at one o'clock to detachments of French and American troops appointed to possess them. The garrison will march out at three o'clock in the afternoon, the cavalry with their swords drawn, trumpets sounding, and the infantry in the manner prescribed for the garrison of York. They are likewise to return to their encampment untill they can be finally marched off.

Article 2nd

Granted.

Article 3rd

Granted.

118

Article 4th

Officers are to retain their side arms. Both officers and soldiers to keep their private property of every kind, and no part of their baggage or papers to be at any time subject to search or inspection. The baggage and papers of officers and soldiers taken during the seige to be likewise preserved for them. It is understood that any property obviously belonging to the inhabitants of these States, in the possession of the garrison, shall be subject to be reclaimed.

Article 5th

The soldiers to be kept in Virginia, Maryland or Pennsylvania, and as much by regiments as possible, and supplied with the same rations of provision as are allowed to soldiers in the service of America; a field officer from each nation, to wit British, Anspach and Hessian, and other officers on parole, in the proportion of one to fifty men, to be allowed to reside near their respective regiments, to visit them frequently and be witnesses of their treatment — and that these officers may receive and deliver cloathing and other necessaries for them, for which passports are to be granted when applied for.

Article 6th

The general, staff and other officers not employed as mentioned in the above article, and who chuse it, to be permitted to go on parole to Europe, to New York, or to any other American maritime posts at present in the possession of the British forces at their own option, and proper vessels to be granted by the Count de Grasse to carry them under flags of truce to New York within ten days from this date, if possible, and they to reside in a district to be agreed upon hereafter until they embark. The officers of the civil departments of the army and navy to be

Article 4th

Granted.

Article 5th

Granted.

Article 6th

Granted.

119

included in this article. Passports to go by land to be granted to those to whom vessels cannot be furnished.

Article 7th

Officers to be allowed to keep soldiers as servants according to the common practice of the service. Servants not soldiers are not to be considered as prisoners and are to be allowed to attend their masters.

Article 8th

The *Bonetta* sloop of war to be equipped and navigated by its present captain and crew, and left entirely at the disposal of Lord Cornwallis from the hour that the capitulation is signed, to receive an aide de camp to carry dispatches to Sir Henry Clinton — and such soldiers as he may think proper to send to New York to be permitted to sail without examination when his dispatches are ready. His Lordship engaging on his part that the ship shall be delivered to the order of the Count de Grasse if she escapes the dangers of the seas — that she shall not carry off any public stores — Any part of the crew that may be deficient on her return and the soldiers passengers to be accounted for on her delivery.

Article 9th

The traders are to preserve their property and to be allowed three months to dispose of or remove them — and those traders are not to be considered as prisoners of war.

Article 10th

Natives or inhabitants of different parts of this country at present in York or Gloucester are not to be punished on account of having joined the British Army.

Article 7th

Granted.

Article 8th

Granted.

Article 9th

The traders will be allowed to dispose of their effects, the allied army having the right of pre-emption. The traders to be considered as prisoners of war upon parole.

Article 10th

This article cannot be assented to, being altogether of civil resort.

Article 11th

Proper hospitals to be furnished for the sick and wounded. They are to be attended by their own surgeons on parole, and they are to be furnished with medicines and stores from the American hospitals.

Article 12th

Waggons to be furnished to carry the baggage of the officers attending the soldiers and to surgeons when travelling on account of the sick —— attending the hospitals — at public expence.

Article 13th

The shipping and boats in the two harbors with all their stores, guns, tackling and apparel shall be delivered up in their present state to an officer of the navy appointed to take possession of them — previously unloading the private property, part of which had been on board for security during the seige.

Article 14th

No article of the capitulation to be infringed on pretext of reprisal, and if there be any doubtful expressions in it, they are to be interpreted according to the common meaning and acceptation of the words.

CORNWALLIS

THO⁵ SYMONDS

Article 11th

The hospital stores now in York and Gloucester shall be delivered for the use of the British sick and wounded. Passports will be granted for procuring them farther supplies from New York as occasion may require. And proper hospitals will be furnished for the reception of the sick and wounded of the two garrisons.

Article 12th

They will be furnished if possible.

Article 13th

Granted.

Article 14th

Granted.

Done in the trenches before York, October 19th 1781

G⁰ WASHINGTON

LE Cᵀᴱ DE ROCHAMBEAU

LE Cᵀᴱ DE BARRAS en mon nom et celuj du cᵗᵉ de Grasse

PART TWELVE

The last days of Cornwallis in Virginia

His return to New York

20th October to 18th November 1781

CHAPTER 64

Miscellaneous correspondence etc

---

1 - Cornwallis to Clinton

Cornwallis to Clinton, 20th October 1781[1]   *74(105): C*

York Town
Virginia
20th October 1781

His Excellency Sir Henry Clinton KB etc etc etc

Sir

I have the mortification to inform your Excellency that I have been forced to give up the posts of York and Gloucester and to surrender the troops under my command by capitulation on the 19th instant as prisoners of war to the combined forces of America and France.

I never saw this post in a very favourable light, but when I found I was to be attacked in it in so unprepared a state by so powerfull an army and artillery, nothing but the hopes of relief would have induced me to attempt its defence, for I would either have endeavoured to escape to New York by rapid marches from the Gloucester side immediately on the arrival of General Washington's troops at Williamsburgh or I would, notwithstanding the disparity of numbers, have attacked them in the open field, where it might have been just possible that fortune would have favoured the gallantry of the handfull of troops under my command. But

---

[1]   Published with three material and other inconsequential differences in Stevens, *Clinton-Cornwallis Controversy*, ii, 205.

being assured by your Excellency's letters that every possible means would be tried by the navy and army to relieve us, I could not think myself at liberty to venture upon either of those desperate attempts. Therefore, after remaining for two days in a strong position in front of this place in hopes of being attacked, upon observing that the enemy were taking measures which could not fail of turning my left flank in a short time, and receiving on the second evening your letter of the 24th of September informing me that the relief would sail about the 5th of October, I withdrew within the works on the night of the 29th of September, hoping by the labour and firmness of the soldiers to protract the defence untill you could arrive. Every thing was to be expected from the spirit of the troops, but every disadvantage attended their labour, as the works were to be continued under the enemy's fire and our stock of intrenching tools, which did not much exceed 400 when we began to work in the latter end of August, was now much diminished.

The enemy broke ground on the night of the 30th and constructed on that night and the two following days and nights two redoubts, which, with some works that had belonged to our outward position, occupied a gorge between two creeks or ravines, which come from the river on each side of the town. On the night of the 6th of October they made their first parallel, extending from its right on the river to a deep ravine on the left, nearly opposite to the center of this place, and embracing our whole left at the distance of 600 yards. Having perfected this parallel, their batteries opened on the evening of the 9th against our left, and other batteries fired at the same time against a redoubt advanced over the creek upon our right and defended by about 120 men of the 23rd Regiment and marines, who maintained that post with uncommon gallantry. The fire continued incessant, from heavy cannon and from mortars and howitzers throwing shells from 8 to 16 inches, untill all our guns on the left were silenced, our works much damaged, and our loss of men considerable. On the night of the 11th they began their second parallel about 300 yards nearer to us. The troops being much weakened by sickness as well as by the fire of the besiegers, and observing that the enemy had not only secured their flanks but proceeded in every respect with the utmost regularity and caution, I could not venture so large sorties as to hope from them any considerable effect, but otherwise I did every thing in my power to interrupt this work by opening new embrazures for guns and keeping up a constant fire with all the howitzers and small mortars that we could man. On the evening of the 14th they assaulted and carried two redoubts that had been advanced about 300 yards for the purpose of delaying their approaches and covering our left flank, and during the night included them in their second parallel, on which they continued to work with the utmost exertion. Being perfectly sensible that our works could not stand many hours after the opening of the batteries of that parallel, we not only continued a constant fire with all our mortars and every gun that could be brought to bear upon it but a little before day break on the morning of the 16th I ordered a sortie of about 350 men under the direction of Lt Colonel Abercrombie to attack two batteries, which appeared to be in the greatest forwardness, and to spike the guns. A detachment of Guards with the 80th company of grenadiers under the command of Lt Colonel Lake[2] attacked the one, and one of light

---

[2] Gerard Lake (1744-1808) had spent his entire service in the 1st Regiment of Foot Guards (the Grenadier Guards). Commissioned an ensign on 9th May 1758, he saw service in German campaigns and was promoted to lieutenant on 3rd June 1762. At the beginning of 1776 he became a captain, a rank which carried with it a lt colonelcy, and was appointed to the household of the Prince of Wales, maintaining a close relationship with him, at least in the early years. In 1780 he came out to North America and formed part of the Brigade of Guards sent south under O'Hara, taking part with it in the winter campaign and the operations in Virginia. Paroled at Yorktown (see vol

infantry under the command of Major Armstrong[3] attacked the other, and both succeeded by forcing the redoubts that covered them, spiking eleven guns, and killing or wounding about 100 of the French troops, who had the guard of that part of the trenches, and with little loss on our side. This action, tho' extremely honourable to the officers and soldiers who executed it, proved of little publick advantage, for the cannon, having been spiked in a hurry, were soon rendered fit for service again, and before dark the whole parallel and batteries appeared to be nearly complete. At this time we knew that there was no part of the whole front attacked on which we could show a single gun, and our shells were nearly expended. I therefore had only to chuse between preparing to surrender next day or endeavouring to get off with the greatest part of the troops, and I determined to attempt the latter, reflecting that, tho' it should prove unsuccessfull in its immediate object, it might at least delay the enemy in the prosecution of further enterprizes. Sixteen large boats were prepared and upon other pretexts were ordered to be in readiness to receive troops precisely at ten o'clock. With these I hoped to pass the infantry during the night, abandoning our baggage and leaving a detachment to capitulate for the town's people and the sick and wounded, on which subject a letter was ready to be delivered to General Washington. After making my arrangements with the utmost secrecy, the light infantry, greatest part of the Guards, and part of the 23rd Regiment embarked at the hour appointed and most of them landed at Gloucester, but at this critical moment the weather, from being moderate and calm, changed to a most violent storm of wind and rain and drove all the boats, some of which had troops on board, down the river. It was soon evident that the intended passage was impracticable, and the absence of the boats rendered it equally impossible to bring back the troops that had passed, which I had ordered about two o'clock in the morning. In this situation, with my little force divided, the enemy's batteries opened at day break. The passage between this place and Gloucester was much exposed, but, the boats having now returned, they were ordered to bring back the troops that had passed during the night, and they joined us in the forenoon without much loss. Our works in the mean time were going to ruin, and not having been able to strengthen them by abbatis nor in any other manner but by a slight fraizing, which the enemy's artillery were demolishing wherever they fired, my opinion entirely coincided with that of the engineer and principal officers of the army that they were in many parts very assailable in the forenoon and that by the continuance of the same fire for a few hours longer they would be in such a state as to render it desperate with our numbers to attempt to maintain them. We at that time could not fire a single gun; only one eight inch and little more than 100 cohorn shells remained; a

V, p 79, note 11), he became principal equerry to the Prince of Wales and an MP. From 1796 to 1799 he went on to serve as a lt general commanding in Ireland, where he gained a reputation for harshness in suppressing the United Irishmen and the rebellion in the south. In January 1801 he landed at Calcutta as Commander-in-Chief in India and from 1803 to 1805 was involved in the Second Anglo-Maratha War, the climax of his military career. Having been created a baron in 1804, he returned to England in 1807 and was elevated to a viscountcy. Shortly afterwards, having contracted a violent cold, he died at his residence in Lower Brook Street, London, and was buried at Aston Clinton, Buckinghamshire. (*ODNB*; *Army Lists*)

[3] Commissioned an ensign in the 36th Regiment on 9th April 1756, Thomas Armstrong was promoted to lieutenant in the 64th Regiment on 4th December 1767 and to captain there on 2nd February 1770. He transferred to the majority in the 17th Foot on 5th October 1778. He was now attached to the light infantry, which consisted of the light companies of the British regiments under Cornwallis's immediate command, together with the light company of the 82nd Regiment. (*Army Lists*)

diversion by the French ships of war that lay at the mouth of York River was to be expected[4]; our numbers had been diminished by the enemy's fire but particularly by sickness; and the strength and spirits of those in the works were much exhausted by the fatigue of constant watching and unremitting duty. Under all these circumstances I thought it would have been wanton and inhuman to the last degree to sacrifice the lives of this small body of gallant soldiers, who had ever behaved with so much fidelity and courage, by exposing them to an assault, which from the numbers and precautions of the enemy could not fail to succeed. I therefore proposed to capitulate, and I have the honour to inclose to your Excellency the copy of the correspondence between General Washington and me on that subject and the terms of capitulation agreed upon. I sincerely lament that better could not be obtained, but I have neglected nothing in my power to alleviate the misfortune and distress of both officers and soldiers. The men are well clothed and provided with necessaries and I trust will be regularly supplied by the means of the officers that are permitted to remain with them. The treatment in general that we have received from the enemy since our surrender has been perfectly good and proper; but the kindness and attention that has been shewn to us by the French officers in particular, their delicate sensibility of our situation, their generous and pressing offers of money both publick and private to any amount, has really gone beyond what I can possibly describe and will, I hope, make an impression on the breast of every British officer whenever the fortune of war should put any of them into our power.

Although the event has been so unfortunate, the patience of the soldiers in bearing the greatest fatigues, and their firmness and intrepidity under a persevering fire of shot and shells that I believe has not often been exceeded, deserved the highest admiration and praise. A successfull defence, however, in our situation was perhaps impossible, for the place could only be reckoned an intrenched camp, subject in most places to enfilade, and the ground in general so disadvantageous that nothing but the necessity of fortifying it as a post to protect the navy could have induced any person to erect works upon it. Our force diminished daily by sickness and other losses and was reduced, when we offered to capitulate, on this side to little more than 3,200 rank and file fit for duty, including officers' servants and artificers, and at Gloucester about 600 including cavalry. The enemy's army consisted of upwards of[5] 8,000 French, nearly as many Continentals,[6] and 5,000 militia.[7] They brought an immense train of heavy artillery, most amply furnished with ammunition, and perfectly well manned.

The constant and universal chearfullness and spirit of the officers in all hardships and danger deserve my warmest acknowledgements, and I have been particularly indebted to Brigadier General O'Hara and to Lt Colonel Abercrombie, the former commanding on the right and the latter on the left, for their attention and exertion on every occasion. The detachment of the 23rd Regiment and marines in the redoubt on the right, commanded by

---

[4]   The words from 'a diversion' to 'expected' are substituted for 'there was a danger of the French ships of war that lay at the mouth of York River coming up'.

[5]   'upwards of' is substituted for 'about'.

[6]   After 'Continentals' the following is deleted: 'in both of which are included about 900 artillery men'.

[7]   After 'militia.' the following sentence is deleted: 'They mounted in their first parallel 35 pieces of cannon from 18 to 24 pounders and fourteen mortars of 9 and 13 inches, in the 2nd parallel 36 pieces of heavy cannon.'

Captain Apthorpe[8], and the subsequent detachments commanded by Lt Colonel Johnson deserve particular commendation.

Captain Rochfort, who commanded the artillery, and indeed every officer and soldier of that distinguished corps, and Lieutenant Sutherland, the commanding engineer, have merited in every respect my highest approbation; and I cannot sufficiently acknowledge my obligations to Captain Symonds, who commanded His Majesty's ships, and to the other officers and seamen of the navy for their active and zealous co-operation.

I transmit returns of our killed and wounded[9]. The loss of seamen and town's people was likewise considerable.

I trust that your Excellency will please to hasten the return of the *Bonetta*, after landing her passengers, in compliance with the article of capitulation.

Lt Colonel Abercrombie will have the honour to deliver this dispatch and is well qualified to explain to your Excellency every particular relating to our past and present situation.

I have the honour to be with great respect, sir,
Your most obedient and most humble servant

CORNWALLIS

§ - §

2 - Between Cornwallis and Washington

Cornwallis to Washington, 27th October 1781[10]   *92(71): Df*

York
27th October 1781

His Excellency General Washington

Sir

Many of our officers having repeated their representations to me that they apprehend that they lose the benefit of the capitulation on that head by signing their paroles in the form

---

8   Charles Apthorpe had spent his entire service in the 23rd Regiment (Royal Welch Fusiliers). Having entered the regiment as a 2nd lieutenant on 19th April 1774, he was promoted to lieutenant on 2nd March 1776, to captain lieutenant on 8th November 1778, and to captain on 9th August 1780. (*Army Lists*)

9   *returns..*: published in Tarleton, *Campaigns*, 445.

10 This and Washington's following reply are published with no differences in Ross ed, *Cornwallis Correspondence*, i, 126-7.

proposed by your commissary of prisoners, I am under the necessity of requesting that you will be pleased to reconsider that subject. I think it will appear to your Excellency that if they are to be subject to be recalled without substantial and previously specified reasons, their situation will be no better than that of officers on parole by indulgence from captors to whom they had surrendered without making any terms. I take the liberty of inclosing a form of parole which we intended to offer[11] and which I thought would have satisfied you as being conformable to the capitulation, but I am by no means tenacious of this form and shall be contented if you will be pleased to order to be specified in the paroles the reasons (consistent with the capitulation) that will subject officers to recall, that their situation may be more precisely defined.

I have the honour to be etc

[CORNWALLIS]

Washington to Cornwallis, 27th October 1781   *270(8): ALS*

Camp near York
27th October 1781

My Lord

In answer to your Lordship's letter of this date I can only express my surprize that any of your officers object to a clause which is essential in every parole, and repeat that, however inclined I am to comply with your Lordship's wishes, I find myself in the impossibility of doing so on the present occasion.

I request therefore that your Lordship will be pleased to communicate my final determination to the gentlemen who have made difficulties on the subject and exhort them to sign the form of parole which has been already adopted if they are desirous of going to New York and Europe.

I have the honor to be
Your Lordship's most obedient humble servant

G⁰ WASHINGTON

§ - §

---

[11] *form of parole..:* no extant copy.

3 - Cornwallis's parole, 28th October 1781[12]
93(24): CS

I, Charles Earl Cornwallis, Lt General of His Britannick Majesty's forces —

DO acknowledge myself a prisoner of war to the United States of America, and having permission from his Excellency General Washington agreeable to capitulation to proceed to New York and Charlestown or either and to Europe —

DO pledge my faith and word of honor that I will not do or say any thing injurious to the said United States or armies thereof or their allies untill duly exchanged.

I do further promise that whenever required by the Commander in Chief of the American Army or the Commissary of Prisoners for the same, I will repair to such place or places as they or either of them may require.

GIVEN under my hand at York Town
28th day of October 1781

CORNWALLIS

§ - §

4 - Between Cornwallis and Lafayette

Cornwallis to Lafayette, 25th October 1781   *92(66): Df*

York
25th October 1781

Major General Marquis de Lafayette

Sir

I am sorry to be under the necessity of troubling you again on the subject of our two flag vessels that were seized in the bay by the French fleet and which Mr Cook, one of our deputy commissaries of prisoners, has reported to me are still detained.

---

[12] The paroles of Cornwallis's aides-de-camp, Major Alexander Ross and Lieutenant Henry Haldane, are couched in identical terms (93(26) and 6(389)).

The cartel settled between General Greene and me for the Southern District having been communicated and acquiesced in by you as the American commanding officer in this quarter, I took the liberty of applying to you some time ago for your good offices in protecting those flag vessels that were necessarily employed in carrying the cartel into execution, and I am perfectly satisfied by your letter dated at Williamsburgh inclosing a letter written by order of the Count de Grasse[13] that it was your intention that those vessels should be held as sacred, but as your applications for their release have not been effectual and as their detention is a breach of the common rules of war, I must request that you will be pleased to state the case to General Washington and I trust that he will see the necessity of joining his requisition to yours that those vessels may be delivered up.

I have the honour to be etc

[CORNWALLIS]

Lafayette to Cornwallis, 26th October 1781   92(68): LS

October 26th 1781

Lt General Earl Cornwallis

My Lord

I shall inclose your Lordship's letter of the 25th to his Excellency the Commander in Chief with the state of facts, which is left unsealed for your Lordship's reading.

I hope General Washington will put the matter under the eyes of Count de Grasse, which, added to my repeated and present application to the admiral, will convince your Lordship of my having given to the flags all that protection which is proper from a land officer, and that I have even wished irregularities to be overlooked.

The moment Count de Grasse's answer is known, I shall lay it before your Lordship. And I do assure you, my Lord, that I am more than ever desirous to observe that mode of conduct which has hitherto marked our correspondence.

I have the honor to be
Your Lordship's most obedient servant

LAFAYETTE

---

[13] *your letter..:* see pp 83-5.

31st October 1781

Lt General Earl Cornwallis

My Lord

The inclosed letter from Count de Grasse will convince your Lordship that irregularities have been committed by the cartel vessels and that any further interference as a land officer is out of my power.

But as the exchange of the officers and men on board those vessels has been candidly made between you and me, I am to assure your Lordship that, in case the vessels are sent up the river, the exchanged will be returned or, in a different supposition, shall be regularly accounted for.

I have the honor to be
Your Lordship's most obedient servant

LAFAYETTE

Enclosure
Extract, de Grasse to Washington, undated　　　　　　　*92(75): C*

Je vois la reclamation que le Lord Cornwallis a fait de deux especes de parlementaire que j'ay arrêté, l'un sortant de la Riviere de James, et l'autre qui étoit charge de differents officiers et de quantité de malades. Ces batimens étant sans papiers en regle, ils sont non seulement confiscables mais même dans l'exactitude ils pourroient etre regardes comme forbans et traités comme cela, n'étant pas permis a qui que ce soit d'étre a la mer sans être muny de papiers en regle. Voila ce qui m'a authorisé a en faire la confiscation et elle est même en réprésaille sur un parlementaire francois venant avec ses papiers en regle de la côte de Guinée et trouvé dans le Golfe de Gascogne devant aller en Angleterre. Il y fut conduit et declaré de bonne prise, mais je n'ay point regardé ce trait d'authorité. Je ne regarde seulement que ces deux parlementaires sont sans papiers, sans liste de prisonniers échangés, sans passeports quelconque et ils ne peuvent jamais etre regardés comme parlementaires, puis qu'ils n'ont jamais pû me prouver papiers justificatifs de quelle nation ils étoient.

2e, vu parlementaire ne doit point avoir de marchandises a son bord, le premier avoit des pieces de mature propres a des mats de frigate, le second, quantité de marchandises seches, souliers, toiles, quincaillerie etc, tous motifs qui m'authorisent a les retenir sans crainte d'enfraindre les droits des gens, que je respecte plus que personne au monde, puisque j'ay proposé aux officiers commandants aux colonies d'établir le même cartel dans ces parages que celuy que nos roys respectifs ont établi en Europe.

I note the complaint which Lord Cornwallis has made about two flag vessels which I have seized, one coming from James River, the other laden with various officers and a great number of sick. Not having papers in order, these vessels may not only be seized but, strictly speaking, be regarded as pirates and treated as such, given that no one is permitted to be at sea unless furnished with papers in order. That is my authority for the seizure and it is even in reprisal for a French flag vessel coming with its papers in order from the coast of Guinea and encountered in the Bay of Biscay bound for England. It was escorted there and declared a lawful prize, but I have not taken this precedent into account. I note only that these two flag vessels have no papers, no list of exchanged prisoners, and no passports whatever, and that they may never be regarded as flag vessels since they have never been able to authenticate to me papers verifying the nation to which they belonged.

Secondly, given that a flag vessel is not to have merchandise on board, the first had lengths of masts suitable for masts of a frigate, whereas the second had a quantity of dry goods, shoes, linen, hardware etc — all being grounds for my detaining them without fear of infringing the laws of nations, which I respect more than anyone in the world, for I have proposed to the commanding officers in the colonies that they should establish the same cartel in those parts as our respective Kings have established in Europe.

§ - §

5 - Thomas Nelson Jr to Cornwallis

Nelson to Cornwallis, 20th October 1781   *90(36): ALS*

October 20th 1781

Rt Hon Lt General Earl Cornwallis

My Lord

I have been informed that a number of the refugees from this State and also Negroes are attempting to make their escape by getting on board the *Bonetta* sloop of war. As they will endeavour to lie concealed from your Lordship's notice till the vessel sails, I have thought it necessary to make this communication to you that you may take measures to prevent the State and individuals from sustaining an injury of this nature.

I have the honour to be
Your Lordship's obedient and humble servant

THO^S NELSON Jr

Nelson to Cornwallis, 21st October 1781[14]   *90(38): ALS*

October 21st 1781

The Rt Hon Lt General Earl Cornwallis

My Lord

I have received your verbal message respecting two citizens of this State, the Reverend Mr William Andrews[15] and the Reverend Mr Harrison[16], who joined the British army after its arrival here and who are now delivered up into the hands of the civil power. The laws of this country have fixed the mode of proceeding against persons guilty of such conduct and we are ignorant of any power which has a right to supersede their force. By these laws, enacted by their own representatives, they shall be fairly and impartially tried and they must abide their sentence.

I am informed that Lt Colonel Simcoe has refused to deliver up a certain Christopher Robinson[17] who now bears a commission in his corps but who deserted from the actual

---

[14] Published with no differences in Ross ed, op cit, i, 125.

[15] An Irishman, the Reverend William Andrews was rector of the Anglican church at Portsmouth and had arrived in Virginia in 1773 after ministering for a few years in New York. A wavering loyalist, who at a 4th July celebration in 1780 had publicly denounced the Declaration of Independence as 'improper and impolitick', he had been appointed chaplain to the garrison at Portsmouth in 1781. Now falling captive at the capitulation of Yorktown, he would be allowed to go home before being indicted in March 1782 for high treason by the justices at Norfolk. He would not, however, stand trial, receiving soon a gubernatorial pardon for 'the treason of which he was not convicted', and take passage for England. In October 1783, while at Chelsea, he presented to the royal commission a claim for compensation in respect of his confiscated property in Virginia and two years later was residing in Glasgow. (Otto Lohrenz, 'William Andrews', *Southern Studies*, xxiv (1985); Otto Lohrenz, 'The advantage of rank and status: Thomas Price, a Loyalist parson of Revolutionary Virginia', *The Historian*, lx (1998); Coldham, *Loyalist Claims*, i, 13, 337)

[16] The Reverend William Harrison was an Anglican clergyman in Dinwiddie County who had resigned his benefice several months before being appointed chaplain to the garrison at Gloucester. Ambivalent in his politics, he had previously served as chairman of his county's committee of safety. Now falling captive, like Andrews, at the capitulation of Yorktown, he too would be allowed to go home, but when he was brought before the examining court of Dinwiddie County on an indictment for high treason, he was acquitted, 'no evidence appearing against him'. He did not return to the ministry full-time, but took up residence in Petersburg, where he was elected to the Common Council, to the Board of Aldermen, and finally to the office of Mayor. (Otto Lohrenz, 'The Right Reverend William Harrison of Revolutionary Virginia, First "Lord Archbishop of America"', *Historical Magazine of the Protestant Episcopal Church*, liii (1984); Otto Lohrenz, op cit, *The Historian*, lx (1998))

[17] Christopher Robinson (1763-1798) would escape the clutches of Governor Nelson, being among those spirited away from Virginia in a flag vessel. Commissioned an ensign in the infantry of the Queen's Rangers on 26th June 1781, he had been born into a family prominent in the public life of Virginia and had attended the College of William and Mary at Williamsburg. At the close of the war he would be placed on the British half-pay list and settle in New Brunswick before moving on to Quebec. In 1792 he took up residence at Kingston, when Simcoe, now Lt Governor of Upper Canada, appointed him Surveyor General of Woods and Forests there. In 1794 he was licensed to practise law and two years later was returned to the House of Assembly as the Member for Ontario and Addington, promoting in due course a bill, which was not enacted, 'to enable persons migrating into this province to bring their Negro slaves into the same'. He died cut off from most his family in Virginia, one of the few Robinsons there to be of the loyalist persuasion. (*DCB*; WO 65/164(31) (National Archives, Kew))

service of the State. The articles of capitulation cannot justify this detention and I shall by no means acquiesce in it. It is my wish to treat those men whom the fortune of war has put into our power with that civility which their situation claims and it would give me pain to be constrained in any instance to act in a different manner. Your Lordship in the case under consideration has, I imagine, the power of preventing it and I flatter myself you will at once see the propriety of exercising this power.

I have the honour to be
Your Lordship's obedient and very humble servant

THO^S NELSON Jr

§ - §

6 - Martelli to Cornwallis

Martelli to Cornwallis, 21st October 1781[18]   *92(64): ALS*

A bord de *L'Experiment* en rade de York
le 21 8bre 1781

Milord

Vous desirés une garde a bord de votre parlementaire pour empecher les Americains d'aller y troubler vos operations. Je viens, d'après votre demande transmise par Monsieur de Grandchain, d'ordonner une garde de 4 hommes et un caporal pour s'y transporter et prendre la consigne de l'officier qu'il y trouvera de votre part, et qui puise connoitre ceux qui doivent aborder ou non. Veuillés bien leur faire donner un emplacement pour se coucher. J'ay fait pourvoir a leur nourriture.

J'ay l'honeur de vous le repeter, milord, je seray toujours empressé de saisir les occasions ou je pourray vous prouver qu'on ne peut ajoutter au respect avec lequel j'ay l'honeur d'etre, milord,

Votre tres humble et tres obeissant serviteur

MARTELLI CHEVALIER

---

[18]   Published with omissions and minor errors in Ross ed, op cit, i, 126.

TRANSLATION

On board *l'Expériment* in York road
21st October 1781

My Lord

You desire a guard on board your flag vessel to prevent the Americans from going and disturbing your operations there. In compliance with your request, transmitted by Monsieur de Grandchain[19], I have just ordered a guard of four men and a corporal to be transported there and to take orders from the officer of yours he will find there and who may know those who are to go on board or not. Please have a bunk provided for them to sleep in. I have taken care of their provisions.

I have the honour to repeat, my Lord, that I shall always be most ready to seize every opportunity for proving to you that it is not possible to add to the respect with which I have the honour to be, my Lord,

Your very humble and very obedient servant

THE CHEVALIER MARTELLI[20]

§ - §

---

[19] De Grandchain was a French naval officer who had been one of three commissioners appointed by the enemy to finalise the articles of capitulation before the lines of York. He represented the French fleet, the Vicomte de Noailles the French army, and Lt Colonel John Laurens the American revolutionary forces. (Thomas Balch, *French in America during the War of Independence of the United States 1777-1783* (Ardent Media, 1972))

[20] Apart from commanding the man of war *l'Expériment*, with which he would take part in the engagement off Saints Passage between Guadeloupe and Dominica in April 1782, Martelli has not been identified.

PART THIRTEEN

Cornwallis in New York

19th November to 14th December 1781

His passage to England

15th December 1781 to 17th January 1782

CHAPTER 65

Letters to or from Clinton, Germain, Amherst or de Rochambeau

---

1 - Between Cornwallis and Clinton

Clinton to Cornwallis, 2nd August 1781[1]   ***68(59): CS***

New York
2nd August 1781

Lt General Earl Cornwallis

My Lord

I was last night honored with your Lordship's letters of the 24th and 27th ultimo[2] by Captain Stapleton, and it gives me no small concern to observe by the tenor of them that you are displeased with the opinions I took the liberty of giving in my letter of the 29th May[3] respecting the probable consequences of your retreat from Cross Creek to Wilmington and march from thence to Petersburg, and with what I said to your Lordship in my letters of the

---

[1] Annotated: 'Received from Captain Smith at New York, 19th November 1781', and published with inconsequential differences in Stevens, *Clinton-Cornwallis Controversy*, ii, 109.

[2] *your Lordship's letters..*: see pp 11-18.

[3] *my letter..*: see vol V, p 118.

141

8th and 11th of last month[4] on your design of abandoning the Williamsburg Neck and retiring with your army to Portsmouth. Therefore, as it was not my intention to give offence and is extremely my wish to be properly understood by your Lordship, I request your attention for a few moments to the following elucidation of my sentiments on both those subjects.

The high opinion I entertained of your Lordship's military talents, and the respect I had for your situation as second to myself, induced me from the moment you took charge of a separate command to leave you at full liberty to act in it as you judged best for the King's Service. And I am persuaded your Lordship is not insensible that I constantly pursued this line of conduct towards you during all your operations in the Carolinas, aiming at no other merit than that of diligently attending to your wants and supplying them, whilst I was content to remain here myself upon the very confined defensive to which I was reduced by the large detachments I had sent to the southward in support of your progress.

Although your Lordship was, as you have observed, subjected by this means to a certain degree of anxiety and responsibility, it does not appear that I was exonerated of my share of them. I could not therefore but be personally and anxiously interested in your successes and disappointments. And tho' I have a respect for your Lordship's judgement and am apt to doubt my own when it differs from it, yet it is certainly a duty I owe to my station as Commander in Chief to express my dissent from any measure your Lordship adopts, when I apprehend that the consequences may be prejudicial. This, my Lord, being the case with respect to the move taken notice of in my letter of the 29th May (and I most sincerely wish experience had convinced me I was mistaken), I immediately communicated to your Lordship my sentiments of the event and how I thought it might have been obviated. In these it seems I am not so fortunate to have your concurrence; but I must confess they are not the least altered by your Lordship's arguments, being still of opinion that, under the circumstances in which you describe your troops to be, you could have fallen back from Crosscreek to the Pedee with much greater ease and safety than you could have marched double the distance to Wilmington thro' a country which you report to be entirely hostile. And I should suppose Lord Rawdon might have moved to the Pedee without interruption to join you with every refreshment your army wanted, as there does not appear to have been at that time an enemy between that river and Camden. And before you reached the Pedee, the country would probably have been so opened that your orders for that purpose might have got to his Lordship with as much expedition and safety as your note did from Guildford after the battle.

And with respect to your Lordship's subsequent move, I hope you will pardon me if I continue to dissent from the policy of the measure, tho' you happily surmounted the danger of it, as I fear the advantages resulting from your junction with the Chesapeak army will not compensate the losses which immediately followed your quitting Carolina, notwithstanding General Greene's wishes to the contrary, which I apprehend meant nothing more than a gasconnade to boast the success he expected from a second action with your Lordship's army in case it had directed its steps towards him instead of Virginia.

I hope your Lordship will likewise excuse me for expressing the uneasiness I feel at the observation you make respecting my opinion of the Virginia force, because it seems to convey

---

[4] *my letters...:* see vol V, pp 140-3.

an insinuation which I am not conscious of deserving. And I trust that as I know myself to be incapable of wresting opinions to serve particular purposes, it will appear that what I have said at different periods on that or any other subject has been perfectly consonant and candidly what I thought. I beg leave therefore to contrast with each other what I have said, in this and my other letters, on the force of Virginia, and I request your Lordship will be pleased to point out the impropriety which gave rise to that observation.

In the letter your Lordship quotes[5] I say: 'I should not have thought even the one under Major General Phillips in safety at Petersburg, at least for so long a time.' In the one of June 8th[6]: 'Your Lordship will see by La Fayette's letter that you have little more opposed to you than his corps and an unarmed militia.' And in that of June 11th[7]: 'where, as appears by the intercepted letters of Washington and La Fayette, they are in no situation to stand against even a division of that army. And your Lordship may possibly have opposed to you from 1,500 to 2,000 Continentals, and (as La Fayette observes) a small body of ill armed peasantry — full as spiritless as the militia of the southern provinces and without any service.' At the period alluded to in the first letter General Phillips was at Petersburg with only 2,000 men, uncovered by works. Fayette was opposed to him with his own corps, Steuben, Muhlenberg etc and all the militia of the province, and expected to be soon joined by Wayne with the Pennsylvania line. I therefore certainly had cause to be apprehensive for General Phillips's corps in case Greene had, on hearing of your Lordship's move from Wilmington, fallen back and, calling La Fayette to him, placed himself with their united force between your Lordship's and the Petersburg army, ready to strike at either as it suited his purpose. But when the other letters were written, my opinion of the Virginia force was formed from the rebel letters just intercepted, which fully describe the state of their arms and their numbers. I therefore cannot discover that they shew I thought at different periods more or less favorably of it, but as I was warranted to do by matter of fact and the intelligence I received.

To give a full and satisfactory answer to your Lordship's letter of the 27th July will perhaps take up more time than you or I can well spare, but as your Lordship appears to be greatly affected by the contents of my letters of the 8th and 11th ultimo, I think it a duty I owe to your feelings and my own to say something in explanation of them. I must therefore beg your Lordship's patience while I state the substance of my correspondence with General Phillips and yourself concerning the stations to be held and operations to be carried on in Chesapeak etc, which I presume will at least prove that I spared no pains to explain my desires to your Lordship, tho' I have perhaps unhappily failed in making them understood.

My instructions to General Phillips, as quoted by your Lordship, gave him power to take possession of York Town or Old Point Comfort as a station for large ships if the Admiral should disapprove of Portsmouth and require one. In my letters to that general officer of 24th

---

5 *the letter your Lordship quotes*: of 29th May, vol V, p 118.

6 *the one of June 8th*: see vol V, p 123.

7 *that of June 11th*: see vol V, p 95.

of March and 11th of April[8] I desired his opinion respecting the post of Portsmouth and such others as he proposed to establish on James River, with their importance considered either as assisting your Lordship's operations or connected with those of the navy, and after having received that opinion, I told him that Portsmouth was by no means my choice and left him at liberty to change it if he saw proper. And the substance of the conversations with him, as extracted by your Lordship, go more fully into the advantage of a naval station, pointing particularly to the one at York — being led to the consideration of its utility by the French having two winters ago sheltered their ships under works thrown up there. And, as I have already mentioned to your Lordship, General Arnold has since told me that from the description given him of it by Lt Colonel Simcoe he judged 2,000 men would be ample for its defence.

From hence, my Lord, I presume it will appear that I very early entertained thoughts of a station in Chesapeak for large ships; and I referred your Lordship in my letter of the 29th May to my correspondence etc with General Phillips (in your possession) for my ideas on that and other operations which I had in view, leaving you at liberty, however, to follow them or your own as you judged best for the King's Service. Having therefore afterwards seen by your Lordship's dispatch of the 26th of May[9] that you had considered the papers referred to and that, tho' you did not think it expedient to attend to Mr Alexander's proposal and the expedition against the stores at Philadelphia, you had the same objections to Portsmouth which had been before stated and was inclined to think well of York as a proper harbour and place of arms, I naturally concluded that your Lordship had entirely concurred with me not only as to the propriety of laying hold of a naval station somewhere on the Williamsburg Neck but as to the place. And I of course supposed that your Lordship would set about establishing yourself there immediately on your return from Richmond, which I expected would be in three or four days after the date of your letter. Wherefore, imagining you were considerably advanced in your works (for I had no letter afterwards from your Lordship until the one you honored me with of the 30th June[10]), I ventured to solicit you for a part of your force to assist me in the operations I proposed carrying on in this quarter during the summer months, when those of the Chesapeak must have probably ceased. And in doing this, as I was totally in the dark with respect to what was then doing in the Chesapeak, I endeavored as much as lay in my power to avoid all possibility of interrupting the moves you might be engaged in or any object you might have in view, as will, I doubt not, be manifest from the following extracts from my letters to your Lordship, which I beg leave to submit once more to your consideration.

29th May — 'I would rather content myself with ever so bare a defensive until there was an appearance of serious operation against me than cramp yours in the least.'

June 8th — 'You will see by Fayette's letter you have little more opposed to you' etc. 'Your Lordship can therefore certainly spare 2,000, and the sooner they come the better' etc.

---

8   *my letters..*: see vol V, pp 11 and 53.

9   *your Lordship's dispatch..*: see vol V, p 88.

10   *one... of the 30th June*: see vol V, p 104.

'Had it been possible for your Lordship to have let me know your views and intentions, I should not now be at a loss to judge of the force you might want for your operations. Ignorant, therefore, as I am of them, I can only trust that, as your Lordship will see by the inclosed intercepted letters my call for a reinforcement is not a wanton one, you will send me what you can spare as soon as may be expedient, for should your Lordship be engaged in a move of such importance as to require the employment of your whole force, I would by no means wish to starve or obstruct it but in that case would rather endeavor to wait a little longer until my occasions grow more urgent or your situation admits of your detaching, of which, however, I request to be informed with all possible dispatch.'

NB: This letter was written immediately after I had known the enemy's designs of attacking this place and should therefore be considered as thoroughly descriptive of the nature of my wishes for a reinforcement.

June 11th — 'I shall of course approve of any alterations your Lordship may think proper to make with respect to the stations I proposed taking in York or James Rivers' etc. 'Thus circumstanced, I am persuaded your Lordship will be of opinion that the sooner I concentrate my force the better.   Therefore (unless your Lordship after the receipt of my letters of the 29th May and 8th instant should incline to agree with me in opinion and judge it right to adopt my ideas respecting the move to Baltimore or the Delaware Neck) I beg leave to recommend it to you, as soon as you have finished the active operations you may be now engaged in, to take a defensive station in any healthy situation you chuse (be it at Williamsburg or York Town).   And I would wish in that case' (i.e after you have secured such a station) 'that, after reserving to yourself such troops as you judge necessary for an ample defensive and desultory movements by water etc, the following corps may be sent me in succession as you can spare them.'

June 15th[11] — 'I delay not a moment to dispatch a runner with a duplicate of my letter of the 11th instant.   And as I am led to suppose (from your Lordship's letter of the 26th ultimo) that you may not think it expedient to adopt the operations I had recommended in the upper Chesapeak and will by this time probably have finished those you were engaged in,' (in which surely the securing defensive stations is obviously implied) 'I request you will immediately embark a part of the troops stated in the letter inclosed (beginning with the light infantry) and send them to me with the greatest dispatch.   I shall likewise in proper time solicit the Admiral to send some more transports to the Chesapeak, in which your Lordship will please to send hither the remaining troops you judge can be spared from the defence of the posts you may occupy, as I do not think it adviseable to leave more troops in that unhealthy climate at this season of the year than what are absolutely wanted for a defensive and desultory water excursions.'

June 19th[12] — 'I am, however, persuaded they will attempt the investiture of the place. I therefore heartily wish I was more in force that I might be able to take advantage of any false movements they may make in forming it.   Should your Lordship have any solid

---

[11]   See vol V, p 97.

[12]   See vol V, p 135.

operation to propose or have approved of the one mentioned in my former letters, I shall not, as I have already told you, press you for the corps I wished to have sent me – at least for the present, but if in the approaching inclement season your Lordship should not think it prudent to undertake operation with the troops you have etc, I cannot but wish for their sake, if I had no other motive, that you would send me as soon as possible what you can spare from a respectable defensive. And that your Lordship may better judge what I mean by a respectable defensive, it is necessary to inform you that other intelligence besides Monsieur Barras' letter[13] makes it highly probable that Monsieur le Grasse will visit this coast in the hurricane season and bring with him troops as well as ships. But when he hears your Lordship has taken possession of York River before him' etc (which in other words certainly means: your defensive is required to be more particularly respectable as le Grasse is expected to come soon with a considerable armament to the Chesapeak, where he will probably seize a station for his large ships in York River, but as it appears to be your Lordship's intention to take possession of that post, I think he will, upon hearing you have done so, relinquish the design and join the force assembling against this place). 'In the hope that your Lordship will be able to spare me 3,000 men I have sent 2,000 ton of transports' etc. 'But should your Lordship not be able to spare the whole' etc.

These letters, my Lord, are each a link of the same chain and collectively or separately were intended to speak the same language, the simple and obvious meaning of which I humbly presume to be this.

I find your Lordship does not think it expedient to undertake the operations I proposed, and you have none of your own in contemplation; and it being probable you have made your arrangements for changing the post of Portsmouth, which you dislike, and have finished your defensive on the Williamsburg Neck, which we both approve of, I request that, of the 7,000 men which (as far as I can judge without having lately received any returns) you have, you will reserve as many as you want for the most ample defensive, and desultory water expeditions, and then send me the rest (according to the inclosed list) in succession as you can spare them.

It is true, indeed, that several of these letters were not received by your Lordship until some time after you received those of the 11th and 15th owing to the unexpected tedious voyage of the *Charon* that carried them (and you must be sensible that it would have been imprudent in me to have risked duplicates of them by the boat in which Ensign Amiel was dispatched), but if your Lordship will be pleased to recur to those you received by him, I am persuaded you will find that the letter of the 11th refers you to those of the 29th May and 8th of June, which (it is expressly implied) your Lordship was to read before you executed the order contained in that of the 15th. And your not having received them would (I should suppose) have fully warranted at least the suspension of your resolution of repassing James River until you had stated to me your situation and heard again from me.

After this very candid and ample explanation, my Lord, I have only to assure you that it was not my intention to pass the slightest censure on your Lordship's conduct, much less an unmerited or severe one. We are both amenable to the censure of a much higher tribunal

---

[13] *Monsieur Barras' letter*: see vol V, p 128-9.

should either of us unhappily commit errors that deserve it. Nor had I the smallest right to doubt your Lordship's readiness to comply with my desires if you had understood them. The dispatch with which you prepared to execute what you thought my wish, and the alacrity you afterwards shewed, together with the ample manner in which you equipped the expedition I ordered, convince me you are inclined to do so. I had therefore only to lament that your Lordship had mistaken my intentions and to endeavor to obviate the inconvenience as speedily as possible. This, perhaps, was done in more positive language than I had been accustomed to use to your Lordship, but I had no other object in view than to make myself clearly understood – which I am happy to find has been the case, and that my messenger was in time to prevent the consequences I apprehended.

I have the honor to be
Your Lordship's most obedient and most humble servant

H CLINTON

Clinton to Cornwallis, 27th August 1781[14]   68(72): CS

New York
August 27th 1781

Lt General Earl Cornwallis

My Lord

I had the honor to receive your Lordship's letter in cypher of the 17th instant[15] by the *Swallow* dispatch boat, which arrived here the 23rd, in answer to which I must confess that I conceived your letter of the 27th ultimo[16] gave me reason to suppose it was your intention to send me the troops you could spare as soon as you finished the evacuation of Portsmouth. And I was impatient for their arrival for the reasons I have already communicated to you, as 'tis probable they would have been of infinite use had they come in time, for, on the arrival of the 2,500 raw German recruits, which I mentioned in my last[17], and in the hope of reinforcement from your Lordship, I had assembled my little army in such a manner as to be able to avail myself of any opportunity which might be given me by the enemy, who had foraged within six miles of my lines on the 17th. This small movement was made on the 18th. They fell back on the 19th, passed the Croton, afterwards crossed the Hudson at King's Ferry, and are now encamped in the neighbourhood of Chatham.

---

[14] Annotated: 'Received from Captain Smith at New York, November 19th 1781', and published with inconsequential differences in Stevens, op cit, ii, 142.

[15] According to the copy, the letter was dated the 16th. See p 24.

[16] *your letter..*: see p 13.

[17] *my last*: of 11th August, p 23.

I cannot well ascertain Mr Washington's real intentions by this move of his army, but it is possible he means for the present to suspend his offensive operations against this post and to take a defensive station at his old post of Morris Town, from whence he may detach to the southward. On this account therefore, and because the season is approaching when operation may recommence in the Chesapeak, I request your Lordship will be pleased to keep with you all the troops you have there, and I shall send you such recruits, convalescents etc as can go by this sudden opportunity, which are all that I can at present spare, as this move of the enemy may be only a feint and they may return to their former position, which they certainly will do if le Grasse arrives. But towards the latter end of next month, when the effects of the equinox are over (for I am persuaded the Admiral will not approve of any water movement 'till then), if this post should not be threatned, I propose to reinforce the Chesapeak army with all the troops which can possibly be spared consistently with the security of this important post.

General Leslie has been here some days. He will himself explain to your Lordship the cause of his coming. I was much concerned to find him in so bad a state of health on his arrival, but as it is now much altered for the better, he embarks tomorrow to proceed to Chesapeak on his way to Charlestown.

If your Lordship from your knowledge of the state of South Carolina should be of opinion that any troops may be spared from thence, I beg leave to suggest that the sooner you give orders for their joining you the better.

I have the honor to be
Your Lordship's most obedient and most humble servant

H CLINTON

Clinton to Cornwallis, 30th August and 1st September 1781[18]   68(74): CS

New York
August 30th 1781

Lt General Earl Cornwallis

My Lord

I am this moment honored with your Lordship's dispatches of the 20th, 22nd and 24th instant[19], which were delivered to me by Lt Colonel Du Buy[20], and as my letters of the 2nd

---

[18] Annotated: 'Received from Captain Smith at New York, November 19th 1781', and published with inconsequential differences in Stevens, op cit, ii, 143.

[19] *your Lordship's dispatches..*: for those of the 20th and 22nd, see pp 25 and 27. There is no extant copy of that of the 24th.

[20] *Lt Colonel Du Buy*: as a major Johann Christian du Buy had commanded the Regiment von Bose during the winter campaign. He had since been promoted to Quartermaster General of the Hessian forces.

and 27th[21] have already spoken very fully to the subjects they chiefly treat of, it becomes unnecessary for me at present to give your Lordship any further trouble thereon.

General Leslie will have the honor to communicate to your Lordship my wishes respecting Carolina, as I have given him such instructions relative to the service in that quarter as my present limited information enables me to do. However, as I cannot but suppose that the operations in Virginia and Carolina will still have a considerable connection with each other, and that your Lordship, by applying to the officer commanding the King's ships, will have the same means of communication that I shall, I must request that you will still retain the direction of the Southern District until I can determine upon it or shall find it expedient to comply with your Lordship's wishes, which I shall not fail to pay the earliest attention to, for, your Lordship having hitherto had the entire management of the civil and military transactions in the Carolinas and being in consequence better qualified than any other person to judge of what may be hereafter proper to be done there, it will be necessary I should receive your opinions upon them before any change takes place or I can frame definitive orders for General Leslie's guidance. Your Lordship will be therefore pleased in the mean time to make such additions to the instructions I have now given him as you shall find requisite.

I am concerned to find your Lordship under the necessity of employing so many troops in working on the fortifications, having entertained hopes that you were supplied with a sufficient number of Negroes for that and other drudgeries.

Mr Wier having informed me that the commissary with your Lordship has received your orders to buy rum for the troops, I have the honor to acquaint you that as there is a considerable quantity of that article in the stores here, a supply of it will be sent you from hence, which will of course come cheaper than any which may be purchased in Virginia.

I hope your Lordship will find every thing you want sent you by this opportunity, except money, of which only £10,000 can possibly be spared at present; but, a considerable sum being expected by the first fleet from England, I shall on its arrival send your Lordship a further supply.

Sir Samuel Hood arrived here from the Leeward Islands on the 28th with 14 sail of the line, 3 frigates and a fire ship, and has brought with him the 40th and 69th Regiments to reinforce this army, the latter of which, however, continues to do duty on board the fleet. On the evening of the same day I received undoubted information that Monsieur Barras' fleet sailed from Rhode Island the morning of the 25th, their destination not known. Mr Washington's force still remains in the neighbourhood of Chatham and I do not hear that he has as yet detached to the southward.

I have the honor to be
Your Lordship's most obedient and most humble servant

H CLINTON

---

[21] *my letters of the 2nd and 27th*: they immediately precede this.

September 1st PS

As your Lordship informs me in your letter of the 22nd that the works you have thought proper to construct at York will not probably be finished before the expiration of six weeks, I am to suppose you will not think of commencing solid operation before this time. Therefore, unless Mr Washington should send a considerable part of his army to the southward, I shall not judge it necessary until then to detach thither. I should wish, however, in the mean time to be informed from your Lordship what number of troops you think will be required for the defence of your works, what force you will afterwards have to take the field with, and what you will want in addition, supposing that you shall not have a greater force acting against you in Virginia than what may be expected from the present appearances.

HC

Clinton to Cornwallis, 14th, 15th and 18th October 1781[22]   *68(93): C*

New York
14th October 1781

Lt General Earl Cornwallis

My Lord

I had the honor to receive your Lordship's letter of the 29th ultimo on the 8th instant and that of the 3rd on the 12th, and am happy to hear that mine of the 24th and 25th have reached you.[23]

At a council of war of the general officers held the 10th instant it was resolved I should submit the three following plans to your Lordship's consideration. They occurred to us as secondary objects only (in case we should find it absolutely impracticable to go directly up to York or by landing at Monday's Point effect a junction with you by the Gloucester side and be thereby obliged to try James River).

First — To land at Newport News, and the troops to advance from thence on the James River road to some favorable position in communication with that river, where we are to wait until we hear from your Lordship or circumstances may make it proper for us to cooperate with you in effecting a junction of the two armies, which we at present think will be best done without your lines in preference to an attempt of doing it within, for reasons we think obvious.

---

[22] Annotated: 'Received from Captain Smith at New York, November 29th [*19th?*] 1781', and published with inconsequential differences in Stevens, op cit, ii, 185.

[23] For the letters referred to, see pp 35-8.

Second —— To attempt a junction with you by a combined move, we moving up James River to James Town, and your Lordship up the York River to either Queen's Creek or Cappahosick Ferry, and effect the junction as near Williamsburg as we can, thereby putting ourselves in a situation to attack the enemy should it be thought adviseable.

Third —— To save as great a part of your Lordship's corps as possible by bringing them off to James Town, and a naval force will be ready to protect them. This, we think, may be done by our giving jealousy to the enemy from Newport News or Mulberry Island whilst your Lordship, moving up the river with as many troops as your boats will carry, or marching up the Gloucester side, crosses the river and lands either at Queen's Creek or Cappahosick and makes the best of your way to James Town.

The above is our opinion of what is best to be done in case we do not hear from your Lordship, but should we receive other ideas from you, we shall of course be governed by them.

By this your Lordship will perceive our wishes are to effect the junction first by York, next by Gloucester, and, in case either of these are absolutely impracticable, by the James River. First, landing at Newport News and taking a position ready to cooperate with your Lordship in case you should recommend a combined effort to effect a junction that way; or to endeavor to effect it near Williamsburg, the two armies moving up the James and York Rivers about the same time, we landing at James Town and your Lordship where you judge best; and when our junction is formed, bring on a general action with the enemy should that on consultation be thought adviseable. But in case all these should fail, our last object will be to save as many of your Lordship's troops as we can and leave the post at York afterwards to make the best terms they can for themselves.

The *Torbay* and *Prince William* having arrived on the 11th, our fleet at present consists of 25 sail of the line and two fifties with a large number of frigates. They are now ready and I expect we shall certainly sail in a day or two.

PS 15th October

Had the wind been fair to day, the fleet would have fallen down to the Hook, but I expect the whole will sail to morrow.

PS by the duplicate, *London* at the Hook, 18th October

The fleet is assembled, the troops embarked on board, and the whole will go to sea, if the wind continues fair, to morrow morning as the tide will not suit before. The Admiral and I entreat that we may receive all possible information from you and the Commodore of your situation and the exact position of the enemy's fleet, to meet us off Cape Charles.

I was honored with your Lordship's letter of the 11th[24] on the 16th instant.

---

[24]   *your Lordship's letter..:* see p 39.

I have the honor etc

H CLINTON

[*Subscribed*:]

Original forwarded by Captain Stapleton on the 15th. Duplicate by the *Resolution* whale boat, Robertson.

Clinton to Cornwallis, 30th November 1781[25]   *68(96): ALS*

New York
November 30th 1781

My Lord

After the conversation I had with your Lordship (before I sent your letter[26] to be published), in which we seemed so perfectly to agree, I must beg your Lordship's pardon for again troubling you on the subject. But being informed, perhaps officiously, that some people here suppose there are passages in that letter which convey an idea that you had been compelled by my orders to take the post of York tho' it was not your own preference, that you had [represented] the defects of the ground and were detained there contrary to your own judgement, and likewise that I had promised the exertions of the navy before my letter of the 24th of September[27], I am persuaded your Lordship will readily excuse my requesting a more formal avowal of your sentiments lest I should have then mistaken them, because if that should unfortunately be the case, I may perhaps be under the necessity of taking measures to obviate your letter's being viewed in the same light in England.

I have the honor to be, my Lord,
Your Lordship's most obedient humble servant

H CLINTON

---

[25] Published in Stevens, op cit, ii, 217. There are no differences.

[26] *your letter*: of 20th October, p 125.

[27] *my letter..*: see p 35.

New York
2nd December 1781

His Excellency Sir Henry Clinton KB etc etc etc

Sir

Yesterday afternoon I was honoured with your Excellency's letter dated the 30th November.

I do not recollect that any conversation passed between us the other day before the publication of my letter relative to my reasons for taking possession of the posts of York and Gloucester; but in my answer[29] to your dispatches dated the 8th and 11th July[30] directing me so positively to possess a harbour in the Chesapeak for line of battle ships your Excellency will see that after finding that works on Point Comfort could not protect a naval force in Hampton Road I thought that I acted in strict obedience to your orders by taking possession of these posts[31]. I thought it unnecessary to enter into a minute detail of the disadvantages of the ground either on my first examination of it in the month of June or on my return to it in August, because on the first occasion, as I have already had the honour of explaining to your Excellency, I did not, after seeing it, entertain for a moment an idea of occupying it, not thinking myself at liberty by the instructions under which I then acted to detain the greatest part of the force in Virginia for the purpose of securing a harbour for ships of the line[32], and on my return to it in August I thought it then became my duty to make the best of it I could, having no other harbour to propose in its place[33].

In regard to the promise of the exertions of the navy previous to your letter of the 24th of September[34], I can only repeat what I had the honour of saying to your Excellency in the conversation to which you allude, that without any particular engagements for the navy before that date all your letters held out uniformly hopes of relief, and that I had no reason from any of them to suppose that you had lost sight of the possibility of effecting it, and that under

---

28   Published with inconsequential differences in Stevens, op cit, ii, 219.

29   *my answer*: of 26th July, p 13.

30   *your dispatches..*: see vol V, pp 140-3.

31   After 'posts' the following words are deleted: 'as forming the only port in the Chesapeak in which we could hope to be able to give protection to ships of the line.'

32   See Cornwallis to Clinton, 30th June, vol V, p 106.

33   Note 29 above refers.

34   *your letter..*: see p 35.

these hopes after serious[35] reflection I did not think that it would have been justifiable in me to abandon these posts with our numerous sick, artillery, stores and shipping or to risk an action which in all probability would[36] in its consequences have precipitated the loss of them.

My letter from York dated the 20th of October was written under great agitation of mind and in great hurry, being constantly interrupted by numbers of people coming upon business or ceremony, but my intention in writing that letter was to explain the motives that influenced my own conduct and to narrate the incidents that preceeded the extremity that forced us to surrender.

I have the honour to be etc

CORNWALLIS

Cornwallis to De Lancey, 4th December 1781   74(137): C

New York
December 4th 1781

Major de Lancey
Adjutant General

Dear Sir

I inclose to you some memorandums explaining to you as fully as possible some matters of business which I have before mentioned in a cursory way to the Commander in Chief. His Excellency seemed at that time to entertain some doubts of the propriety of his ordering the Commissary General to pay such receipts of the commissaries of captures as might be presented at this place, but was rather inclined to refer them to the commissary at Charlestown. I hope the reasons which I have stated in the inclosed paper may remove any objections that might have occurred to him. It will give me the greatest satisfaction to know that they have done so before I leave America, as this is a point in which I not only engaged my own honour but, as far as it was in my power, the honour of Great Britain.

General Robertson having informed me that his allowing more than a dollar a day to Mr St George would involve him in an inconvenient precedent, I beg leave to recommend him for another dollar from some other fund. I mentioned to the Commander in Chief the case

---

[35] Before 'serious' are deleted 'much and frequent'.

[36] 'in all probability would' is substituted for 'might'.

of the unfortunate Major Stockden[37] and the important services which he rendered in the Jerseys. He is an object of charity and his Excellency seemed inclined to order him some allowance.

I am etc

CORNWALLIS

Enclosure
Memorandum for Clinton   *74(139): Df*

Memorandums from Lord Cornwallis to be laid before the Commander in Chief

When the troops received provisions or forage from the publick stores through the Commissary General's Department, receipts were granted in the usual manner; but when they lived upon the country, which was in general the case on account of the distance of the operations of the army from the magazines, Lord Cornwallis thought it right that all provisions, forage and other articles made use of by the troops but not intended to be paid for to the proprietors should become a clear saving to the publick and therefore directed the commissaries of captures to collect supplies for the army but to grant receipts only to known friends or to doubtful characters, inserting in the latter that their payment would depend upon the past and future conduct of the possessors, and into which it was intended strictly to enquire, but an assurance was given to the former that their receipts should be paid when presented at the Commissary General's Office. The people of the country were likewise told that receipts granted by the cavalry or by commanding officers of foraging parties or other detachments would be treated in the same manner as those granted by the commissaries. This mode was practised in North Carolina and in Virginia untill the army took possession of York. In the beginning of August Lord Cornwallis published an order[38] that the inhabitants of York, Elizabeth City and Warwick Counties should on or before a fixed day repair to Head Quarters to deliver up their arms and to give a military parole that they would not in future act against His Majesty's interest, promising protection to those that obeyed and payment for whatever part of their property might be wanted for the use of the troops, and notifying that the corn and cattle of those that did not obey would be seized for the use of the army and,

---

[37] Born in Princeton, New Jersey, Richard Witham Stockton (1733-1801) had been commissioned a major in the 6th Battalion, New Jersey Volunteers, on 3rd December 1776. While commanding a mixed force of the brigade out of Bennet's Neck, he was surprised on 18th February 1777 and captured with some sixty of his men. Humiliatingly he was made to march with them in irons through the streets of Philadelphia. It was an act deprecated by Washington, who wrote, 'The major has, I believe, been very active and mischievous, but we took him in arms as an officer of the enemy and by the rules of war we are obliged to treat him as such, not as a felon.' When exchanged almost two years later, Stockton found that his battalion had been reduced, with part being incorporated into the 3rd, and that he had been retired on half pay. At the close of the war he removed to Saint John, New Brunswick, where he remained on half pay until his death. (Thomas Coates Stockton, *The Stockton Family of New Jersey and Other Stocktons* (Carnaham Press, 1911); Nan Cole and Todd Braisted, 'A History of the 6th Battalion, New Jersey Volunteers' and 'New Jersey Volunteers — List of Officers, 1776-1783', *The On-Line Institute for Advanced Loyalist Studies*, 5th December 2005; Treasury 64/23(30) and WO 65/165(15) (National Archives, Kew))

[38] *an order*: of 9th August, p 108.

if taken, that they would be otherwise punished as might be thought proper. In consequence of this publication large supplies of cattle and forage were easily procured from the country and receipts or certificates were granted for whatever belonged to quiet inhabitants. The military chest at York being very low, few of those certificates or receipts could be paid in money,[39] but to satisfy the people of the country who became impatient for payment, to support the publick credit and to encourage the vent of British goods it was notified to the merchants by order from Lord Cornwallis that they might, if they thought proper, take those receipts in payment for goods and depend upon being paid the amount of those that were regularly indorsed as soon as a sufficient sum of money arrived from New York, and to avoid disputes in future it was directed that their value should be certified on the back by Lt Colonel Hamilton and Mr Hubbard[40], two gentlemen well acquainted with the common rates in that part of Virginia. It is supposed that many receipts granted during the operations of Lord Cornwallis's corps and that are entitled to payment will never be presented, and it is likewise imagined that if the whole were presented and paid, their amount would bear a small proportion to the value of the number of rations actually issued to that army. And as no part of that difference can have become the perquisite of individuals, the saving to the publick must be very considerable, for to prevent this perquisite a number of receipts which had been granted by the regiments in the usual form to the Commissary General, but in fact for provisions found in the country, were taken up from him at Wilmington and it was directed that no receipts should be given in future to that department unless for articles furnished from the publick stores. The constant supplies of fresh meat to the hospitals are included in those receipts, and it is supposed that part of the usual stoppage for provisions from the soldiers would be sufficient (if thought necessary) to pay the whole.

The necessaries of the soldiers being worn out by the fatigues of the winter, Lord Cornwallis ordered a quantity of shoes to be issued from the Provincial Stores to the troops while at Wilmington and some trowzers to the Regiment of Bose, which he promised should not be charged against them.

On account of the constant duty and the uncommon fatigue that the soldiers underwent during the siege of York, Lord Cornwallis ordered some cocoa and sugar to be issued to them at the publick expence, and which he requests the Commander in Chief will be pleased to order to be paid.

---

[39] After 'money,' the following words are deleted: 'and even if the military chest had been better provided it did not then appear expedient to allow a large sum of money to go into the country for many reasons,'.

[40] A prominent lawyer before the revolutionary war, James Hubard of Williamsburg had been an early supporter of protests against the closure of Boston harbour and had been elected to the town's committee of safety in 1774 and 1775. He nevertheless remained a loyalist at heart, opposed to breaking the constitutional ties with the Crown. Accordingly he declined to be appointed by the revolutionaries as a Judge of the Admiralty Court in July 1776 and refused to take the test oath in 1777. As a result he was briefly imprisoned and his law practice destroyed. By 1780 he and his large family were living in greatly reduced circumstances. When Cornwallis reached Williamsburg in late June 1781, Hubard openly aided the army, conduct which had led to his being spirited away to New York in the *Bonetta* after the capitulation, presumably to save him from the halter. Already ill, he would die in May 1782. (Kevin P Kelly, 'The White Loyalists of Williamsburg', *The Colonial Williamsburg Interpreter*, xvii, 2 (1996); Coldham, *Loyalist Claims*, 243)

For reasons which Lord Cornwallis has had the honour to communicate to the Commander in Chief it was promised to Mr David Ross to pay for the provisions and forage taken from his different plantations for the use of the troops. A similar promise was made to Mrs Byrd[41] and to Major Monro[42] for some of his friends in North Carolina, and Mr St George was promised to receive some indemnification for losses sustained by him from the rebels on account of his loyalty.[43] Their different accounts are inclosed and Lord Cornwallis begs leave to recommend them to the Commander in Chief for payment.

Captain Branston (not yet arrived from Virginia) of an independent North Carolina company made application to Lord Cornwallis for an allowance which he said had been promised by Government to himself as well as some other North Carolina loyalists. Lord Cornwallis has referred him to the Commander in Chief and he takes this opportunity of recommending him to his favour as a man of great zeal and loyalty.

De Lancey to Cornwallis, 5th December 1781

71(43): ALS

December 5th 1781

My Lord

I had the honour to receive the papers your Lordship sent for the approbation of the Commander in Chief, which I shall take the earliest opportunity of laying before him and do myself the honour to communicate his answer to your Lordship as soon as possible.

I have the honor to be with great respect
Your Lordship's most obedient servant

OL DE LANCEY
Adjutant General

---

[41] Mary Byrd, whose plantation north of James River Cornwallis had occupied in late May, was the widow of William Byrd III, who had committed suicide at the age of forty-eight on New Year's Day, 1777. Having inherited probably the largest estate in Virginia, he had dissipated it to a large extent by his death. Mary was a daughter of Charles Willing of Philadelphia and a first cousin of Benedict Arnold's wife Peggy (née Shippen). (Tyler, *Encyclopedia*, i, 161-2; *The Cornwallis Papers*)

[42] James Monro had been nominated for a majority in the North Carolina Highland Regiment but it was never embodied. He nevertheless joined Cornwallis at Hillsborough. He was presumably a Scottish settler in North Carolina, though at some period he had resided in Nansemond County, Virginia. In 1782 he removed to England and two years later was living in London. At the close of the war he was placed on the Provincial half-pay list. (Clark, *Loyalists in the Southern Campaign*, i, 426; Coldham, op cit, 255; Treasury 64/23(32) (National Archives, Kew))

[43] *Mr St George..*: according to 74(143), he 'was plundered by the rebels'.

De Lancey to Cornwallis, 6th December 1781

74(144): ALS

Head Quarters
December 6th 1781

Lt General Earl Cornwallis

My Lord

I laid the letter your Lordship honoured me with, together with the papers it enclosed, before the Commander in Chief, and in consequence of your Lordship's expressing a wish to know his Excellency's determination before you left America I am commanded to inform you that orders will be immediately given to have the business settled in the manner your Lordship has proposed.

I have the honour to be with great respect
Your Lordship's most obedient servant

OL DE LANCEY
Adjutant General

Clinton to Cornwallis, 2nd and 10th December 1781[44]

68(98): LS

New York
2nd December 1781

Lt General Earl Cornwallis

My Lord

As your Lordship is pleased in your letter of this day to revert to the circumstance of your quitting the Williamsburg Neck and repassing the James River, so contrary to the intentions I wished to express in my letters of the 11th and 15th June[45] and those referred to by them, and which I thought they would have clearly explained, your Lordship will I hope have the goodness to forgive me if I once more repeat that I am of opinion, if those letters had been properly understood by your Lordship, you would at least have hesitated before you adopted that measure, for I humbly presume that it will appear upon a reperusal of them that it was my desire to recommend to your Lordship the taking a healthy defensive station either at Williamsburg or York and, after keeping what troops you might want for the ample defence of such a post and desultory movements by water, to send me such a proportion of the corps (mentioned in a list) as you could spare, taking them in the succession they are there placed in. Your Lordship on the contrary understood these as conveying a positive order to send me 3,000 men (by which you say your force would have been reduced to about 2,400 rank and

---

[44] Published with inconsequential differences in Stevens, op cit, ii, 240.

[45] *my letters..*: see vol V, pp 95-8.

file fit for duty, having, it is presumed, above 1,500 sick) and was pleased to tell me in your answer[46] that you could not, consistent with my plans, make safe defensive posts at York and Gloucester, both of which would be necessary for the protection of shipping, and that you should immediately repass James River and take measures for complying with my requisition.

I own, my Lord, that my opinion of the obvious meaning of the letters referred to continues still the same and I am sorry to find by the letter you have now honored me with that it differs so widely from your Lordship's. It is plain, however, we cannot both be in the right.

My letter of the 11th July[47] directs your Lordship to fortify Old Point Comfort in the mouth of James River with the intention of securing Hampton Road, which the Admiral recommended as the best naval station and requested I would occupy, but your Lordship's letter of the 27th[48] informs me you had examined Old Point Comfort with the officers of the navy and the engineers, and that you were all of opinion a post there would not answer the purpose, and that you should in compliance with the spirit of my orders seize York and Gloucester, being the only harbour in which you could hope to be able to give effectual protection to line of battle ships. Supposing therefore of course that your Lordship approved in every respect of York and Gloucester from the preference you had thus given them to the post I had recommended, I did not oppose the choice you had made, having never received the least hint from your Lordship that the ground of York was unfavorable or liable to be enfiladed till after you had capitulated.

With respect to your Lordship's having been influenced in your conduct by the hopes of relief (which you say was uniformly held out to you in all my letters), your Lordship cannot be insensible that the possibility of effecting it must have entirely depended upon the exertions of the navy, which as I was not authorised to promise before the 24th September[49], I am persuaded your Lordship will readily acknowledge that, if your letter of 20th October[50] implies I had done so before that period, the implication cannot be supported by any thing I wrote previous to my letter of that date, which you received on the 29th.

As, therefore, my letters of the 2nd and 6th September[51], which promise only my own exertions, did not reach your Lordship before the 13th and 14th of that month and you did not before then know of Sir Samuel Hood's arrival or of Mr Graves having more than seven sail of the line to combat Monsieur le Grasse's force, which on the 29th August you had heard consisted of at least 25 sail of the line, your Lordship consequently could have no hopes

---

46 *your answer*: of 30th June, vol V, p 104.

47 *My letter..*: see vol V, p 142.

48 *your Lordship's letter..*: see p 13.

49 See Clinton's letter of 24th September, p 35.

50 *your letter..*: see p 125.

51 *my letters..*: see pp 32-4.

of relief before that time. And with respect to your escape to New York immediately on the arrival of General Washington's troops at Williamsburg, which your letter of 20th October implies you were prevented from undertaking by the receipt of mine of 24th September, I must beg leave to observe that, if it had been ever practicable after the time your Lordship mentions (which I am free to own I do not think it was), it must have been between that period and the time of the enemy's force appearing before your lines. It may therefore be presumed you could not have been prevented by any thing I said in that letter, as you did not receive it until after the latter event took place. But I readily admit, my Lord, that none of my letters could give you the least reason to suppose that an attempt would not be made to succor you.

Your Lordship will, I am persuaded, also forgive me if I again take notice of the too positive manner in which you are pleased to speak of the opinion I gave you about the sailing of the fleet, as my words[52] were, 'There is every reason to hope we shall start from hence about the 5th October', and in my letter of the next day[53], for fear that should appear too positive, I say, 'It is supposed the necessary repairs of the fleet will detain us here to the 5th of next month, but your Lordship must be sensible that unforeseen accidents may lengthen it out a day or two longer.'

With regard to entrenching tools, the want of which your Lordship so much complains of, I can only say that by the returns made to me by the Adjutant General it appears that 2,500 had been sent to the Chesapeak by the engineer since General Arnold's expedition inclusive, and that the first moment a requisition was made for more (which was not before the 23rd August) I ordered an additional supply to be sent, which were prevented from going by the arrival of the French fleet. I own, however, that I was not at that time very uneasy on this score, as I supposed it possible for your Lordship to have collected a sufficiency from the neighbouring plantations any time before the investiture was begun.

December 10th

I had wrote thus far, my Lord, immediately after the receipt of your Lordship's letter of this date[54], but considering that it was possible you might not have adverted to the implications which your letter of the 20th of October may be thought to bear from the great agitation of mind and hurry in which you tell me it was written, I was unwilling to give you at that time more trouble on the subject in the honest hope that your Lordship's candor will induce you most formally to disavow your having any such intentions by writing that letter in case you find on your arrival in England that the passages of it which I have taken notice of are understood as I suspect they may be, and I therefore intended to have sent this letter to a friend to be delivered to you in London. But upon reconsidering your letter of the 2nd instant, which I have had more leisure to do since my public dispatches were closed, I am of opinion that it is properer your Lordship should receive my answer to it here.

---

[52]   *my words*: in Clinton's letter of 24th September, p 35, but see note 64 on p 36.

[53]   *my letter..*: see p 37.

[54]   *letter of this date*: i.e, that of the 2nd.

I have the honor to be
Your Lordship's most obedient and most humble servant

H CLINTON

PS

Having forgot to speak to the part of your Lordship's letter of the 2nd instant when you say, 'I do not recollect that any conversation passed between us the other day before the publication of my letter relative to my reasons for taking possession of the posts of York and Gloucester,' I beg leave to do it here.

It is true, my Lord, no conversation passed from your Lordship on that subject, but when in the conversation alluded to I mentioned that I had directed you to examine Old Point Comfort and fortify it, but that, disapproving of that post, you had seized York and that therefore York was your Lordship's preference, as you were pleased not to make me any answer, I took it for granted you agreed with me.

§ - §

2 - From Germain or Amherst to Cornwallis

Germain to Cornwallis, 4th June 1781[55]   *6(215): LS*

N° 4   Whitehall
                                                                 4th June 1781

Earl Cornwallis

My Lord

His Majesty's Ship *Galatea*, which arrived with a convoy from Charles Town on the 19th of last month, brought me a letter from Lord Rawden inclosing a note from your Lordship to him written on the 17th of March at the town of Guildford[56], which your Lordship made famous by the glorious victory you had gained there over the rebel forces commanded by General Greene. I immediately communicated the agreeable intelligence to the King, and it is a great happiness to me to be in consequence of it again commanded to signify to your Lordship His Majesty's royal approbation of your able conduct, unremitted exertions, and

---

[55]   According to 65(27), Cornwallis received this dispatch at New York on 19th November. It is published with no differences in Stevens, op cit, ii, 10.

[56]   *a note..*: see vol IV, p 46.

ardent zeal for His service, and to convey to you His royal congratulations upon your happy and provident escape from a danger that twice approached you so nearly as to destroy two horses under you.

The rapidity of your movements thro' a country so thinly inhabited and so little cultivated is justly matter of astonishment to all Europe as well as to the rebels in America, and altho' they appear to make every possible exertion to oppose your progress and conduct their enterprizes in Carolina with more spirit and skill than they have shown in any other part of America, His Majesty has such confidence in your Lordship's great military talents that he entertains no doubt of your fulfilling his utmost expectations in the course of the campaign, especially as, from the happy defeat of the French fleet from Rhode Island by Admiral Arbuthnot and the arrival of a considerable reinforcement in the Chesapeak under Major General Phillips, the rebels' hope of succor must be frustrated, the loyalists encouraged, and any troops that Greene might be able to assemble exposed to the attack of two armies.

I was indeed much alarmed, upon reading the copy of Sir Henry Clinton's instructions to General Phillips[57] to return with the greatest part of his force to New York if he did not receive orders from your Lordship, lest you might not speedily have had an opportunity of communicating with him, but your late victory at Guildford will, I trust, have opened the country more to you and afforded you an occasion of taking him and his whole force under your command and employing it as a cooperating army untill the southern provinces are reduced or the season becomes too intemperate for active service, for it is the King's firm purpose to recover those provinces in preference to all others and to push the war from south to north, securing what is conquered as we go on, and not by desultory enterprizes taking possession of places at one time and abandoning them at another, and I have signified His Majesty's pleasure to Sir Henry Clinton to this effect.

The Assembly of Georgia has shown so much loyalty and attachment to the King and the Constitution and set so good an example to the other provinces which may be restored to the King's peace that great attention is due to the safety and comfort of the inhabitants, and care must be taken to guard them from the effects of the enmity of the rebel partizans which their meritorious conduct will probably excite. Many murthers have already been committed on the frontier settlers, and plantations destroyed, which has occasioned Sir James Wright, the Governor, to embody sixty of the militia, who mount, arm, and supply themselves with provisions at no very exorbitant rate and who he proposes to employ in parties keeping a continual watch upon the frontiers. As this measure promises to keep the province in quiet and makes no demand upon your force, the King has approved it, and I am commanded to signify to your Lordship His Majesty's pleasure that you do order the said corps to be paid according to its establishment and continued on foot untill the province of South Carolina is restored to the peace of the King.

I am, my Lord,
Your Lordship's most obedient humble servant

GEO GERMAIN

---

[57] *instructions..*: of 10th and 24th March, vol V, pp 7 and 11.

Whitehall
19th June 1781

Lt General Earl of Cornwallis

My Lord

I have had the honour to receive your Lordship's letter of the 18th of April past[59] by Captain Broderick and I lost no time in laying it before the King.

His Majesty has been graciously pleased, in consideration of your Lordship's very earnest recommendation of Major Tarleton and of his many eminent services, to promote him to the rank of lt colonel by brevet. And I believe I may venture to inform your Lordship that the King intends, before Captain Broderick returns to America, in compliance with your Lordship's wishes in his favour, to promote him to the rank of major.

The situation of Lieutenant MacLeod of the artillery has been considered, and as it appears he is within five of the rank of captain in his own regiment and that two of the persons standing in the regiment before him are like him on service in America, one at Gibraltar, and the other at Minorca, the King does not approve of giving him the brevet of captain, as such promotion cannot but be a matter of much disgust to the senior lieutenants.

And as His Majesty does not approve of taking the engineers into the line of the army or of changing their services, your Lordship's recommendation of Lieutenant Haldane for a lieutenantcy in the Guards cannot therefore take place. Every possible attention is wished to be paid to your Lordship's desires in favour of your officers, but I hope your Lordship will see the impropriety, and indeed impossibility, of giving them effect in the two last mentioned instances.

I have the honour to be, my Lord,
Your Lordship's most obedient and most humble servant

AMHERST

§ - §

---

58   Annotated: 'Received at New York, 19th November 1781'.

59   *your Lordship's letter..*: see vol IV, p 117.

3 - Cornwallis to de Rochambeau

Cornwallis to Rochambeau, 25th November 1781[60]　　　　　**_92(81): Df_**

Nouvelle York
Novembre 25 1781

Son Excellence le Comte de Rochambeau etc etc etc

Monsieur

Après un trajet très désagreable je suis arrive ici le 19 de ce mois.

L'Amiral Digby a eu la bonté de promettre de faire partir le _Bonetta_ sans perte de tems et d'envoyer à son bord tous les François qui sont à présent prisonniers ici. Un nombre suffisant de prisonniers americains seront envoyés pour naviguer et seront chargés de vous livrer les autres parlementaires le plutôt qu'il sera possible, et si ce nombre n'egale pas le nombre des notres qui arrivent dans ces parlementaires, l'Amiral se tiendra responsable de vous rendre compte du reste à votre satisfaction. Le parlementaire nommé le _Cochran_ fera voile dans peu de jours; celui nommé l'_Andrew_ n'arriva qu'hier mais, ayant fait eau dangereusement dans deux places, ne peut pas sortir avant d'être reparé; et nous n'avons pas encore reçu des nouvelles de celui nommé le _Lord Mulgrave_.

Capitaine Dundas se charge de quelque fromage et de porter anglois, que je vous prie de me faire l'honneur d'agréer.

C'est avec des sentimens de la plus vive reconnoissance qui ne seront jamais effacés que je presente à votre Excellence mes très humbles remerciments pour toutes vos bontés et politesses. Il me fera le plaisir le plus sensible de saisir toutes les occasions qui pourront se presenter de montrer la consideration et l'estime la plus parfaite avec laquelle j'ai l'honneur d'être, monsieur, etc

[CORNWALLIS]

---

[60] Published with two inconsequential errors in Ross ed, _Cornwallis Correspondence_, i, 128-9.

TRANSLATION

New York
November 25th 1781

His Excellency le Comte de Rochambeau etc etc etc

Sir

After a very tiresome passage I arrived here on the 19th instant.

Admiral Digby has kindly promised to dispatch the *Bonetta* without loss of time and to send on board her all the Frenchmen who are now prisoners here. A sufficiency of American prisoners shall be sent to navigate and be charged with delivering up to you the other flag vessels as soon as it can be done, and if these men are not equal in number to ours coming in these flag vessels, the Admiral will hold himself responsible for accounting for the rest to your satisfaction. The flag named the *Cochran* will set sail in a few days; the one named the *Andrew* arrived only yesterday, but having sprung a dangerous leak in two places, it cannot leave until it is repaired; and we have as yet no news of the one named the *Lord Mulgrave*.

Captain Dundas has taken charge of some English cheese and porter, which I beg you will do me the honour of accepting.

With sentiments of the warmest gratitude which will never be effaced, may I express to your Excellency my very humble acknowledgements for all your acts of kindness and courtesy. It will give me most heartfelt pleasure to seize every opportunity that may offer for demonstrating the respect and most perfect esteem with which I have the honour to be, sir, etc

[CORNWALLIS]

§ - §

CHAPTER 66

Miscellaneous letters etc

---

1 - Stewart to Cornwallis

Stewart to Cornwallis, 19th September 1781   **_71(30): ALS_**

Private   Flood's Plantation
19th September 1781

Lord Cornwallis

My Lord

I wrote to you the 9th[1], giving you an account of the action of the 8th[2], since which nothing particular has happen'd. I sent off my wounded, at least as many as I could get convey'd, in waggons the 9th in the morning towards Monk's Corner and followed with the army that evening to Martines. The 10th in the morning I met Lt Colonel McArthur with a detachment of three hundred men at Ferguson's Swamp. I remained there that day and forwarded my wounded and sick to the Corner, to which place I came early next morning. I was their joined by General Gould, who now commands the army. Green (after having sent off his two remaining three pounders and one he got from me with his amunition waggons by the way of McCord's Ferry), I afterwards found, moved down as far as Martines, but on hearing that I was reinforced, he immediately went off and is now gone some days across the Santee. He crossed at Lawrences Plantation, and had we every thing in proper order for pursuing him he might be drove out of the province. His loss has chiefly fallen on the

---

[1]   *I wrote to you the 9th*: the letter miscarried. A copy is published in Davies ed, *Docs of the Am Rev*, xx, 226-9.

[2]   *the action of the 8th*: the Battle of Eutaw Springs.

Virginia and Maryland lines, and Washington's cavalry is almost all cut to pieces. There are two circumstances in that action which I shall regrate as long as I live: the one was my not having cavalry to profit of the totall rout of their infantry; the other is my rooting partys being out and not having joined me till the action was over, notwithstanding I sent to them on the first notice of the advance of the enemy, which was three hours before the action began. Had I knowen of the enemy's advancing towards me the evening before the action, the rooting partys would not have been out, but my first information of it was from two deserters that came to me about six o'clock the morning of the action, but you know well how difficult information of the enemy's movements are to be got, particularly when you are in a part of the country where every one is against you, which is the case on the Santee. They are almost all with Marrion and Mayam[3]. I assure you the action was bloody and obstinate, and had I not my self rallyed the left wing of the army, carried them on, and exposed myself much, the consequences to my little army, I beleave every one allows, might have been fatal. That and the flank battalion unexpectedly coming upon the flank of the column *or mob* that had forced my left compleated the business and occassioned a totall panick and rout in the enemy. Your Lordship will be so obliging as to transmit home such parts of my publick letter as you think proper, and I'm sure from the friendship you have always showen me you will use your good offices with the King and His Ministers in my favor if you think I deserve it. And I hope it will appear to your Lordship that I should have some mark of His Majesty's favor for beating Mr Green so compleatly, tho it has cost me a good many men, as you would see by the returns. My prisoners taken from me[4] was owing to the left flank breaking, and their noumerous cavalry profiting of it, and my only having fifty cavalry to cover the forming of my infantry when they were obliged to give way, and Colonel Washington own'd to me after the action that they had above five hundred swords men in the field.

General Leslie not yet being arrived keeps us all in the dark as to the plan to be pursued for ensuing campaign. I hope your Lordship has order'd me to act as a brigadier. It would be hard on me to have the command of an army, as I have had for near these three months past, and not to have the appointments of a brigadier general. The wound in my arm is not yet well, but I'm averse to quit the field if I can avoid it, as General Gould wishes me with him. Forgive my troubling you with this long letter and you'll oblige, my Lord,

Your Lordship's most obedient and obliged humble servant

ALEX^R STEWART

---

3   Colonel Hezekiah Maham (1739-1789), who had been serving under Marion, was commissioned in June 1781 to raise a corps of mounted state troops with a complement of 160 rank and file. He never succeeded in completing the corps, which by early November would have only 70 men fit for service. In March 1782 the corps, which was attached to Marion's brigade, was amalgamated with a similar one which Peter Horry had attempted to raise. Maham was given the command, but he was soon taken ill and withdrew to his plantation. Taken prisoner there by loyalists, he was paroled, which terminated his military service. Possessing an irritable temper, which led him after the war to force a deputy sheriff to eat and swallow papers being served on him, he is chiefly remembered for devising the Maham tower, which in April 1781 compelled Fort Watson to surrender. He served several terms in the South Carolina legislature. (*The Greene Papers*, viii-x, *passim*; N Louise Bailey et al, *Biographical Directory of the South Carolina Senate, 1776-1785* (University of South Carolina Press, 1986), ii, 1035-7; Johnson, *Traditions*, 291; Lee, *Memoirs*, 332)

4   *My prisoners taken from me*: Stewart means British troops made captive.

[*Subscribed*:]

General Gould has appointed me to act as brigadier till your pleasure is knowen.

I hope you'll order me to join your army.

Stewart to Cornwallis, 26th September 1781   6(399): ALS

Private
St Clair's Plantation
26th September 1781

Lord Cornwallis

My Lord

I had the honor of writing you both a publick and private letter with an account of the action at the Ewtaws on the 8th of this month. The Commandant of Charlestown wrote me he had a vessell ready to dispatch it to your Lordship but for fear it should be taken beged I would send a duplicate[5], which I now do along with this letter. I hope you received both my publick and private letter safe, and I shall be anxious untill I hear that my conduct, and that of the few gallant troops under my command, meets with your Lordship's approbation. I assure you the action was bloody and obstinate and I hope you'll think the troops behaved well to beat so superior a force. Green's army suffer'd much, were certainly amazingly panick struck to run as they did, leaving their two six pounders behind them. I'm sure the consequances of that action must be very favorable to the situation of this province. Washington's dragoons is almost totally annihilated; only one officer escaped being either killed or wounded. I'm informed by a serjeant of one of the Maryland line that deserted to me that the day before the action the regiment he belonged to was 350 strong and the morning after the action they could not find above fifty of them. Their other Continental regiments likewise suffer'd much. Their militia run away from the field of battle and never stoped till they got home. Your Lordship will see by the returns[6] that I suffer'd a good deal, was unfortunate enough to have the rooting partys of the flank battalion and Buffs taken prior to the action, I'm afraid owing to the officers staying to fight instead of making the best of their way to camp. They had arms with them, and each man had four rounds of amunition. Our left likewise gave way, upon which occasion some prisoners were made by Lee's dragoons being ready to fall upon them. My front line consisted of the flank battalion on the right, next them the Buffs, 63rd, 64th, Cruger's battalion, and Provincial light infantry. The reserve consisted of Allen's corps, 84th detachment, New York Volontiers and fifty mounted infantry, which was all the mounted I had. As to any militia I had, they did not fire a shot the whole day. When the left of the line was broke, matters were in a very critical situation. I myself got them rallyed and put in pretty good order after they had retired about three hundred yards. I told them, if they would follow me, I would insure them success. I instantly charged the

---

[5]   *a duplicate*: not extant.

[6]   *the returns*: see Tarleton, *Campaigns*, 513.

rebels in front, and the flank battalion under Major Marjoribanks[7] attacking them in flank at the same instant, we totally routed them, retook some of our own guns who was in their possesion, and took their two six pounders. I should have taken every gun they had, but their two three pounders had been disabled early in the action and had been sent back with the three pounder they got on our left giving way. Your Lordship may perhaps think that I should have retired upon my first getting information of the enemy advancing, as they were so superior in numbers, but that in my opinion would have been a most dangerous and impracticable step, as by the time my army was formed they were within four miles of me. They had a very numerous body of horse. I should have lost all my rooting partys. The waggon and artillery horses were scatter'd about grasing and were not got together untill about half an hour before the action began. I therefore hope your Lordship will agree with me that a retreat would have been impracticable and impossible. You may perhaps be surprised that my intelligence was so bad as to allow Green's army to get within seven miles of me without knowing it. I do assure you I had five different spys that promised to inform me the moment he came across the Congaree, but not one of them ever came back to me and I'm told some of them joined the rebels, and my first information of him being on this side the Congaree was from two deserters who left him seven miles of[8] the night before the action, and they did not come into me till the morning of the action about 6 o'clock. After the action was over and Green had retired, I was surprised to receive a flag from him beging a cessation of arms, which I instantly refused as I did not know what he might do in that time. Had I body of cavalry any way near their number, I should certainly have destroyed all his infantry. I hope Green will find it difficult to recruit his army. They acknowledge to have had fifty officers killed and wounded. From that you may calculate the number of men they must have lost if in proportion. I hope, my Lord, my conduct will meet your approbation, and when you consider that with not 1,200 fighting men I beat between four and five thousand, they will little blame lay at my door. I stay'd two days on the field of battle, burrying my dead and taking care of my wounded, and then sent of as many of the wounded as I could get carriages to transport them on, and retired to Ferguson's Swamp without Green's daring to fire a shot at me, where I was met by Colonel McArthur with near three hundred men, who had been posted at Monk's Corner for the preservation of the stores for the support of my army. General Gould joined me at the Corner two days afterwards and now commands the army. As I'm not accustomed to write accounts of battles, your Lordship will be so good as to publish such parts of my publick and private letters as you think proper, as I'm sure my character is very safe in your hands, and I'm sure from the friendship you have always honor'd me with, if you think I have any merit in this affair, you will do me every justice with His Majisty and the Ministers in your power and, if I have been of use to my country, that I shall reep some benefit from it. Allow me to trouble your Lordship to forward the enclosed in your dispatches, as a wife and five children will have some anxiety

---

[7] John Marjoribanks (pronounced 'Marshbanks') was major in the 19th Regiment, which had arrived at Charlestown from Ireland at the beginning of June. Commanding the flank battalion at the Battle of Eutaw Springs, he had made a signal contribution to winning the day. Mortally wounded, he would die on 22nd October and be buried 'on the Santee Canal Road about half a mile below the church' (Biggin Church?). As late as 1821 an old headboard was still to be seen marking his resting place. Much lamented, he was respected by both sides to the conflict, not only for his bravery, but also for his humanity and kindness. (Boatner, *Encyclopedia*, 350-6, 679, 680; James, *Marion*, 137; Garden, *Anecdotes* (1st series), 264; Garden, *Anecdotes* (2nd series), 103)

[8] *of*: off.

about me. The wound I received is almost well. It has never obliged me to quit the field.

With respect and regard I have the honor to be, my Lord,
Your Lordship's much obliged humble servant

ALEX STEWART

[*Subscribed*:]

I hope your Lordship has been so good as to order me to act as brigadier general with the appointments.

Enclosure
Stewart to his wife, 27th September 1781   *71(32): ALS*

Santee River
27th September 1781

Mrs Stewart
Stair House
Near Air
North Britain

My dearest Catherine

I have wrote you two or three letters since the action I had with General Green in which I totally defeated him, but in case any of them should miscary, I send this to my Lord Cornwallis to Virginia to forward in his dispatches. The slight wound I got in my left arm is almost quite well, so I beg you'll not be uneasy about it. It is only a *mark d'honeur*. Douglass Hamilton[9] is well but prisoner. Blair is well. We had but one officer killed in the Buffs, which will make the vacancy of an ensigncy, which I have recommended Blair for.[10] Love to all with you. If Lord George Germain has any friendship for me, he'll now have an opportunity of making my fortune for life. Adieu. All happiness attend you.

Ever your affectionate husband whilest

A STEWART

---

[9]   Douglas Hamilton had been commissioned a lieutenant in the 3rd Regiment (the Buffs) on 2nd June 1778. (*Army Lists*)

[10]   Blair would be commissioned an ensign in the 3rd Regiment (the Buffs) with effect from 8th November 1781. (WO 65/164(6) (National Archives, Kew))

Camp at Goose Creek
29th November 1781

Earl Cornwallis

My Lord

How mortified I am to find I'm not to have the honor of serving under you in America. Overpower'd by numbers as you were in Virginia prevents me of that pleasure, which I most sincerly feel and regrate.

I wrote you my publick letter after my defeating Green at the Ewtaws, which no doubt will have reached you ere this. I likewise wrote you several private letters, in which I beg'd of you to correct my publick letter as you thought proper and only to let appear to the publick such parts of it as you thought right, as I was certain from the friendship you have always honor'd me with during our long acquaintance that you would do me every justice in your power. I hope His Majesty will be pleased to do something for me. If he does not, my fate will be cruel indeed. I shall be obliged to sell my commission after serving so long, and all this brought about, not by my own folly, but by money engagements with an unfortunate elder brother, who ruined himself and brought me in for a large sum, which was hard indeed for a man who has a wife and five children, when[11] I did write Lord George Germain (who before I left England was perfectly acquainted with my situation as to money matters) that I might have leave to dispose of my commission and retain my rank in the army and get a new corps. This has been done for Colonel White[12], who never did his country any service. I have taken the liberty to mention this to you, as I'm sure you'll do every thing in your power to forward it for me, particularly so, as I was under your command when I gain'd the action at the Ewtaws. You'll no doubt have seen Mr Green's letter giving an account of that action[13]. I assure you it was bloody and obstinate. When our left gave way, in rallying it I was obliged to expose myself much. The moment I had got the line in order, I placed my self at their head and charged the enemy, the flank battalion at the same time charging them in flank. They gave way in all quarters and their infantry never stoped till they got behind a swamp seven miles from the field of battle, leaving us entierly masters of the field and of all the canon they then had on it. The other two pieces had been dismounted early in the action and sent off, otherwise I should likewise have had them. I received a slight wound in my left arm and had my horse shot in two places. I remained all that day and the next on the ground, taking care of my wounded and sending as many as I could to Charlestown, but was obliged to leve fifty behind, not having waggons to transport them. Green soon after the action sent me a flag, beging a cecesstion of arms that he might have leave to dress such

---

[11] *when*: used in the sense of 'at which time'.

[12] White has not been identified.

[13] *Mr Green's letter..*: of 11th September, it is published in *The Greene Papers*, ix, 328. The version to which Stewart refers had been modified for public consumption and appears in Tarleton, *Campaigns*, 513.

wounded as he had left behind and to burry his dead, which I refused, yet he has the assurance to say in his letter that he left a picket on the field. In short, his letter is full of lies. On my retreat I met McArthur at Ferguson's Swamp. I then halted that day and afterwards retired to Colleton House, where I was joined by General Gould and the 30th Regiment. Green, on my forming a junction with McArthur, retired to the High Hills of Santee, where he has remain'd ever since with numbers of wounded and sick. I had not, as you'll see by the returns, above 1,200 effective men in action, and I really beleave I killed and wounded him near that number. He acknowledges by his account to 59 officers killed and wounded. He must have had men in proportion, but they never give the full numbers. General Gould continued with the command of the army for some little time but was soon taken ill of a fever and went down to Charles Town. I have therefore had the honor to command ever since. General Leslie is arrived, but I have not had the honor of seeing him. Green is dayly expecting reinforcements, when he'll probably draw nearer us. Craig is withdrawn from Wilmington and arrived at Charlestown. I received your obliging letter of the 16th July from Suffolck[14] but never received any other from you, tho' you mention having written me. I had the honor of writing your Lordship on the 16th July[15] when Lord Rawdon left the command of the army to me at Orangeburgh, but I'm informed all my letters must have miscarried and I'm informed by Colonel Balfour that the private letters I wrote you after the action were all lost in the *Hope* sloop of war. I have therefore troubled you with this long scrawle, which I hope you'll have goodness enough to excuse.

With the greatest respect and regard I have the honor to be, my Lord,
Your Lordship's much obliged humble servant

ALEX[R] STEWART

§ - §

2 - Craig to Balfour or Cornwallis

Craig to Balfour, 22nd and 24th October 1781   *6(391): ALS*

Willmington
22nd October 1781

Dear Sir

An officer is this moment arriv'd from the *Solebay*, which is now at the barr, and the time allotted is so short that, in the number of things which unfortunately occurr to be transacted in that time, I am afraid I shall forget many. You must therefore excuse me.

---

14   *your obliging letter..*: see vol V, p 299.

15   Although Stewart assumed command of the army on 16th July, he does not appear to have notified Cornwallis until 15th August. See his letter of that date, p 75.

You judge most justly that our prisoners are an exceeding heavy load on us, and I know few inconveniencies I would not submit to to get rid of them, except that of furnishing a guard of fifty men. *That* I really cannot afford and it would have taken at least *that* to have sent them as propos'd in the transports. I had therefore laid aside all thoughts of that scheme, when the arrival of the *Solebay* gave me fresh hopes of getting rid of them by prevailing on the officer who commands her to take them on board, but on looking over I find a very considerable number to be still in the small pox and, the remainder having been with them, I could not think of running even the chance of introducing an infection on board a King's ship. I have therefore now laid aside that scheme and mean to send as many as we can safely divide among the victuallers and Quarter Master General's vessells, which I can send, keeping only such as at a very short allowance of tonnage can in case of need transport us from this.

I send Mr Burke[16] and all the Continental officers. With regard to the former I must beg to make a remark that he is by far the man of the greatest abilities and one of the most violent in this province, a man whose principles will, I believe, never interfere with his projects and who, if exchang'd, is capable of doing infinite mischief in these parts, where I assure you the turn for Torryism or rebellion is pretty near on a parr or in point of numbers certainly in favour of the former. In this situation his being exchang'd is a matter of infinite consequence to the kind of war carrying on here, and I must most strenuously request to put an absolute negative if possible but at all events to delay it as long as possible.

I look on the present appearance with regard to the observation of the cartel[17] to be the most fortunate circumstance in the world for me, as *our war* depends in a great measure on seizing the most violent men and those of most influence. This has ever been a capital point with me and I really believe I have two thirds of them, but if according to the cartel I am oblig'd to send them home on parole, the trouble and hazard of seizing them is thrown away, for if they even pay so much attention to their paroles as not to take arms (which is not often the case), it is folly to suppose that by intelligence, advice and influence they do not do infinitely more mischief than if in arms, especially as the very circumstance of their being on parole affords them the most convenient oppertunities. This I have most particularly experienc'd here, and as it is not possible for me to send all, I have kept the worse, I mean those whose presence at home might be most prejudicial to our friends. I have sent you all the Continental officers, except two who were parol'd by Fanning to come down here but have not thought proper to observe their words yet. I also inclose you a news paper

---

16 Born in Ireland, Thomas Burke (*c.* 1747-1783) had been elected the revolutionary Governor of North Carolina on 25th June, having previously served as a delegate to the Continental Congress. He was captured on 12th September during a raid on Hillsborough led by David Fanning and Hector McNeil. Transported to Charlestown, he was soon paroled to James Island, but fearing that he was held hostage and that his life was in danger, he decided that his parole was nullified and escaped in January 1782, resuming the governorship of North Carolina. Criticised even by revolutionaries for allegedly violating his parole, he was, according to one historian, a broken and alienated man by the time his term in office ended three months later. (Boatner, *Encyclopedia*, 144-5; *The Greene Papers*, ix, 365n; DeMond, *Loyalists in NC*, 147)

17 *the observation of the cartel*: Greene had suspended its execution. See his letter to Cornwallis of 26th August, p 78.

containing a correspondence between Mr Martin[18], who has succeeded Mr Burke, and myself. I hope you will approve my part of it.

I have no accounts from Virginia but of pretty near the same date as your own. Nothing material on shore had then happen'd. It is certainly a very important and, I may add, awfull moment. The fate of the war hangs on it. I am naturally sanguine, but I cannot help thinking I shall not be deceiv'd when I expect the turn will still be favourable. I have taken every possible precaution to procure the most early intelligence of the decisive event, however it may turn out, but I think you will hear it before me.

With respect to myself I feel so much the unreasonableness of expecting positive directions that I am content to take my share of the censure which with us ever attends misfortune. I have vessells enough to carry me off. I have my eye on the passage by land, and I am fortifying myself in a manner to defy every thing but heavy canon and all the apparratus of a siege because it will be attended with no expence and I forsee cases in which a delay here may be of infinite consequence.

Our situation with respect to provisions is the only thing that gives me pain. Instead of 28 days by the two last vessells we have got only fourteen of flour. I suppose you are yourselves short in that article, but it is to us a grievous disappointment, as when it arriv'd, we were on a short allowance of bread made of peas, oatmeal and flour mix'd and had not above 15 days of that left. The inhabitants of the town are likewise suffering much for want of flour, the corn of last year being all consum'd and that of this not yet gather'd and will be very scarce when it is. The extreme attention which, with the sincerest thanks, I acknowledge you have shewn to all our wants hitherto convinces me you will give us every possible relief in this article, and if you could add a vessell of oats, to be laid by as a certain magazine of forage in cases of necessity, it would be of infinite service to us, as I really cannot bring myself but with difficulty to give corn to our horses when I know hundreds of inhabitants to be suffering for the want of it.

It will be a proof to you how little we fear him that I have neglected all this while to inform you that General Rutherford is advanc'd within twenty five miles of us with a very considerable body. Report makes him 2,000 strong. However, as I know he has been collecting forces from every part, and from other circumstances, I believe him to have about 1,000 or 1,200. They are on the other side the NW and their only view is to subdue the Tories. Distress them they will, but as they are *admirably expert at swamping*[19], they will catch but very few, I hope. They cannot exist long where they are for want of provisions,

---

[18] As President of the North Carolina Senate, to which he had been elected in 1778, Alexander Martin (1740-1807) had become acting Governor, as prescribed in the revolutionary constitution, after Thomas Burke (see above) was captured. He had previously served as Colonel of the 2nd North Carolina Continental Regiment, but following the Battle of Germantown he was charged with cowardice. Tried by court martial, he was acquitted but nevertheless resigned his commission on 22nd November 1777. Besides going on to serve in the North Carolina Senate, he had recently sat on the Board of War and on its successor, the Council Extraordinary. He would be elected Governor in his own right in 1782 and continue to play a prominent part in public affairs for most of his remaining life. He died at 'Danbury', his plantation in Rockingham County, and was buried there. ('Alexander Martin: Writings and Biography', US National Archives and Records Administration; *Appletons'*)

[19] *swamping*: hiding out in swamps.

tho' their eating up all that country, which is another of their objects, will likewise distress us much in point of forage. If they cross the NW and Black River and come into Duplin it will be of more consequence to us and may perhaps induce me to try what we can do with them, tho' I cannot go out with above a fourth of his numbers. I should not be much alarm'd at meeting him, tho' I have even some reason to believe he has some of Grene's people with him. This I am not, however, certain of, especially as I hear nothing of Sumner, who commanded Grene's detach'd men. I may in confidence put a question to you: for what am I trying, at a great risk sometimes, to draw his attention so as to oblige him to detach, if his necessary weakness occasion'd by it is not taken the advantage of? He cannot be strong enough to detach against us (which he has certainly done) and hold his ground against our army in South Carolina at the same time. I must own I am against the general idea of letting all stand till the grand point in Virginia is settled. On the contrary, I think the very great importance of that situation is a reason why we ought to exert ourselves more than ever so as to be more at hand to profit from good success or by previous advantage retard the ill effects of a misfortune.

Colonel Fanning having been wounded, I have receiv'd but an imperfect report from him of his surprising Hilsborough and the subsequent action. However, it was really a gallant attempt and merited the success it met with. The loss of the Highlanders and his people in the action with Butler was very great and serves to shew a degree of spirit in our cause that has never been shewn in any other part of America. They lost near seventy men. A Colonel Kay[20], who met them at the Raft Swamp, and Colonel McDougal[21], who jointly manag'd rather than commanded them from thence, have also very great merit. The latter distinguish'd himself much in the action with Butler. The route they came from Hilsborough here is upwards of two hundred and thirty miles thro' a country which it is scarce possible to have an idea of without seeing it. Their difficulties, from every circumstance of want of provisions, fatigue and the danger of being intercepted, were such as requir'd great resolution to contend with, and at last they would have fail'd in their hopes of reaching this had we not march'd out to support them, which was without any previous communication with them, and I only guess'd at their route from my knowledge of their usual method of conducting

---

[20] Archibald McKay was Lt Colonel of the Cumberland County loyalist militia. By mid 1782 he would have fled to Charlestown, where he was paid as a refugee militia officer till its evacuation. (Clark, *Loyalists in the Southern Campaign*, i, 353, 496, 498, 500; DeMond, *Loyalists in NC*, 147)

[21] Archibald McDugald (1756-?) was a Scot who was brought in 1767 to Cumberland County, North Carolina, where he went on to acquire considerable property and live in affluence. In January 1779 he attempted to make his way to the Crown forces in Georgia, but was taken up and confined on a prison ship in Charlestown harbour for ten months. He proceeded to escape, reached Savannah, and was commissioned an ensign in John Hamilton's Royal North Carolina Regiment, with which he served till the end of the war. Left behind with the bulk of the regiment at Wilmington when Cornwallis marched for Virginia, he was on 27th September seconded to the colonelcy of the Cumberland County loyalist militia and sent into the interior to embody them. Having recently arrived back at Wilmington, as Craig now describes, he was sent again to Cumberland, where Cornwallis's capitulation and Craig's evacuation of Wilmington left him no option but to disband his men. At the close of the war, having had his property in North Carolina confiscated by the revolutionary authorites, he moved to Nova Scotia and was placed on the Provincial half-pay list. In 1787-8 he visited London to pursue with the royal commission his claim for compensation, which was supported by testimony from Balfour, Craig and Hamilton as to his service. (AO 15/121(254), (255), (256), Treasury 64/23(17), and WO 65/165(11) (National Archives, Kew); Clark, op cit, i, 353, 372-3; DeMond, op cit, 147; Nan Cole and Todd Braisted, 'Claims & Memorials', *The On-Line Institute for Advanced Loyalist Studies*, 22nd April 2006)

themselves. General Butler, having mounted between four and five hundred men, march'd so rapidly to get possession of the pass at Livingston's Creek that he reach'd it within three or four hours after they had join'd me. Indeed his march was so rapid that I could not conceive it to be him, and I must candidly confess that error prevented our destroying his corps compleatly, for he as little expected to see us as I did him. On the appearance of forty or fifty of his horse I took it for a Colonel Brown[22], who I knew to have about that number, and order'd the cavalry supported by about 60 infantry to push them, which they did for two or three miles and fell in with about two hundred more who were very advantageously posted. These they drove also but then return'd in consequence of my orders. Even then it might perhaps not have been too late could I have got the better of my prepossession that Butler could not have march'd the distance in the time, We had one man of my troop wounded.

When the militia return'd, I sent Major Manson with 150 men to accompany them as far as the Brown Marsh. We had intelligence that General Butler with near six hundred men was still waiting with a determination to intercept them in their return. Major Manson, getting intelligence of his situation and being apprehensive that if he heard of his being with the militia he might retire further, determin'd to lose no time but attack him the moment he could reach him, which happen'd to be at 12 o'clock at night. The rebels had accounts of his coming and were prepar'd for his reception, notwithstanding which, and notwithstanding the misinformation of his guide, which occasion'd the whole body of militia that were with him (except about fifty) to be useless, yet the spirit of the officers and men under him overcame every difficulty of numbers and situation. The rebels were compleatly dispers'd, leaving twenty dead and five and twenty prisoners. They had also a number of wounded who in the darkness of the night got off. We took between 30 and 40 horses, but the militia the next day got upwards of a hundred more who were runing loose in the woods. We had a serjeant and four men wounded, one of which is since dead. Captain Holloway of the Orange County militia[23] with one private man was kill'd.

All this, as you may imagine, has exasperated the people against the Tories to an amazing degree and they have made every exertion possible to collect the present force to subdue them. I have not heard lately but I am afraid the Highlanders have suffer'd – however, more in their property than their persons. A trifling advantage, in which they did not lose five men, gave the turn to their spirits and dispers'd them in a moment. My Bladen County friends, who are all natives (at least the lower part), took their share of the panick and ran away on the firing of their own centinels, but this among them is of no signification. They will assemble again as soon. Fanning, who for spirit and activity is the best among them, is recovering and has collected again about three hundred men. I have sent to him to take the

---

22 Thomas Brown (?- 1815) was a leading revolutionary in Bladen County and had been appointed to the lt colonelcy of its revolutionary militia in September 1775, an office which he still held. He had also represented his county in the Commons House of the revolutionary assembly. Militarily he had spent almost his entire service in attempting to suppress loyalism in or near his locality, as evinced in October and November 1780, when he led a party of militia against Captain Jesse Barefield (see vol III, p 92, note 56) in the Little Pee Dee region. He had now been captured by Craig, who mentions it in the postscript to his letter. At Aspen Hall, a private residence some four miles from Pittsboro, there are some rare antiques and portraits from Brown's family. (Hay ed, *Soldiers from NC*, 503, 614; William Thomas Sherman, 'Calendar and Record of the Revolutionary War in the South: 1780-1781' (Internet, 23rd April 2006); Robinson, *NC Guide*, 439)

23 Of the Holloways living in Orange County, the one who was killed has not been identified.

oppertunity of Rutherford being down here to lay waste the counties from whence his men come, which will dissipate his *army* in a moment. I am only afraid of his not getting my message, as our communication is exceedingly difficult. However, I trust a good deal to his good sense, which, tho' plain, is not deficient in point of strength.

I have reason to believe Rutherford has kill'd in a shamefull manner a Captain Andrews of the Bladen militia.[24] The men he has treated pretty well, only because he wants to exchange them. If Andrews's fate is ascertain'd as now reported to me, I shall regret much that I think the shooting a captain of theirs in return is a step of too much importance from its consequences for me to take on me, otherwise my conscience would, I declare, be perfectly quiet on the occasion. On the other side the NW, I mean in Duplin etc, the proceedings of scoundrels in small parties is more horrid than can well be conceiv'd, and it is impossible to lay hold of them. I inclose you an order[25] which I mean to issue tomorrow or next day and which affects some of the first people in the province. They ought to use their influence to prevent outrages which they affect to condemn.

The situation of the militia, by the by, is deplorable in respect to cloathing. Many of them are absolutely without coats, and a season of the year is approaching when they must suffer considerably. Blankets is another article of which they have not one among them. The only encouragement I have been able to give them hitherto has been good words and a pair of shoes each, and I assure you I sometimes wonder myself at the confidence they repose in the former — but seriously, among them *I* am almost on a parr with *Old Wallis*.

Of ninety six men which I victuall'd this morning of Governer Martin's corps, thirty four were officers, every one of which has a Negro and a horse, and believe me the proportion will, I am afraid, ever hold the same. The Highlanders settled here, tho' most loyal in their principles and certainly most active in their exertions to shew it, will hardly ever be brought to inlist at all — but, I may I am confident assert, *certainly* not under the officers now appointed. The reasons are *to us* very apparent. Why not then (but I confess there are other people to be convinc'd of it as well as me) employ them in their own way? I can, I think, almost promise that, with a post at Cross Creek, seven hundred young Highlanders without families might be form'd into a corps, but it must be only for a short period, so that the return to their farms is held up to them, and not to go out of the province. In the present mode, where every *little art* of recruiting is daily practis'd, they look on themselves as the mere instruments of the raising of people who were their comrades a month ago. I leave you to judge how the Highland pride, which is a most laudable quality when properly exercis'd, feels on such an occasion.

I am very much concern'd to be oblig'd to give a more unfavourable report of the healthiness of our men than I have hitherto done. We have had more sickness and lost more

---

[24] *Rutherford has kill'd..*: Craig was apparently mistaken. Samuel Andrews was a captain in the Great Swamp company of Hector McNeil's Bladen County loyalist militia. Unsupported after the evacuation of Wilmington, he and other members of the company would flee to Charlestown, where they arrived in the week ending 16th February 1782. He is not to be confused with his namesake, Major Samuel Andrews, who commanded the company. (Clark, *Loyalists in the Southern Campaign*, i, 355, 411; DeMond, *Loyalists in NC*, 237)

[25] *an order*: not extant.

men within this month past than during the whole time of our being here before. It is true very few men have died but such whose constitutions were absolutely worn out, but the number of our sick just now is considerable. Much of it is to be attributed to the sudden and violent change of the weather, but I believe still more to the quantity of rum with which we abounded here. I am endeavouring to lessen the effects of both as much as possible, and as the surest means of doing so to the latter I have order'd all the women and children of Lord Cornwallis's army away by this oppertunity.

I did propose leaving my accounts open to the last of December. However, I will now close them to the 24th October and send them to you the first oppertunity after.

Let me once more return you my sincere thanks for your general attention to our wants and request a continuance of them. I am never asham'd to make or repeat a request that I am confident the person receiving it must think reasonable. The fifty cavalry appointments you have been good enough to send us will about compleat the independant troop, and as I suppos'd them to be design'd principally for that use, I have not touch'd them for my own, but I would beg to mention that mine has been employ'd in exceeding active service ever since the raising of them and never receiv'd a single article but boots. Those that have leather breeches bought them themselves and caps and spurs were procur'd at my expence. The former are of soft leather and totally unfitt for the purpose. As they have no additional pay for serving on horseback, I think they ought to receive every other encouragement of cloaks, breeches etc, and by the time an oppertunity offers they will be entitled to new boots — *all which as usual is humbly submitted.* They are only thirty, of which about a third have been kill'd and wounded already.

I am with great sincerity, dear Colonel,
Your ever faithfull and much oblig'd servant

J H CRAIG

[*Subscribed*:]

24th

The victuallers and every thing are now under weigh to go down the river. I have forgot to mention that I have several colonels of militia and other prisoners here yet, whom I keep for particular reasons, particularly a Colonel Brown of Bladen County and a Colonel Traverse[26] of Cumberland, both men of great influence.

The universal cry among the common people is: 'We must conquer, submit or die. We cannot subsist without salt.' The quantity we destroy'd in New Berne and the small space to which we reduce their works now has made it so scarce as to be fifty hard dollars per bushell in the Back Country. There is not at present an object that employs my mind so much as the destruction of Beaufort and the salt works between that and New River, but if you look at the

---

[26] There are three Traverses and one Travis listed in Hay ed, *Soldiers from NC*, but none appears to have come from Cumberland County.

map you will see the difficulty from the situation to accomplish it with our very small force. However, it is so capital an object that I shall carefully watch any possible opening. There are more prizes carried into Beauford than I believe in all the other ports to the southward of New York put together. Anthony was murder'd by an officer who went to press his horse just before we reach'd New Berne. None of my parties that are gone to watch Rutherford are yet return'd. I begin to doubt his numbers being even what I suppos'd them when I began my letter.

Let me add one more entreaty for at least leather breeches and new boots for my troop. Helmets and cloaks they equally deserve,

Your ever faithfull

JHC

Craig to Balfour, 6th and 7th November 1781   6(401): ALS

Willmington
6th November 1781

Dear Sir

I dispatch a whale boat just to inform you of our situation here. General Rutherford has contriv'd to collect together about 1,500 men, all militia, tho' in some degree better appointed and better furnish'd with ammunition than usual, and is now encamp'd on the opposite side of the NE nearly opposite Heron's Bridge. He seems powerfull in cavalry and last Saturday receiv'd two field pieces from Halifax. At first I thought his only object was to eat up the country, but I now find their intention is to secure to themselves the honour of receiving *us prisoners when hunger obliges us to capitulate*, to accelerate which they confidently report 3 or 4 French frigates are to cruize off the barr. Tho I place not the smallest dependance on this latter circumstance, yet it is right you should be apprized of the possibility of it. I have still a post at the bridge, which would defy them all without cannon, but now they are provided with that article I am not clear whether I can keep it long, especially as it becomes difficult to supply them with provisions and I cannot venture to risk any considerable store there. If I withdraw the post, I shall endeavour to destroy the bridge.

It is a little mortifying, my dear Colonel, to be once more block'd up, but it must for the present be submitted to. I am not, however, the least alarm'd for us, so little so, that even if Mr Rutherford acts sensibly and attacks us, as he certainly, I think, ought to do, I mean not to abandon the town, execrable as it is in every idea of defence. I will attempt to save the property of the inhabitants at almost any risk. The numbers with which I could go out are so very small that I dare not venture it, especially as his great strength of cavalry would make it extremely hazardous if I left the smallest opening to the town, which I could scarce avoid. Had I the 4 or 500 men more I have so long wish'd for, I would hope to give the province a blow they would not easily recover, but for God's sake don't send them without provisions. On that article I can only say we are all on two thirds' allowance. Our bread is a mixture of flour, india meal and rice, and of this and any other species I have about twenty five days only, and in order to make the most of our india corn I have been oblig'd to put all my cavalry horses (but ten of each troop) on an island. These twenty are all I forage. In short, we must look up to you for another supply in twenty five days or our case will be desperate. I would likewise request some oats, as corn will be very scarce.

Our friends above have, as I mention'd in my last, suffer'd in their property, but very little in their persons, few being taken. They are still staunch and exerting themselves. Fanning, who is just recovering from his wound, is again the terror of the country. Seven of his men lately kill'd a Colonel Mabane[27] (a Continental colonel much esteem'd) and six others. Many of the militia of the lower parts have from terror join'd Rutherford, at which I am very glad, as they will never do him any good, I am confident, and would distress me much were they here on the score of provisions. I have about 200 here with me, but almost without arms and, what is much worse, without cloathing. I do not think myself authoris'd to purchase any for them, tho' I think it would be a measure of justice as well as utility. I wish I had directions on this head.

The last news which I can depend on from Virginia was of about a month ago or not so much. Every thing was then well, the enemy waiting to starve Lord Cornwallis out, who was too strong to be attack'd. Washington has a *world* of militia with him, not less as reported than 20,000. Tarleton and Simcoe had each made a sally in which they carried their point, tho' *as usual* with a great loss of men. To ballance this account the rebels in Rutherford's camp fir'd last night a feu de joye. I have not been able yet to learn on what account but imagine it was for the suppos'd surrender of his Lordship.

7th

The easterly winds which have prevail'd here lately give me great hopes the Corke fleet will be arriv'd, and the southerly one which now blows makes me extend my hopes to the seeing part of them here soon. If we should not be so fortunate within the time limited in the former part of my letter, I do not know what we shall do, for it is absolutely not to be got about here on any terms. It is with some difficulty at present I can even supply the hospital with fresh provisions.

We are in the greatest want imaginable of blankets and barrack bedding. Our men have also suffer'd much for want of hospital bedding.

We have a flying report here of another action, in which Green is said to have been wounded. If so, I suppose I shall hear from you. You may imagine that we are not without our little hurries when we have 1,500 men so near us. I have only time to add that

I am with great truth, dear Colonel,
Your ever faithfull

J H CRAIG

---

27   Robert Mebane of Orange County had been a lt colonel in the North Carolina Continental line. Taken prisoner at Charlestown, he was exchanged in June 1781 under the cartel with Greene and became involved in suppressing loyalist operations in North Carolina. (Heitman, *Historical Register*, 387; Wheeler, *Reminiscences*, 330-1)

Charlestown
3rd December 1781

My Lord

May I request your Lordship for one moment to reflect on the mortification under which a man must labour who has every reason to apprehend he has incurr'd the displeasure of the person in the world to whom he looks up with the greatest reverence and esteem, whose approbation he would prefer to that of all mankind besides, and the attainment of which has been the object of his most unwearied endeavours for these ten months past. This, my Lord, is the situation of mind in which I presume to address you. Conscious of having spar'd no pains to forward your Lordship's views and having every reason to be thankfull for the little successes with which my endeavours have been croun'd, I presum'd enough on your Lordship's generosity to have hop'd you would have excus'd the liberty I intended to have taken in asking your protection to my pretensions to succeed to the vacant lt colonelcy of the regiment I belong to. With the most mortifying regret I find myself oblig'd to abandon those hopes and instead of them must confine myself to the most humble request that you would be assur'd I should ever esteem it my greatest ambition as well as duty to pay the most implicit deference to your Lordship's directions, and that I am as incapable of deviating in the smallest tittle from them as I am of hearing with indifference that your Lordship has express'd yourself much displeas'd with me for staying so long at Willmington. I know, my Lord, that Colonel Balfour's letters to you as well as my own miscarried by which you would have been inform'd that I remain'd by his and Lord Rawden's directions, but tho' I know this will sufficiently exculpate me to your Lordship, yet I feel the most extreme anguish to find I could ever for a moment be thought capable of neglecting your instructions and to think I am at present the object of your displeasure on that account. To be satisfied that I had remov'd this unfavourable impression in your Lordship and was restor'd (if I ever possess'd it) to your Lordship's good opinion will be as wellcome as my succession to the promotion for which I intended solliciting your Lordship's patronage, but if your Lordship's goodness carries you so far as to confirm the former by one syllable in support of my pretensions to the latter it will lay me under everlasting obligations of gratitude, tho' it can never increase the sentiments of respect and esteem with which I am, my Lord,

Your Lordship's most obedient and most devoted servant

J H CRAIG

§ - §

3 - The exchange of Cornwallis for Henry Laurens[28]

John Laurens to Cornwallis, 5th November 1781[29]   **_92(77): ALS_**

5th November

The Rt Hon Earl Cornwallis etc

My Lord

I accompanied General Washington on his visit of leave in order to have a more particular conversation on the subject which your Lordship did me the honor to propose by Major Ross. That gentleman will have explained the public reasons that oppose my wishes. I am nevertheless inclined to believe that Congress will consent to the exchange which we have in view. If your Lordship therefore agrees to take measures on your part, I will endeavour to have an official letter sent into New York previous to your departure for Europe.

I entreat your Lordship to accept my best wishes and the sentiments of respect with which

I have the honor to be
Your Lordship's most obedient and most humble servant

JOHN LAURENS[30]

---

[28] For completeness these papers extend to 15th August 1782.

[29] This and Cornwallis's following reply are published with one inconsequential difference in Ross ed, _Cornwallis Correspondence_, i, 127-8.

[30] The son of Henry Laurens (see vol I, p 279, note 61), John Laurens (1754-1782) was born in Charlestown, South Carolina, and educated there and in Europe. Having been admitted to the Middle Temple in London in 1772, he began to study law but returned to North America in 1777 and became one of Washington's aides, displaying much tact and skill. He fought at Brandywine, Germantown, and Monmouth before going south and taking part in military operations there with the rank of lt colonel on the Continental establishment. Taken prisoner in the capitulation of Charlestown, he was soon exchanged and dispatched by Congress as a special envoy to solicit aid from France. Arriving back in Philadelphia on 25th August 1781 with $500,000 and two cargoes of military supplies, he went on to take part in the siege of Yorktown and was one of the commissioners appointed to settle the articles of capitulation. While his political and diplomatic dexterity suggested that he was destined to go far in public life, his military reputation has left much to be desired. Wedded to the outdated idea that military glory lay in exposing himself needlessly or recklessly to danger, he took risks with the lives of himself and his men. Not content that the war was won with the surrender of Cornwallis, he would become involved in the small-scale and senseless warfare that continued in South Carolina. On 27th August 1782 he would be killed near Combahee Ferry while leading on his men in a typically reckless manner. Politically adept, militarily he was a fool and paid the price for it. (_DAB_; Moultrie, _Memoirs, passim_; McCrady, _SC in the Rev 1775-1780_ and _1780-1783, passim_)

Cornwallis to John Laurens, 25th November 1781   92(79): Df

New York
November 25th 1781

Lt Colonel Laurens etc etc etc

Sir

I am very sorry that I had left York before General Washington and yourself did me the honour to call at my quarters. I this day received by Lt Colonel Dundas your letter of the 5th. If you will procure an official letter to be sent to me saying that I am at liberty as soon as Mr Laurens is released in exchange for me, I will on my arrival in England take every measure in my power to forward that business.

I beg you will accept my acknowledgements for your civility and attention to me and the other British officers, and believe me to be with great esteem, sir,

Your most obedient and most humble servant

[CORNWALLIS]

Carleton to Cornwallis, 15th August 1782   7(3): ACS

New York
August 15th 1782

Rt Hon Earl Cornwallis

My Lord

I received the inclosed letter from General Washington, to which I was enabled to make the answer which your Lordship will also find inclosed and which I have extracted from a letter written by Admiral Digby and myself to General Washington. I have as yet heard nothing further on this subject, but some proper notice will, I presume, be soon taken of it, of which I shall by the first opportunity acquaint your Lordship.

I am with great regard
Your Lordship's most obedient and most humble servant

GUY CARLETON[31]

---

[31] Born at Strabane to an Anglo-Irish family, Sir Guy Carleton (1724-1808) had served as a field officer during the Seven Years' War before becoming Governor of Quebec from 1768 to 1778. In 1775-6, while concurrently Commander-in-Chief in Canada, he had defeated an invasion by American revolutionaries. In May 1782 he arrived at New York to supersede Sir Henry Clinton and would remain in command until the evacuation. Between 1786

Enclosure (1)
Washington to Carleton, 30th July 1782[32]   *92(83): C*

Head Quarters
30th July 1782

His Excellency Sir Guy Carleton

Sir

In pursuance of Act of Congress directing me 'to remand immediately Lt General Earl Cornwallis to the United States unless the Hon Henry Laurens Esq be forthwith released from his captivity and furnished with passports to any part of Europe or America at his option or be admitted to a general parole', I have to request your Excellency that orders for this purpose may be communicated to Lt General Earl Cornwallis by the first conveyance, informing him that, as this order is strictly conformable to the tenor of his parole, I have the fullest expectation of his immediate return to the United States unless the conditions mentioned in the Act of Congress are complied with.

I have the honor to be, sir,
Your Excellency's most obedient and most humble servant

G^O WASHINGTON

Enclosure (2)
Extract, Carleton and Digby to Washington, 2nd August 1782   *92(85): C*

With respect to Mr Laurens we are to acquaint you that he has been enlarged from all engagements without any condition whatever, after which he declared of his own accord that he considered Lord Cornwallis as freed from his parole. Upon this point we are to desire your Excellency's sentiments or those of Congress.

§ - §

---

and 1796, having been created Baron Dorchester, he would again serve as Governor of Quebec. He died at Stubbings House, his estate near Maidenhead. (*ODNB*; Boatner, *Encyclopedia*, 174-9, 182-4)

[32] This and enclosure (2) are published with no differences in Ross ed, op cit, i, 140.

4 - A return of officers taken by capitulation
(2(32): DS)

A comparative view of the British and German officers taken by capitulation at York Town, 19th October 1781, with the American officers taken by capitulation at Charlestown, 12th May 1780

RETURN of officers under the capitulation of York Town to be exchanged, exclusive of those left behind with the men		Supposed to remain of American prisoners taken at Charlestown by capitulation, 12th May 1780	
Lt general	1	Brigadier generals	2
Brigadier general	1	Colonels	10
Colonels	2	Lt colonels	11
Lt colonels	14	Majors	14
Majors	12	Captains	81
Captains	58	Lieutenants	62
Lieutenants	93	Ensigns	17
Ensigns	32	Regimental surgeons	3
Adjutants	2	Mates to regiments	1
Quarter masters to regiments	4		
Regimental surgeons	3		
Regimental mates	1		
	Value		*Value*
1 lt general	1044	2 brigadier generals	400
1 brigadier general	200	10 colonels	1100
2 colonels	200	11 lt colonels	792
14 lt colonels	1008	13 majors	364
12 majors	336	79 captains	1264
58 captains	928	50 lieutenants	300
93 lieutenants	558	16 ensigns	64
32 ensigns	128	3 regimental surgeons	18
2 adjutants	12	1 regimental mate	4

4	quarter masters to regiments	24		
3	surgeons to regiments	18		
1	mate to regiments	4	Taken at Blandford, 10th May 1781, Virginia	
			1 major	28
			2 captains	32
			5 lieutenants	30
			Taken by Colonel Simcoe's and on parole at Philadelphia	
			3 lieutenants	18
			Remains of New York prisoners	
			4 lieutenants	24
			1 ensign	4
			Ballance in favor of the Americans	28[33]
		4460		4460

NB: Exclusive of the within comparative view, provision is made for the exchange of Lt General Burgoyne, and as all the British and German officers taken in the Carolinas since the capitulation of Charles Town have been exchanged down to July last and no American officers that have been taken since the above capitulation are included, it may reasonably be supposed that the ballance of officers is in our favor.

JOS LORING[34]
Commissary General of Prisoners

§ - §

---

[33] *28: 18.*

[34] A native of Massachusetts, Joshua Loring (1744-1789) had once served as a lieutenant in the British Army. Shortly after retiring in 1768, he was appointed High Sheriff of Massachusetts. A firm loyalist, he accompanied the British garrison to Halifax when Boston was evacuated in 1776. Early in 1777, undoubtedly through the influence of his wife, who had become William Howe's mistress, he became Commissary General of Prisoners. Proscribed and banished by the revolutionary authorities in Massachusetts, he died in England. (Boatner, *Encyclopedia*, 659; Sabine, *Biographical Sketches*, ii, 27-8)

5 - Macleod to Cornwallis

Macleod to Cornwallis, 24th November 1781   *71(34): ALS*

Charles Town
November 24th 1781

Lt General Earl Cornwallis
New York

My Lord

If my wishes for your Lordship's health and happiness should prove troublesome, you are to attribute them to the number of obligations already conferr'd, which encourage me to forward these by letter when denied the satisfaction of personally expressing them. Seperated from your Lordship, I am afraid, for a *long* time, it would add much to my uneasiness that you embark'd for Europe without some acknowledgement of my gratitude, without some assurances that your favor and esteem, however thrown away upon an undeserving, have not been lavish'd on an insensible.

Among the many uncomfortable ideas arising from the alteration of our course[35], the possibility of your Lordship's being unsuccessfull[36] was one of the most painfull to us all. I myself, however, have still, notwithstanding former disappointments, some faith in copper bottoms. It is on that faith I build my hopes of your reaching New York. As for us, considering ship-situation and the inflexible *north-westers*, we think ourselves fortunate in attaining any part of the coast. General Lesslie and our Commandant (who would not have cursed the fates which had conducted the *Cochran* here) have done every thing to compensate for those adverse ones which have blown us hither. Two ships are order'd to be fitted out immediatly for us, but a winter's passage, the chance of a West India visit and at the best an arrival in the land of strangers (for your Lordship will probably be half way to England) are not strong incentives for my undertaking *individually* to buffet the ocean a second time these three months — indeed *at all*, if it can be permitted me to embark from hence for England.

As General Lesslie and Colonel Balfour both write, I shall leave every circumstance relative to Charles Town to them and, having trespass'd long enough upon your Lordship's time already, conclude as I began, with wishing you ease and tranquillity and a reestablishment of health and constitution. In the continuation of my wish you must pardon me for being a little selfish — I cannot express how happy I shall be in again seeing you at the head of an army and not covet[37] the pleasure of being *one* in it.

---

[35] *alteration of our course*: from New York to Charlestown.

[36] *being unsuccessfull*: in reaching New York.

[37] *not covet*: i.e cannot not covet.

May I take the liberty to beg my remembrances to General O'Hara, Major Ross and my friends Broderick and Haldane and to be believed, my Lord, with every degree of respect and affection

Most earnestly and sincerely yours

J MACLEOD

§ - §

6 - The passage of Cornwallis to England

Certificate on capture by privateer, 17th January 1782　　　*7(1): DS*

We the subscribers, the master of and passengers on board the *Greyhound* transport from New York in North America, do hereby certify that, haveing been made prize on the fourteenth day of this instant January by the *Boulogne* privateer of and from Saint Maloes, [we] proceeded in the said ship under the direction of le Sieur Julien Duroutois, first lieutenant of the said privateer, in order to reach the ports of Morlaix or Saint Maloes, which by reason of the violence of the winds and weather it hath been impossible to effect, and as all the crew belonging to the *Greyhound* were removed on board the privateer and the people who were put on board of her from the privateer are quite insufficient to navigate her and she could not have resisted the violence of the winds and weather, which has now lasted three days and two nights, unless they had been assisted with the utmost exertions of the master and all the other persons on board the *Greyhound* who were capable to assist but who are thereby now become so exhausted and fatigued that they as well as the officers and men belonging to the said privateer are not able to continue them much longer, and as there is not quite one butt of water on board the said ship and it would be attended with the most iminent danger to the lives of all the persons who are board the said ship if, with the wind now blowing and which has the appearance of continuing and increasing, to approach to the coast of France, we therefore, in order to the preservation of our lives and the lives of all the persons who are on board of her, have earnestly requested the said Julien Duroutois to put into a near port in England to procure necessary assistance, and the said Julien Duroutois, being convinced of the necessity of so doing and the crew belonging to the privateer unanimously consenting and concurring with him, hath agreed thereto. We in consideration thereof do hereby undertake and promise that it shall in no wise be of prejudice to the owners or marinners of the said privateer concern'd in the capture but that the said ship shall be actually and faithfully reserved for their benefit and deliver'd to the said Julien Duroutois to proceed to Saint Maloes or Morlaix unless it shall hereafter be agreed upon that the same shall be sold and disposed of for their benefit in England, and we and each of us do hereby declare that we hold ourselves bound and promise upon our parole of honour that we will hereafter consider ourselves to be in the same situation as prisoners as we should have been if we had arrived in France on board the said ship.

Witness our hands near the Ram Head on the coast of England
the seventeenth day of January Anno Domini 1782

CORNWALLIS

CHEWTON
Aide de camp

A ROSS
Aide de camp

H HALDANE
Aide-de-camp

THO^S TONKEN
Captain, Navy

ALEX^R MERCER[38]
Captain, Engineers

J SIMPSON
Secretary to the King's Commissioner

HENRY STORK[39]
Major

JOSEPH CLARKE
Master

[Endorsed:]

I do hereby certify and acknowledge that, in consideration of the necessities and distress set forth in the within certificate and from a conviction of the great danger which would attend my attempting to gain a port on the coast of France, I have, with the concurring opinion of my crew and in confidence of the stipulations contracted in the said certificate, voluntarily agreed to the request to go into an English port for the purpose therein mentioned.

JULIEN DUROUTOIS[40]
Captain

FRANÇOIS FONTAINE[41]
First mate

§ - §

---

[38] Alexander Mercer had been serving as the commanding engineer at New York. Commissioned an ensign in the Corps of Engineers on 17th March 1759, he was promoted to lieutenant on 23rd June 1762, to captain lieutenant on 1st April 1771, and to captain on 25th May 1772. (Clinton, *American Rebellion*, 538; *Army Lists*)

[39] No major named Henry Stork or bearing a variant of the surname has been identified. He does not appear in the *Army Lists* or in Raymond's 'British American Corps'.

[40] Julien Jean Duroutois would in later years become captain of the packet *Franklin* owned by Benjamin Dubois of Saint-Malo. In January 1791 he would be made an honorary member of the New-York Marine Society for rescuing shipwrecked Americans. (Dorothy Twohig etc eds, *The Papers of George Washington: Presidential Series* (Letterpress edition by the University Press of Virginia), v (January-June 1790), 9n)

[41] François Fontaine has not been identified.

PART FOURTEEN

Supplementary papers

CHAPTER 67

Papers undated or written before 1780

1 - Preparations mainly for the civil administration of South Carolina

Elliott to Russell, 22nd December 1779   *1(33): C*

22nd December 1779

Captain Russell[1]

Sir

By the General's desire you have, enclosed, the following papers in order that you may lay the same before him as time and circumstances may require, viz:

---

[1] Born in Cork, Peter Russell (*c.* 1738-1808) was a captain lieutenant in the 64th Regiment who was serving as an assistant secretary to Clinton. Now about to embark for Charlestown, he has left a journal of the campaign which was edited by James Bain Jr and published in the *American Historical Review*, iv (April 1899), 478-501. A colourful character who in his earlier years was addicted to gambling, he had served as a junior officer in the 14th and 94th Regiments during the Seven Years' War before incurring gambling debts at Martinique, evading his creditors, and purchasing a 482-acre tobacco plantation 42 miles west of Williamsburg, Virginia. There he remained for almost eight years until he again lost at gambling and had to sell up. Returning to England, he was beset by demands to pay his Martinique creditors and ended up in the Fleet Prison, being discharged in October 1774 under the Insolvent Debtors Relief Act. On 19th December 1780 he would be promoted to a captaincy in the 64th but sell his commission nine months later at an inflationary price of £2,000. On 1st January 1782 he was appointed by Clinton the Superintendent of the Port of Charlestown and three months later was commissioned a captain in the Royal Garrison Battalion. In May 1782 he took passage with Clinton for England. In later life he became Receiver and Auditor General in Upper Canada with seats on the Executive and Legislative Councils. When Simcoe took leave of absence from the office of Lt Governor, he served in his place as administrator from July 1796 to August 1799. He died at York (Toronto), having amassed a land holding of several thousand acres. (*DCB*)

N° 1	Proclamation to be published on landing
2	Reasons assigned for proposing regulations, proclamations etc
3	Heads of civil regulations and military proclamations proposed for any town or place that may in future submit or be conquered
4	Proclamation appointing a Superintendent and regulating trade
5	Heads of proclamations to establish civil regulations and instructions to the officers appointed
6	Copys of the Commissioner's proclamations which may be found necessary in point of forms when the General acts as Commissioner
7	Endorsed forms used at the Superintendent's Office in New York, to be given to the Superintendent when N° 4 is published.

Besides the enclosed papers, I must beg leave to observe that it will be necessary for the General to publish a proclamation relative to Negroes, ordering all such as may come in to give in their names, together with their masters' names and former places of abode, to the Mayor and aldermen, who must have orders to send them to the person appointed to enroll them, where they must receive a certificate thereof. All Negroes found without having such a certificate (except those belonging to the inhabitants in town, who ought to have one from their masters) must be imprisoned. This will prevent the bad effects found at New York and put it in the General's power to make the proper use of them in labouring for the different departments.

When a proclamation is issued for new corps or enlistment, it will be proper to insert a promise of lands.

Every publication proposed at present is in the General's name as Commander in Chief, but when he receives his appointment as Commissioner, most of them must be entitled accordingly, but particular attention must be paid to the issuing a proclamation similar to two clauses in N° 6, one for allowing prizes to come into port, and the other in relation to the exportation of prize goods and others. A Court of Admiralty must be established and a judge etc appointed.

Before the General receives his appointment as Commissioner, it will be absolutely necessary, upon his taking possession of any town where he proposes keeping possession, for the benefit of men of war and privateers as well as to secure necessary supplys, immediately to apply to the Admiral to give orders to the fleet to allow all prizes to enter the harbour unmollested and also merchantmen coming with supplys having proper licences and documents from Custom Houses, altho for other ports in America or the West Indies, likewise to come into harbour unmollested. And the General must give similar orders to the Superintendent.

Be so good to write me when the General chuses to have supplys sent from this port.

I am etc

[ANDREW ELLIOTT]

Enclosure Nº 2
Elliott's reasons for proposing civil regulations, etc   *1(40): C*

When Georgia was taken, His Majesty's Commissioners' powers were in force, and their instructions to the land and sea commanders of any expedition to declare any place or province that might submit or be conquered at His Majesty's peace was agreeable to Act of Parliament and became at once valid. No such powers as were then vested in the Commissioners now subsist, altho' there can be no doubt the Commander in Chief, when the public good requires it, may with freedom take upon him to exert similar powers, which would certainly be confirmed by Parliament.

In the case of Georgia no similar instance can arise, as that province was so thinly inhabited that the getting possession of Savannah was getting, in a manner, possession of the whole province, so that it was proper enough to make trial of establishing a civil government at once. A Governor, Council etc were soon sent out from Great Britain, and civil government immediately established. Altho' it could only even there be done in a lame manner, yet the consequences attending that lameness in the civil line could not be so conspicuous as it would have been in an old well settled province, where the courts of law might be called on immediately to decide on mortgages, property etc when one or more of the parties might be in rebellion. This alone would greatly retard a general settlement with the colonies. Besides, where an army is to act in a province, until that province in general submits, it will be found improper to restore a capital to His Majesty's peace, as the military powers in the place so restored to His Majesty's peace can then only enforce the civil and mercantile laws, when their assistance is called for by the proper civil officers.

In a province still in rebellion, every place in that province that is conquered or has submitted ought to continue under the direction of the Commander in Chief till the greatest part of the province submits; otherwise, great delays, many disputes etc between the military and civil will arise, and every necessary step the service requires the General to take that may encroach upon the civil power will be deemed oppressive and arbitrary. Small as the army and the number of inhabitants were in Georgia, and critical the situation of both, which would of course allow of but one object, yet it is probable some inconveniency of this nature may have happened from the too speedy reestablishment of government; and if much prudence, and much subduing of the passion of retaliation, has not been exerted by the civil, many future inconveniencies will appear.

In this light the inclosed plan is offered as the ground work of establishing at any place that in future may submit or be conquered such a mixture of civil regulations as may not only prevent immediate disorders and future inconveniencies but secure to the inhabitants protection to their persons and property and at the same time give a means of settling such quarrels and disputes about money matters etc as may daily arise amongst them, and, by giving the management of billetting etc to the civil, will even clear the military from the complaints of individuals, who always on such unavoidable occasions think themselves aggrieved, and, by restraining every power from touching on property or giving a legal opening to private passions to exert themselves, will smooth the way to immediate peace and good order when a general reestablishment of government takes place.

In September 1776, when New York was taken possession of, it was found almost clear of inhabitants. Property, houses etc got immediately into confusion. It was not thought necessary to make any regulations in the civil way as a prospect of a general settlement appeared then so near. A Commandant alone could not attend to every thing, and of course matters could not be brought into proper order. In July 1777 a Superintendent of Exports and Imports was appointed to regulate the trade. In May 1778 General Jones[2], by the direction of General Clinton, appointed a police to assist the Commandant. The many daily incurable evils that appear to have arisen from the delay of civil regulations taking place, and the many future inconveniencies that it will occasion, makes it absolutely necessary that civil plans and military proclamations should be provided to go with every expedition to prevent those incurable evils which the least delay of the regulations they ought to establish must always occasion.

Enclosure N° 3
Heads of civil regulations and military proclamations   *1(50): C*
proposed by Elliott

HEADS of CIVIL REGULATIONS for the securing peace and good order in any town
or place in America now in rebellion that in future by conquest
or submission may come under His Majesty's protection — also
HEADS of necessary PROCLAMATIONS for establishing the same

A Commandant to have a Council consisting of three inhabitants, men of abilities, moderation, character and fortune, who must attend the Commandant, when called upon, to decide the disputes that may arise between the military and the inhabitants. All criminal matters to be by the Commandant and Council referred to court martials, and no dispute whatever decided that originated before the submission of the place. Fining, imprisonment, and turning out of the lines to be the punishments to be used to enforce their determinations, and if possible a gaol to be set apart for the civil line.

This Council to be empowered to fix upon barracks for the soldiers, houses and billets for officers, regimental stores, stores, wharves and fuel yards for the Artillery, Commissary General, Quarter Master General and Barrack Department etc, also to point out where and in what manner fuel, fresh provisions, waggons, carts and horses etc may be procured, by the departments that it may concern, with the greatest facility and least inconveniency to the inhabitants under His Majesty's protection. All their proposals for effecting the above, when approved of by the Commandant, he must confirm in garrison orders that all the departments

---

[2]   Daniel Jones was a major general commanding the garrison of New York. On 4th May 1778 he issued a proclamation establishing the office of Superintendent General of Police for the city, to which he appointed Andrew Elliott.

may act accordingly. Three inferior officers under the Council will be necessary to attend the Barrack Office and other departments, to assist in pointing out and seeing that all is done agreeable to the Commandant's orders, and to report thereon to the Council, who will inform the Commandant of what is amiss. A Port Master and assistant, in like manner, for the wharf business, under the same direction, and to report as above.

When impressing horses, carriages etc etc etc is necessary, the orders to be signed by the Commandant and Council, and the rates to be paid for hire etc fixed by them and published.

> NB: By the above method of deciding complaints between the inhabitants and the military there are three civil judges to one military; the barracking, billetting etc etc will be pointed out with more correctness and ease by men who know the size of families, houses, and principles of owners; and as the whole appears to lean so much to the civil, no complaints can be made of military oppression. The necessity of the grievance will appear, and quiet submission follow.

Officers under any name to be appointed to act as a Mayor, with four or six in character of aldermen as the size of the place may require, who are daily to attend in the different districts of the town and determine all such complaints and disputes as would have come before them as aldermen by the charter of the town and imprison for non compliance of determinations. Where a fine is thought necessary, the fine to be determined by the Mayor and aldermen, who are twice a week to meet in a body to hear and decide on such appeals as may be made from the determination of any single alderman when the sum exceeds [blank] pounds sterling. Where any case appears that requires punishment, the delinquent to be confined by the alderman he was first brought before, and at the first meeting in a body, if agreed to by the majority, the affair to be sent to the Commandant and Council to be referred to a garrison court martial. The Mayor and aldermen to be empowered to collect and receive all rents, ferriages, revenues etc that formerly belonged to the corporation, and, as circumstances may require, to raise a contribution on every house, agreeable to the number and circumstances of the occupiers, to enable them to take care of alms houses, relieve private objects, clean the streets, light lamps etc, all which must be under their care. A Treasurer, chosen by the Council, must keep all accounts and pay money by orders signed by the Mayor and two aldermen, his accounts to be examined quarterly by the Mayor and aldermen and then laid before the Commandant and Council. The naming of their assistants and their number to enable the magistrates to perform the above duties must be left to them, to be paid out of public funds.

No inhabitant to be imprisoned, but by order of the General or Commandant, until he is carried before one of the Council, the Mayor or an alderman, any of whom may sign an order for commitment. And no houses or property in towns belonging to persons out in rebellion to be given away for any purpose but upon the express condition of their being immediately resigned by the person or persons who may have been allowed to make use of such property or houses whenever the owner returns to his allegiance in compliance with such proclamations as the Commander in Chief may think fit to issue for that purpose.

> NB: No precaution of this sort having been taken before Sir William Howe's second proclamation was published, in which a restoration of property was promised, the consequences were bad. Many came in; claimed their property; its situation did not

admit of its being returned; character was taken notice of; the owner disgusted, and returned to the rebels, often from necessity. One returning prevented hundreds from coming. All these matters as yet appear of little consequence but will at a general settlement be very disagreeable and therefore ought to be guarded against in future by every Commander in Chief. Sir William Howe's prospects of suddenly finishing the military operations and then leaving the civil to act prevented proper steps being taken till matters were too far gone at New York.

Mercantile disputes to be settled by the merchants, who must monthly elect a committee of seven to meet three times a week to determine on all disputes connected with merchants' accounts, shipping, bills, insurances etc etc. Their report to be sent to the Commandant and Council for their approbation and then to be enforced by their authority if necessary.

NB: Even where the laws are in force, most mercantile disputes are settled by a reference to merchants, as custom and usage is often to be attended to, so that by the above method the Commandant and Council will have little trouble and no doubts or uneasiness in confirming mercantile decisions.

The regulations of trade to be the same as at New York, and the same restrictions in regard to the exportation of every thing fit to eat, drink, or that is wanted for the use of the army and navy. As the powers of the Commissioners that settled the mercantile plan at New York are expired, it will become necessary for the General to issue in his own name a proclamation for that purpose as similar to Sir William Howe's and the Commissioners' as possible. These proclamations having been approved of by administration makes it the surest path for the Commander in Chief to walk in. Both proclamations may be easily blended together to answer any place, leaving out the regulations relating to Long Island and Staaten Island, as the supplies going into the country must be first regulated by situation and disposition of the country and inhabitants, and occasionally enlarged or restrained, as circumstances may require, by orders to the Superintendent of the port from the Commandant and Council.

NB: All the civil regulations proposed by this plan, altho' they appear greatly in favor of the civil, are still left entirely under the controul of the Commandant, and their existence depending upon the Commander in Chief leaves the whole power where it ought to be till civil government is legally established.

Salt ought to be allowed to go with expeditions as it often tempts the inhabitants to run risks in bringing in supplys that money would not have induced them to undertake. A number of merchant ships burthen a fleet; a number of merchants croud the army; and a large supply of goods, hurried into a new acquisition, too suddenly forces open the door of communication with the country, necessary only when the disposition of the people is known and regulations established for granting them supplys of merchandize. If orders are left to allow the merchants to carry British manufactures etc from this[3] as soon as from authority we hear of success, such supplys will soon follow.

---

[3]   *this*: New York.

PROCLAMATIONS

A proclamation offering such terms, restoration of property etc as the General shall think fit in order to encourage submission and return to allegiance, in which should be pointed out what certainly may be expected when the troops are fired upon from houses, barns etc.

A proclamation appointing a Commandant and such officers as shall be thought necessary to execute the civil regulations that may be adopted, together with their powers.

A proclamation to settle trade as at New York (as before mentioned).

NB: The Superintendent of New York may be ordered to give copys of forms used etc in the business of importing and exporting, as they also have been approved of.

MONEY

Had a plan been established for the circulating paper bills of credit at the different places in America that have been taken possession of by His Majesty's troops, the advantages that would have acrued can hardly be enumerated. Great Britain by sending out specie is drained and America realy made rich, and it has put a weapon into the hands of rebellion it could not have otherways obtained. It occasions or may occasion great disadvantages where accident detains the soldiers' pay, and is always attended with risk both from sea and capture; but at New York it is too late to introduce such a plan by order of Government on Government security. Had such a plan at first taken place at New York, Long Island, that now almost requires an army to keep the inhabitants in order, would have been almost sufficiently guarded by the inhabitants themselves had their wealth which they have obtained from the army been in bills of credit in place of specie, as that very wealth would have depended upon clearing the island of rebels and securing its possession to Great Britain. On the success and credit of that kingdom would then have depended the payment of their securities, so that those who are now spys would have been informers, and all from interest real friends to Government, as in this rebellion interested views has done more than principle. If it is agreed that such consequences would have followed the circulation of paper bills of credit, it is certainly an object to be attended to, particularly as it is done with no risk to the money contractors, who in fact may be gainers by the usual loss and destruction of bills, provided they can get such printed as cannot easily be counterfeited; and the Commander in Chief must be applauded by the nation, whose interest alone he consults in giving orders necessary to enforce such a circulation. If a plan of this sort is agreed upon, it must take place by virtue of a proclamation from the Commander in Chief the day any town or place is conquered or submits, as it would then seem a thing of course to the inhabitants, but if any time elapses, it would give them a suspicion of necessity. Merchants, traders and others must be ordered to take as cash bills signed by [blank]. Such bills will then answer all publick departments and these bills when offer'd to [blank] must be taken up in sums not less than £100 sterling, for which the owner of the bills will receive from [blank] a draft on [blank] in London for that amount, and so on in proportion. A proper quantity of circulating cash will be necessary, which may come from the soldiers' pay and other small payments to be made in specie, but bills of credit will equally answer the merchant and of course the departments and country people bringing produce, as these bills will not only be easily got out of the lines but also easily concealed, so that it is to be expected that, in place of the gold and silver that creeps out of the lines from New York, paper bills will there find their way into the country, by which means the possessors are secured friends to Government from interest, and gold and silver kept from getting amongst the rebells.

Simpson's proposals for the civil administration   *4(437): ADS*
      of South Carolina, undated[4]

I have considered the plans, proposed by Mr Elliott for restoring peace and good order in such places in America as by conquest or submission may come under His Majesty's protection, with that attention and deference that is due to his knowledge and experience, upon which I beg leave humbly to suggest the following observations.

As a general submission of the country hath been the consequence of the reduction of Charles Town, a plan of more general jurisdiction will be proper than what is proposed by Mr Elliott, which seems to be only calculated for a town, or at least limits not near so extensive as are now under His Majesty's subjection in this province; and as there are no civil officers of any denomination under the King's authority now in the country, some establishment will be absolutely necessary to prevent that anarchy and confusion which will otherwise infallibly ensue. In a matter so entirely unprecedented any system that can at once be proposed must be very imperfect, especially as so short a time is allowed for consideration. The more simple it is, the more likely is it in my apprehension to succeed in calming the minds and conciliating the affection of the people, who from the necessity of the case and the impossibility to apply an immediate remedy will, it is hoped, remain patient under some inconveniences that are unavoidable until that government can be restored which indiscriminately secures to all persons peace, harmony, security and liberty.

As a ground work I would propose to keep unblended as much as possible the judicial from the executive powers, and that wherever the local institutions of the country (such as roads, dams, bridges etc) can be executed, it should be done by persons appointed in the method the nearest that can be to what is prescribed by the laws. Their fitness for the duty will be what is most material; in general their political opinions will be of no consequence.

I will not take upon me to add any thing to what is recommended by Mr Elliott for the government of the town, altho' the difference of our customs and situation will render some deviations necessary, but for securing the quiet and in some measure administering justice through the country I most humbly propose:

That under the commanding officer of His Majesty's troops, who in all cases, whenever he shall think proper to interfere, must be considered as supreme, there shall be a Commandant for Charles Town, to be assisted with a Council consisting of four persons in the manner proposed by Mr Elliott's plan, and to exercise his functions in the manner suggested therein.

---

[4]   Written shortly after the fall of Charlestown. Simpson became the Intendant General of Police in South Carolina on 23rd June 1780.

That the senior of the council[5] to the Commandant shall be the Intendant General of the Civil Police throughout the whole country, and the junior council Intendants of the Police for Charles Town District.

That there shall be three superintendents of the police for each district in the country, who are to maintain a constant correspondence with the Intendant General of the Police and regulate their conduct by such instructions as they will receive from him or the Commandant or the commanding officer of the army.

That it shall be the duty of the intendants in their several districts to execute the duties usually exercised by Justices of the Peace, church wardens, overseers of the poor, commissioners of high ways, and in general all the peace establishments, always nevertheless remembering that their authority is not to clash with or in any shape controul a military order, which they must always hold themselves in readiness to give effect to, if called upon, to the utmost of their power.

That all disputes between citizens shall be settled by the intendants in their several districts, but any orders they may give may be subject to be reversed by the commanding officer of the army or in Charles Town by the Commandant.

That it shall be in the power of the intendants in their several districts to appoint persons in the nature, and to do the duty, of constables therein, reporting them to the Intendant General, and they shall be allowed the same fees as were heretofore allowed by law to those officers.

That all private disputes between citizens and soldiers shall be referred to an officer in the army and one of the intendants, who, if it arises in Charles Town, are to report to the Commandant, and, if in the country, the officer commanding in the district, and he is to decide thereon, unless it is determined otherwise by the commanding officer of the army.

The intendants of the police shall on no account receive any gratuity or reward for their trouble by way of fees, but in consideration of their trouble they shall receive the following salaries, viz: [*blank*].

It shall be the duty of the intendants diligently to attend to the police of the country; to give immediate information to the military officers and to the Intendant General of every appearance there may be of any publick commotion; to watch over the Negroes and to settle disputes between them and their masters; and to see that none of the masters violate the engagement they undertook when they received the Negroes that had belonged to them who have joined the British Army. And the neglect of their duty will be deemed criminal, and for which they must be accountable.

The militia of the country, under the established laws or such regulations and engagements as already have been or hereafter may be made, is to be solely under the commanding officer in the army and whoever he shall appoint, and no person must presume to interfere with it

---

5   *council*: used in the sense of 'counsel'.

under the pretence of any other authority upon any account whatever unless in the case of immediate self preservation.

J SIMPSON

§ - §

2 - Cornwallis's dormant commission

Germain to Cornwallis, 12th April 1778 **60(2): LS**

Whitehall
12th April 1778

The Earl Cornwallis

My Lord

It having been thought fit (to guard against inconveniences that would arise if any unforeseen accident should happen to Sir Henry Clinton) that you should have a dormant commission giving you the rank of general in America only, I have the honour to transmit to you by His Majesty's command the inclosed commission, which, as it is not to take place but in case of a contingency in order to secure to you in such case the chief command over the foreign generals, is not to be made public if the contingency does not happen.

I am, my Lord,
Your Lordship's most obedient humble servant

GEO GERMAIN

Enclosure
Dormant commission, 10th March 1778 **60(1): DS**

GEORGE R ◯

GEORGE the Third by the grace of God King of Great Britain, France and Ireland, Defender of the Faith etc

To Our right trusty and right wellbeloved cousin and councillor Charles Earl Cornwallis, GREETING

We, reposing especial trust and confidence in your loyalty, courage and good conduct, do by these presents constitute and appoint you to be general in Our army in America only, and We do hereby give and grant you full power and authority to command and take your rank accordingly. You are therefore carefully and diligently to discharge the duty of general in

America only, by doing and performing all and all manner of things thereunto belonging, and We do hereby command all Our officers and soldiers whom it may concern to acknowledge and obey you as general in America only as aforesaid, and you are to observe and follow such orders and directions from time to time as you shall receive from Us or any your superior officer, according to the rules and discipline of war, in pursuance of the trust we hereby repose in you.

GIVEN at Our Court of St James's
the tenth day of March 1778
in the eighteenth year of Our reign

By His Majesty's command

GEO GERMAIN

§ - §

3 - Miscellaneous

Knox to Cornwallis, undated[6]   *277(1): ADS*

Directions for Lord Cornwallis's health

The eruptions which have been troublesome to your Lordship appear to have been a crisis to the complaint you laboured under in the year 1770. I am of opinion there ought to be great attention and circumspection in the use of either internal medicines or external applications, and therefore during the service your Lordship is now engaged in I recommend what follows.

As much regularity in diet and exercise as the service can admit.

That your Lordship should avoid high seasoned and fried meats and eat your food plain dressed with a due proportion of vegitables.

Let your common drink at meals be spruce beer with a moderate quantity of wine after meals.

If the spruce beer agrees with your Lordship, you may try for your eruptions a liquor which is the most effectual remedy for the scurvy I have ever yet known and supplys the deffect of vegetables for the cure of the scurvy, of which I have had convincing prooffs when I was upon service in Canada and shall annex the manner of preparing it to this paper.

---

6   The fact that this document refers to Musgrave as 'Colonel' and to Leslie as 'Major General' indicates that it was written after August 1776 and before Leslie's promotion in late July 1781 to lt general became generally known.

When the eruptions are troublesome, your Lordship may take the powder N° 1 in the prescription[7], going to bed, and drink a gill of the infusion above it. If it does not keep your body open, I have desired something may be added to it to procure that effect.

You may continue it three or four weeks at a time and try at the same time the effect of the liniment N° 2.

During the summer or autumn take the bark draught N° 3 every day before dinner about two hours, and if autumnal intermitting or remitting fevers are common, take it twice a day. When it is inconvenient to get the medicine with bark made, please to supply it by taking near a tablespoonfull of Hincham's Tincture of the Bark out of a glass of water in the morning and the evening, and to keep the body open, rhubarb is the safest medicine in hot countrys.

In case your Lordship serves within the tropics, do not make any sudden change of dieting. You will have a greater demand for thin liquors but avoid going too liberally into the use of sour and weak punch. Believe me, my Lord, wine is the best preservative against the diseases of the climate if used with moderation, and I am persuaded Madeira is the best. On the service I was upon in the West Indies, we who had opportunitys of getting wine had better health, and fewer of them died than of those who were too free in the use of sour punch. I believe Major General Lesslie and Colonel Musgrave[8] can vouch for this fact, as we were together on the same service and in the same family in the West Indies.

RO^T KNOX[9]

PS

The infusion of spruce for the scurvy

Take the small branches of what we call hemlock spruce and is called *pruche blanc*[10] by the French.

Beat them a little and fill up a vessell with them without pressing it down. Pour upon them water sufficient to cover them, and give it a gentle boil, and letting it stand untill it is cold, strain out the liquor through a cloth by pressure.

---

[7] *the prescription*: not extant.

[8] The youngest son of a baronet, Thomas Musgrave (1738-1812) had served as a lieutenant in the 3rd Regiment (the Buffs) at the capture of Guadeloupe in May 1759. As Lt Colonel of the 40th Regiment, he had distinguished himself in 1777 at the Battle of Germantown by throwing himself and 200 of his men into the Chew House and holding up the enemy's advancing right wing. He went on to serve in the West Indies and as the last British Commandant of New York. In later life he served indifferently under Cornwallis in India for some three years before returning to England and commanding for a time the Northern District. In 1800 he inherited the baronetcy. He died a full general at his London home in Bolton Street, Piccadilly, and was buried at St George's, Hanover Square. (*ODNB*)

[9] Robert Knox had taken part as a master surgeon in the expedition which captured Guadeloupe in 1759. He apparently retired on half pay soon after. (Johnston, *Commissioned Officers in the Medical Service*, 29)

[10] *pruche blanc*: 'white pruce', an obsolete expression for 'white spruce'.

Or pour boiling water upon the spruce as above and let it stand for 24 hours in infusion, which in my opinion is the best method of preparing it, after which strain it off for use.

Let the scorbutic person drink a quart or three pints of this every day. I have added a little rum to it sometimes to make it more gratefull to the soldiers with a little molasses.

Profit from hiring out 200 waggons with horses, undated[11]　　　*5(151): D*

A waggon with 4 horses, prime cost	£60 - 0 - 0
⅓ for repairs and loss	£20 - 0 - 0
One driver at 1*s* 7*d* per year per day	£28 - 17 - 11
Expence of a waggon the 1st year	£108 - 17 - 11
Hire of a waggon for 1 year	£223 - 11 - 3
Profit of one waggon for 1st year	£114 - 13 - 4
	× 200
200 waggons — profit	£22,933 - 6 - 8
Waggon master general at 20*s*	£365 - 0 - 0
2 deputies at 10*s*	£365 - 0 - 0
4 assistants at 5*s*	£365 - 0 - 0
20 conductors at 3*s*	£1,075 - 0 - 0[12]
	£2,170 - 0 - 0[13]
	£19,763 - 6 - 8[14]

---

[11]　This document was probably written in late 1780. In a letter of 4th September 1780 to Cruger (vol II, p 177), Cornwallis states that the Government allowance for the hire of a waggon and horses is 12 shillings sterling per day, making £219 per year.

[12]　*£1,075 - 0 - 0*: £1,095 - 0 - 0.

[13]　*£2,170 - 0 - 0*: £2,190 - 0 - 0.

[14]　*£19,763 - 6 - 8*: £20,743 - 6 - 8.

Substance of a plan concisely stated and humbly offered to his Excellency
Sir Henry Clinton by Hector MacAlister for subjecting the Colony
of Virginia to His Majesty's Government

He begs leave to premise a short description of James and York Rivers.

James River is navigable for ships of 17 feet draught of water to Warwick, 5 miles distant from the Falls and about 120 from its entrance into Chesapeak Bay. He does not conceive that its navigation can in any degree be impeded from its banks for 50 miles to Jamestown, which was formerly an island but is now rendered peninsular by a causeway from the adjacent shore. Here the channel runs within 400 yards of the banks, upon which the rebels have a battery. From thence to the Appamattox at its confluence with James River he does not reccollect any narrow place where the aid of land forces will be required to support the water communication, excepting on the northside at Kennon's and on the southside at Flower de Hundred. From the mouth of the Appamattox to the Falls of James River the distance by land is 20 miles — by water 50 — the river narrow and the banks high. On the northside of the Falls stands Richmond, the present seat of usurped government, — on the southside Manchester.

York River is navigable for ships about 80 miles to Cumberland Town, but it becomes intricate and narrow about 40 miles from its mouth. Upon a high bank on its southside stands York Town 25 miles up. From the opposite shore jutts out Glocester Point. Both these places were fortyfyed at the first settlement of the colony and command the navigation of the river. Williamsburg, the capital of Virginia, is 12 miles from York Town and is nearly equidistant from York and James River.

These two rivers form an interstice or neck of country about 150 miles in length and not exceeding, in its greatest breadth, 20 miles.

From these general outlines he, with the utmost diffidence, begs permission to draw three different plans of operation, any one of which may be adopted according to the object in contemplation to be obtained or the force to be employed.

1st, if it be meant to co-operate imediately with the forces acting under the command of Lord Cornwallis in the southern provinces by penetrating the country south of James River towards the borders of North Carolina, the post of communication with the water may be at City Point on the east side of Appamatox, distant 7 miles from Petersburg, from which, being a place of great commerce, the roads branch as from a common center to all parts south of James River.

2ndly, if it be meant to take posession of the southside of James River — in some degree to obstruct a northern and a southern communication and to be in readiness on any imergency

---

[15] Internal evidence suggests that this document was written in the autumn of 1780 before Leslie's expedition to Virginia.

to make a sudden movement to the southward (but with a force inefficient for a more extensive plan) — an army at Manchester may communicate with the water at Bermuda Hundred on the west side of Appamattox.

3rdly, if it be intended to act with a solid force and by vigorous efforts to subject the colony, he humbly conceives that a position at Richmond and a communication with the shipping at Westover or Shirley Hundred, with posts at York Town, Glocester Point and if necessary at James Town, will be productive of the following effects.

Seven entire counties laying between James and York Rivers must submitt without a struggle to His Majesty's Government, as an enemy cannot (without command of the navigation) remain on that peninsular. These counties as well as the country above and about Richmond abound in every kind of produce necessary for the subsistence of an army. The post at Glocester Point will give an easy enterance into the fertile County of Glocester and the country laying between York and Rappahannock. The County of Northampton on the eastern shore of Virginia is a mere granary, from whence an imense quantity of indian corn and oats may be drawn with great facility. A very considerable body of cavalry may be mounted, the country affording an excellent and a numerous breed of horses.

A position at Richmond is covered (two sides of a triangle) by James River and Chicahommony, which issues about 6 miles above Richmond and enters James River 40 miles below it, the greatest part of which being a swamp, it is utterly impassable but by a few bridges that may be either preserved or destroyed. It also covers the communication from Westover to Richmond.

The country above Richmond is quite level and open for 75 miles to the Southwest Mountains, nor is there a single river to pass all that distance. The Rivanna or North River a little above that is fordable in many places. Whereas the enemy in the northern provinces find strong and impenitrable recesses within a few miles of the sea coast, this country affords none within 200 miles.

It is a well authenticated fact that near one half of the value of the whole produce of Virginia was exported from James River. The public warehouses upon this and York River, the repositaries of the staple wealth of the colony, are directly within reach. The navigation of these rivers will be compleatly lock'd up, and the produce of their fertile banks in posession.

Finaly, he humbly conceives there is not another position which can be taken in America that with so small a number of posts, and all in a connection to sustain one another, secures the source of navigation of so extensive a country as this (in any comparison its equal in population and wealth), comprehending from Rappahannock in Virginia and Roanoke in Carolina.

Having presumed thus far to deliver his sentiments respecting the natural advantages imediately consequent upon a position at Richmond, other circumstances will depend on the efforts made by the enemy. However, there are some that are not obvious and which he begs permission to point out.

The enemy from the north and south must respectively either pass York River or James River to form a junction. If that is made between the two rivers, their situation will be so straitned that they must hazard an action, as every place above is accessible. If they do not make a junction, they are liable to be attacked separately, and on whichever side of the two rivers their whole force is collected, the other will be left exposed. In all cases whatsoever, excepting that of the enemy being able to sustain their ground between James and York Rivers above Richmond, the communication between the northern and southern provinces below the Apalachian Mountains will be entirely cutt off, and any which can be carried on beyond these will be tedious and ineffectual. Upon a further extension of military operations, even that may be destroyed by a post at Alexandria. He need not mention that a successfull war may be rapidly spread to the boundary of Powtowmack, as the peninsular of the Northern Neck will fall a very easy conquest.

The posts of James Town, York and Glocester will not only be calculated for internal security but also against any sudden external attempt from a foreign enemy.

If it is thought proper either to accept of or to invite the aid of the Indians, they will find sufficient employment for the rebels inhabiting the country beyond the Blue Ridge.

With respect to a post at Portsmouth, it can be only consequential, as it will afford a harbour to the shipping and cruizers to intercept the navigation of the rebels in Chesapeak Bay. When an army is in the upper parts of the country, it may be maintained with very little force.

§ - §

CHAPTER 68

Papers received by Cornwallis after 1781

---

1 - Balfour to Germain, 1781

Balfour to Germain, 16th January 1781   *109(3): C*

N° 1   Charles Town
                                                        January 16th 1781

Rt Hon Lord George Germaine etc etc etc

My Lord

I am honored with Lord Cornwallis's directions to address myself to your Lordship during his absence from this province and to have the honor of informing your Lordship from time to time of the state of the army and situation of affairs here.

By the last dispatches from Lord Cornwallis, which were dated the 11th instant, the army was then in motion and advancing towards North Carolina, so that his Lordship wou'd reach Bullock Creek between the Catawba and Broad Rivers by the 16th, to which I am happy to add that the troops under his command were at that time in the highest health.

The latest accounts of the enemy inform us that General Greene with his army is at Hayley's Ferry on the eastern banks of the Pedee.

In order to cooperate with Lord Cornwallis's views on Cape Fear River and to afford provisions and other supplies for his army, a small force of about 300 men under Major Craig of the 82nd Regiment will sail from hence with the packet. Captain Barclay in the *Blonde* with the *Delight* and *Otter* sloops of war convoy this corps and will cooperate with the troops upon this expedition, which I trust will be successful and give us possession of Wilmington and this very essential communication.

It is with pleasure I inform your Lordship that many of the principal inhabitants of the province and some who held the chief offices under the late rebel powers have reverted to their loyalty and declared their allegiance to His Majesty's Government.

I have also the satisfaction to acquaint your Lordship that Major Ross and Captain Broderick are arrived with the dispatches, and as the former gentleman has mentioned to me your Lordship's great anxiety to receive frequent information from hence and as there has of late been no elligible conveyance, I have from these motives taken it upon me to change the course of the packet by sending her directly home, to which I have been rather induced as a ship of war is shortly to sail for New York and will take with her the Commander in Chief's dispatches and the mail for that place.

Captain Mallum of the 63rd Regiment, an officer of merit and who is returning to Europe for the recovery of his health, has Lord Cornwallis's directions to deliver this dispatch to your Lordship.

I have the honor to be, my Lord,
Your Lordship's most obedient and most humble servant

N BALFOUR

Balfour to Germain, 18th February 1781[1]   109(16): C

Nº 2

Charles Town
February 18th 1781

Rt Hon Lord George Germain etc etc etc

My Lord

By the letter in which I had the honor to address your Lordship on the 16th of January last you will have been informed of the situation of affairs here to that period, and, by Lord Cornwallis's dispatch dated the 18th of the same month[2], of Lt Colonel Tarleton's unfortunate action on the preceeding day. I am now to give your Lordship such further informations as have been received since, either immediately from Earl Cornwallis, Lord Rawdon and Major Craig or by intelligence through the country.

Notwithstanding the unexpected and untoward event of the 17th ultimo, Lord Cornwallis still continued his forward movements and pressed hard on General Morgan without being able to come up with him, who with his prisoners pushed for the Catawba and, by crossing that river high up, there's cause to believe accomplished his junction with General Greene's army.

---

[1] Published with inconsequential differences in Davies ed, *Docs of the Am Rev*, xx, 62-3.

[2] *Cornwallis's dispatch..*: see vol III, p 47.

It was not till the 1st instant that Lord Cornwallis could pass it. This he then did at a private ford four miles below Beatty's, tho' strongly opposed by a body of militia, who were routed, and General Davidson, who commanded them, killed. On this occasion his Lordship observes, 'The Guards behaved gallantly, crossing the river under a heavy fire without returning a shott until they were over and formed.'[3]

On the same day Colonel Tarleton had the good fortune to defeat another corps of the enemy's militia that had assembled under Colonel Pickins, killing and taking many and entirely dispersing the rest.

In relating these circumstances to your Lordship it is no small satisfaction to add that on both occasions the loss sustained by the King's troops is inconsiderable, and that, except Colonel Hall of the Guards, who is killed, no officer was hurt.

After gaining these advantages Lord Cornwallis proceeded to Salisbury, which town he possessed himself of on the 4th instant.

Hitherto General Greene had remained in his position on the eastern banks of the Pedee and, by thus hanging on the frontiers of the province and having with him a force in cavalry, was enabled to make inroads into the heart of it, which were greatly distressing to the inhabitants and obliged me to detach, beyond the ability of this garrison[4], to cover the communication between this and Camden, prevent the enemy's taking post on this side the Santee, and hinder insults in our vicinities. But on the news of Lord Cornwallis's late successes he called in his out-parties and by a precipitant movement reached the Moravian settlements in North Carolina, where by the last accounts he has taken a station to cover the passage of the Yadkin.

From this view of the situation of both armies we may expect soon to hear of some event of moment, and which I hope will give occasion to congratulate your Lordship.

By my last letter your Lordship was informed of an expedition being then to sail under Major Craig of the 82nd Regiment, the force employed on that service, and the objects of it. I have now the honor to communicate to your Lordship his having taken possession of Wilmington without opposition on the 29th ultimo. But finding that a body of the enemy had posted themselves at Heron's Bridge about 12 miles from that town to cover as well this pass as the shipping in the river and to shew a force for the militia to form on, Major Craig by an immediate and well timed exertion surprized the rebels in this very strong position and by dislodging them from it has cleared that part of the country, gained in cooperation with His Majesty's ships of war possession of their vessels, and taken on board them and in the camp several military stores, the want of which may be much felt shou'd they attempt again to raise any force in those parts.

---

[3] The quotation paraphrases part of Cornwallis's letter of 4th February to Rawdon, vol IV, p 44.

[4] The words from 'beyond' to 'garrison' are annotated: 'not printed'.

Major Craig further informs me that he is exerting every means to put the very essential post of Wilmington into a state of defence and eventually to communicate with the army under Lord Cornwallis.

Governor Bull arrived here in the last fleet from England, and as no directions have been received from Lord Cornwallis for the reestablishing of civil power, and the state of the country being far from admitting it, he has been so obliging as to take upon him the superintendency of the police as the only present means of rendering his extensive knowledge of this province beneficial to Government. Sir Egerton Leigh[5] has likewise accepted a seat at this board, which must derive great assistance from his judicial information.

Conformable to the directions contained in your Lordship's circular letter of the 7th December[6], such spare victuallers, transport and oat ships as were in readiness will proceed home with the *Galatea*, and the rest shall be sent with the next convoy which sails from hence.[7]

I have the honor to be, my Lord,
Your Lordship's most obedient humble servant

N BALFOUR

Balfour to Germain, 25th February 1781[8]   *109(19): C*

N° 3
Charlestown
February 25th 1781

Rt Hon Lord George Germaine etc etc etc

My Lord

Since the date of my dispatch N° 2 Captain Barklay with the *Blonde* arrived here from Cape Fear, where he left every thing in a state of security and the works for the protection of Wilmington nearly perfected. To him I had the honor to communicate your Lordship's

---

5   The son of a Chief Justice of South Carolina, Sir Egerton Leigh Bt (1733-1781) had been a conspicuous member of the province's administration before the revolution. He had held public office, at one time or another, as Judge of the Vice-Admiralty Court, as Surveyor General of Lands, as Attorney General, and as a member of HM Council, which acted as a privy council advising the Governor in the exercise of his functions and as the upper house of the legislature. He would now serve as an intendant of police with an allowance of twenty shillings per day, but not for long, as he would die about the beginning of November. (McCowen Jr, *Charleston, 1780-82*, 20; *Royal Gazette* (Charlestown), 21st November 1781)

6   *Your Lordship's circular letter..*: see enclosures (1) and (2), pp 231-2.

7   The penultimate and final paragraphs are annotated: 'not printed'.

8   Published with inconsequential differences in Davies ed, op cit, xx, 65-6.

circular letter of the 7th of December[9], but as he thinks it will be best to delay the *Galatea* and vessels in Government's service until the *Camilla* and trade are in readiness to proceed with them, they will not probably put to sea these two weeks. I have therefore forwarded the packet from a wish at this juncture to afford your Lordship the earliest information.[10]

No accounts since my last have been received immediately from Lord Cornwallis, but Lord Rawdon has favor'd me with some further intelligence respecting the operations of the army which his Lordship derived from a man who quitted it on the 9th instant and who is come into Camden.

At that period it appears Lord Cornwallis was advanced six miles beyond Salem, the farthest of the Moravian settlements in North Carolina and to the eastward of the Yadkin, which points out by what uncommon exertion and rapid movements his Lordship must have reached that distance in so small a space of time through a strong and intricate country.

By crossing the Yadkin so high up the army has got above Greene's, which by *this* intelligence was advancing on Deep River and some way removed to the rear of Lord Cornwallis's right, General Morgan with his corps being advanced and on the left. With this last there were some hopes Lord Cornwallis wou'd soon be able to come up, and on the whole it will be clear to your Lordship that by this movement the junction of the enemy's force, of which in my last I was apprehensive, is for the present frustrated.

I have thought it my duty, as well from Lord Cornwallis's instructions as the strong desire of rendering every information on a subject so interesting to your Lordship, to be thus particular in a relation not absolutely authenticated, more especially as the army is now advanced to that situation when the first movements must decidedly point out to the enemy its ultimate object.[11]

On receiving from General Arnold the letter of which an extract[12] is inclosed, I did myself the honor to lay the same before Captain Barklay, the senior sea officer here, that he might judge what could be done for relieving the fleet and army in the Chesapeak and forcing the French ships from thence (His Majesty's Ships of War the *Chatham, Assurance, Blonde, Carysfort* and *Galatea* being then here), but I learn from Captain Barklay it has been found inexpedient to attempt any thing in this way.[13]

---

[9]   *your Lordship's circular letter..*: see note 6 above.

[10]   The passage from 'To him' to the end of the paragraph is annotated: 'not printed'.

[11]   This and the following paragraph are annotated: 'not printed'.

[12]   *an extract*: no copy. Of 14th February, it reported that three French ships of war had anchored at Lynnhaven the previous day. It requested naval assistance. (CO5/184(24) (UK National Archives, Kew))

[13]   The French man of war *Éveillé* (64 guns) and two frigates had sailed from Newport, Rhode Island, on 22nd January, evading the blockading British squadron. They took the *Romulus* (44 guns) and some other British vessels in the Chesapeake before retiring and reaching Newport on the 24th February. The rest of the British vessels were saved by moving them up Elizabeth River to Portsmouth. (Boatner, *Encyclopedia*, 1151)

I must not omit informing your Lordship of the arrival of the *Assurance* with the fleet of victuallers from Cork after a passage of twelve weeks, the length of which obliges them to water before they can proceed on their voyage to New York, during which time the *Assurance* will remain at Beaufort, being of too large draft to pass this bar.

I have the honor to be, my Lord,
Your Lordship's most obedient and most humble servant

N BALFOUR

Balfour to Germain, 24th and 27th March 1781[14]　　　　　*109(23): C*

N° 4

Charles Town
March 24th 1781

Rt Hon Lord George Germaine etc etc etc

My Lord

By the inclosed letter to the Commander in Chief[15] your Lordship will see with what astonishing rapidity the army under Lord Cornwallis advanc'd thro' North Carolina and penetrated to the remotest extremities of that province on the banks of the Dan. The greater part of these accounts, I have now the honor to inform your Lordship, are verified by dispatches of the 21st ultimo, 5th and 8th instant[16] this day received from Earl Cornwallis thro' Lord Rawdon, and which enable me to communicate to your Lordship the further operations and successes of His Majesty's arms in these parts.

Lord Cornwallis's unremitting exertions were such as precluded General Greene's being joined by any considerable body of the militia and forced him for a while to retire into Virginia, where his army has gained some small reinforcements.

Having accomplish'd this, Lord Cornwallis moved to Hillsborough in order to erect the royal standard there, refresh his troops, greatly fatigued by uncommon marches, and afford that support to the distressed friends of Government as might enable them to make head and maintain the King's cause against their enemies.

To frustrate objects so essential called naturally for every effort from General Greene, who therefore recrossed the Dan and by his light corps attempted to hinder the assembling of our friends between the Deep and Haw Rivers, but in this endeavour they were impeded by Lt Colonel Tarleton, who on the 2nd instant fell in with a considerable body of those troops, of

---

[14]　Published with one inconsequential difference in Davies ed, op cit, xx, 95-6.

[15]　*the inclosed letter..*: of 3rd March, p 235.

[16]　*dispatches..*: see vol IV, pp 41 and 45.

which ninety were killed in the field and many others in the pursuit, and, I am truly happy to add, with scarcely any loss on our side.

At this time General Greene with his army was in those parts of Guildford County south of Reedy Fork, when Lord Cornwallis found it necessary to cross Haw River in order to protect the loyalists, whom Greene by his station strove to check; but on a corps of six hundred of his militia being forced by Lord Cornwallis to retire with precipitation, General Greene marched without delay for the iron works on Troublesome Creek, which, being to the northward, as your Lordship knows, of Reedy Fork, on which the King's army was moving, indicates either the view of meeting his reinforcements or an intention of retiring a second time into Virginia. However, Lord Cornwallis has at present no design, as I apprehend from his letters, of pursuing him on that route, as his army is in the greatest want of the supplies which have been long waiting for it in Cape Fear River, and which he will receive on his communicating with Cross Creek, which he means to do after passing thro' Guildford County and favoring on his way the exertions of our friends to free themselves from their late oppressions and persecutors.

By his Lordship's letters I learn reinforcements from Pensylvania and Virginia are daily expected by the rebel army, and I must further beg leave to inform your Lordship of the exertions of the enemy to raise a force in this province either, as I apprehend, with a view to distress us by frequent interruption of the communications or on the more enlarged idea, if greatly successful, of drawing back Lord Cornwallis's attention to the more immediate protection of South Carolina.

I do myself the honor to transmit your Lordship the copy of a letter from Captain McNemara of His Majesty's Sloop *Hound*[17], by which will be seen the danger which at present threatens West Florida. On receiving this account I immediately forwarded the same to Governor Dalling and General Vaughn that if possible some aid might be afforded by them to the garrison of Pensacola, and have taken care to send to St Augustine such supplies of ammunition and provisions as we could part with from this, which, together with a strong galley sent there, the presence of Lt Colonel Clarke, and a small reinforcement he takes with him from Savannah, will, I trust, give security to that place.

Agreeable to your Lordship's directions for supplying the West Indies with lumber etc from hence, I have given every encouragement in my power to this trade and now enclose an account[18] of what exports have been made to those islands since November last, but tho' they are not so great as could be wished, I have every reason to believe those from Georgia much more considerable.[19]

---

[17] *a letter..*: no copy. Of 12th March, it reported that McNamara had encountered a fleet supposedly bound from Havana for Pensacola and that de Gàlvez had declared his intention to attack St Augustine afterwards. Jamaica had been informed. (CO5/184(74) (National Archives, Kew))

[18] *an account*: no copy. Of 23rd March, it was prepared by R McCulloh, Deputy Superintendent of the Port of Charlestown. (Ibid)

[19] The penultimate and this paragraph are annotated: 'not published'.

I have the honor to be, my Lord,
Your Lordship's most obedient and most humble servant

N BALFOUR

March 27th 1781

Thus far, my Lord, had I proceeded previous to the accounts of the victory at Guildford being received here. These will be communicated by Lord Rawdon and I have only to congratulate your Lordship on so fortunate an event. However, I conceive it necessary still to forward this dispatch, not only as it contains matters essential tho' extra from this but also a detail of the circumstances which led to so handsome an issue. And as Lord Rawdon has not yet sent a duplicate of his dispatch, I do myself the honor herewith to transmit a copy of Lord Cornwallis's account of the action[20] by each of the two men of war that have charge of the convoy in order as much as possible to secure your Lordship's receiving early these interesting and pleasing advices.

Balfour to Germain, 1st May 1781[21]   *109(30): C*

Nᵒ 5

Charles Town
May 1st 1781

Rt Hon Lord George Germain etc etc etc

My Lord

By Lord Cornwallis's dispatches[22], which are herewith transmitted, your Lordship will be informed that after the action at Guildford General Greene, being obliged to retreat from before the King's army, turned his views towards this province as the more vulnerable point in the absence of Lord Cornwallis.

With this idea, on the 19th ultimo he came before Camden, having with him near 1,500 Continentals and several corps of militia, Lord Rawdon having charge of that post and about 800 British and Provincial troops to sustain it.

For some days General Greene kept varying his position, waiting, as is supposed, to be reinforced by the corps under Brigadier Marian and Colonel Lee, which were on their way, being ordered to join him.

---

[20] *Cornwallis's account..*: see his letter of 17th March to Rawdon, vol IV, p 46.

[21] Published with no differences in Davies ed, op cit, xx, 130-1. An abbreviated version appears in Tarleton, *Campaigns*, 465, with the omissions mentioned in notes 23 to 25 below.

[22] *Cornwallis's dispatches*: see vol IV, pp 104-9.

Judging it necessary to strike a blow before this junction could take place and learning that General Greene had detached to bring up his baggage and provisions, Lord Rawdon, with the most mark'd decision, on the morning of the 25th marched out the greater part of his force to meet him and about 10 o'clock attack'd the rebels in their camp at Hobkirk's Hill with that spirit which, prevailing over superior numbers and an obstinate resistance, conpelled them to give way, and the pursuit was continued for three miles. To accident only they were indebted for saving their guns, which, being drawn into a hollow out of the road, were overlook'd by our troops in the flush of victory and pursuit, so that their cavalry, in which they greatly exceeded us, had an opportunity of taking them off.

My Lord Rawdon states the loss of the enemy on this occasion as upwards of an hundred made prisoners and four hundred killed and wounded, his own not exceeding an hundred, in which is included one officer killed and eleven wounded.

After this defeat General Green retir'd to Rugeley's Mills (12 miles from Camden) in order to collect his troops and receive the reinforcements; but as Lt Colonel Watson of the Guards, who had for some time been detach'd by Lord Rawdon with a corps of 500 men to cover the eastern frontiers of the province, is directed by me to join his Lordship, I am in hopes he will be able speedily to accomplish this and Lord Rawdon be placed in such a situation as will empower him either to make head against the enemy, shou'd they attempt any thing further, or retire with security on this side the Santee, as circumstances may require.[23]

It is to the several letters which (notwithstanding the enemy having well nigh overrun the province)[24] Lord Rawdon has been so good to transmit me that I am indebted for the detail I have now the honor to present your Lordship, and which I trust his Lordship will hereafter conclude in the most satisfactory manner.

With my last dispatch I had the honor to transmit your Lordship the copy of a letter respecting the Spanish invasion of West Florida. The only accounts to which credit can be given that have been received subsequent to those are by an express to a merchant at Augusta, and which inform that on the 10th of February the Spanish fleet arrived at Pensacola, that the army, nearly two thousand, was landed on Rose's Island, and that the ships were cannonading the works on Red Cliffs.[25]

I have the honor to be, my Lord,
Your Lordship's most obedient and most humble servant

N BALFOUR

---

[23] The words after 'accomplish this' are annotated: 'omitted in printing'.

[24] Annotated: 'this parenthesis omitted in printing'.

[25] This paragraph is annotated: 'omitted in printing'.

Balfour to Germain, 1st May 1781   *109(29): C*

Seperate   Charles Town
                                      May 1st 1781

Rt Hon Lord George Germain etc etc etc

My Lord

Lord Charles Montagu having been sent here with an appointment from General Dalling to raise a corps from the rebel prisoners to serve in Jamaica, I did myself the honor to write on that subject to the Commander in Chief, but as his Excellency has been pleased to refer it to Earl Cornwallis[26] and as it is not at present possible to communicate with his Lordship on it, I have taken upon me to sanction the measure, as it was so perfectly conformable to the views held out in your Lordship's letter to Lord Cornwallis of the 9th of November last[27], and which might have been frustrated by a greater lapse of time. I have now the honor to inform your Lordship that Lord Charles Montagu has succeeded in forming a very fine corps of five hundred men, and which, I doubt not, will render good services when employed under him at Jamaica or on the Spanish Main.

I have the honor to be, my Lord,
Your Lordship's most obedient and most humble servant

N BALFOUR

Balfour to Germain, 27th June 1781[28]   *109(38): C*

Nº 6   Charles Town
                                      June 27th 1781

Rt Hon Lord George Germain etc etc etc

My Lord

After the advantage gained by Lord Rawdon on the 25th of April over General Greene's army, of which your Lordship was inform'd by my dispatch of the 1st ultimo, the general state of this province, the almost universal revolt of its inhabitants, and the many parties of the enemy which were every where harassing it rendering it expedient to relinquish the post at Camden, Lord Rawdon therefore quitted that place after having again offered battle to General Greene, who, secured in a strong position behind Sawney Creek, cou'd by no efforts be induced from it.

---

[26] For Balfour's letter of 5th February and Clinton's reply of 9th March, see pp 229 and 238.

[27] *your Lordship's letter..*: see vol III, p 44.

[28] Published with no differences in Davies ed, op cit, xx, 163-4.

On the corps under Lord Rawdon falling back towards this town, the enemy by detachments invested the posts at Mott's House, Congarees and Augusta, having previously taken that at Wright's Bluff. These posts, my Lord, had been established for controuling the country and preserving its communications. Unfortunately, from the superiority of the enemy and the impossibility of immediate relief as affairs were then circumstanced, these garrisons were obliged to surrender, tho' gallantly defended. However, I have the satisfaction to inform your Lordship that the stores in them were but inconsiderable and the amount of regular troops in all not exceeding six hundred, and even they have since been exchanged under a cartel which has lately taken place between my Lord Cornwallis and Major General Greene for the release of all prisoners of war in the Southern District.

Having accomplished these smaller purposes, General Greene combined his force and laid close siege to Ninety Six, the most commanding and important of all the posts in the Back Country, and which was therefore maintain'd by about three hundred and fifty men, exclusive of militia, and put under the charge of Lt Colonel Cruger, an able and zealous officer.

Thus circumstanced was this province when a reinforcement of three regiments from Ireland arrived, and as soon as the necessary arrangements could be made, Lord Rawdon, having under him a corps of near two thousand men, proceeded to the relief of Ninety Six, an undertaking (from the unfavorableness of the climate at this season) which, your Lordship knows, must have been attended with many difficulties and much fatigue, but which the zeal and exertion of the troops enabled them to surmount.

General Greene, on finding this corps approaching him, took the resolution of attempting to storm the garrison as an expedient less dangerous and decisive than coming to action with Lord Rawdon. On the morning of the 19th instant he therefore made the experiment but by the gallantry of the troops was repulsed, having, as acknowledged by the enemy, at least seventy five killed and one hundred and fifty wounded. On this occasion and during the siege our loss was truly inconsiderable, tho' at present I am unable to specify to your Lordship the particulars of it.

Thus disappointed in his views, General Greene the ensuing day raised the siege and retired with his army behind the Saluda to a strong situation within sixteen miles of Ninety Six, at which post Lord Rawdon arrived on the 21st.

The essential service done by the troops under Colonel Cruger in their gallant defence of the post, which was closely pressed by the enemy, and the noble spirit with which they repelled the assault of all Greene's army is much too obvious to require any tribute I cou'd pay to such distinguished merit.

I have the honor to be, my Lord,
Your Lordship's most obedient and most humble servant

N BALFOUR

N° 7   Charles Town
                                                             July 2nd 1781

Rt Hon Lord George Germain etc etc etc

My Lord

By the *Prince William Henry* packet I was honored on the 28th ultimo with the duplicates of your Lordship's letters of the 7th of March and 4th of April last[29], the originals of which have not yet come to hand.

Your Lordship may be assured that no exertions on my part will be wanting for the defence and maintenance of this place, which has lately received from works constructed by the commanding engineer, Lt Colonel Moncrieffe, every additional security which professional abilities can bestow.

Since the date of my dispatch N° 6 I have been honored with two letters from Lord Rawdon, who pursued General Greene to the fords of the Ennoree but, tho' near, was unable to come up with him from the uncommon precipitancy with which the enemy retreated and their having so much the advance on the march. This circumstance, and the great fatigue of the troops in attempting to counteract it, rendering improbable all hopes of overtaking General Greene's army so as to effect any thing decisive, Lord Rawdon is return'd to Ninety Six, and General Greene having passed the Tyger and Broad Rivers, it wou'd from thence seem that the object of his march pointed towards Virginia, which I am the rather inclined to beleive from the intelligence (to which, however, I do not give the fullest credit) which has reached me of his being order'd there to join the force now under Generals La Fayette and Wayne.

The last dispatches which I have received from Lord Cornwallis were dated at Petersburgh the 25th of May[30] and give accounts of his having accomplished his junction with the army under the late Major General Phillips. His Lordship was at that time proceeding in the pursuit of La Fayette, who daily expected to be reinforced by a corps under General Wayne detached by General Washington to his support.

I have the honor to be, my Lord,
Your Lordship's most obedient and humble servant

N BALFOUR

---

[29] *your Lordship's letters..*: for that of 7th March, see Davies ed, op cit, xx, 79.

[30] *The last dispatches..*: only those of 20th May, vol V, pp 274 and 286, are extant.

Balfour to Germain, 1st August 1781

109(45): C

Charles Town
August 1st 1781

Rt Hon Lord George Germain etc etc etc

My Lord

This opportunity being by the Spanish flag of truce which carries home Governor Chester[31], it wou'd perhaps be violating its strict neutrality to write your Lordship particularly on the state of affairs here. This deficiency, however, is amply supplied, as Captain Benson will have the honor to deliver this to your Lordship.

He has been for some years a major of brigade and since the capture of this town always employ'd in the most confidential situations, so that I can venture to refer to his thorough knowledge of the civil and military state of this province the enquiries you may think it necessary to make on these heads. And permit me to assure your Lordship that shou'd he be honored with any mark of your approbation, it will be bestowed on a most deserving officer.

I have the honor to be, my Lord,
Your Lordship's most obedient humble servant

N BALFOUR

Balfour to Germain, 13th August 1781

109(46): C

Charlestown
August 13th 1781

Rt Hon Lord George Germain etc etc etc

My Lord

I have now only to acknowledge the honor of your Lordship's letter of the 4th of June last, for as my Lord Rawdon is going home, it wou'd be needless for me to trouble your Lordship on the affairs of this province and its military transactions, as in these particulars his Lordship is undoubtedly possesed of the fullest and most perfect information.

I am sorry it has not yet been in my power to forward your Lordship's dispatches to Lord Cornwallis[32] owing to no man of war remaining in the harbour and the impossibility from thence of a suitable conveyance for them.

---

[31] Formerly in the military line, Peter Chester (1717/18-1799) had been appointed Governor of West Florida in December 1769. With the arrival of Major General John Campbell at Pensacola in 1778, he began to play a subordinate role in the province's administration, and when the town fell to the Spanish in May 1781, he was taken prisoner. Presumably on parole, he was now making his way to retirement in England, where he would eventually die at his house in New King's Street, Bath. (*ODNB*)

[32] *your Lordship's dispatches..*: of 4th June, p 161.

I have the honor to be, my Lord,
Your Lordship's most obedient and humble servant

N BALFOUR

Balfour to Germain, 12th October 1781   109(48): C

Nº 8   Charlestown
                                                         October 12th 1781

Rt Hon Lord George Germain etc etc etc

My Lord

Intelligence having been receiv'd that most of the pacquets and vessels which for some months past have sail'd from hence for Britain are fallen into the enemy's hands, it must have been consequently long since your Lordship cou'd have received official and authentic information of the state of public affairs here, which being at present truly essential, I have thought it necessary to hire a vessel and send her express with these dispatches.

I was in hopes by Lord Rawdon your Lordship before now wou'd have received the fullest account of the situation of this country, to which his compleat knowledge was in every way adequate, and I therefore thought it unnecessary to trouble you on that subject by the pacquet which carried his Lordship, but as I have since learn'd with infinite regret, as well from public as private considerations, that she has been captured by the French and that he is now a prisoner to that nation, I do myself the honor to enclose the extract of a letter to the Commander in Chief[33] from whence will be seen what military transactions have occurred here from the date of my dispatch Nº 7 to the period of his Lordship's departure.

Those subsequent to that are contain'd in Lt Colonel Stewart's public letter of the 9th ultimo to Lord Cornwallis[34], copies of which and its several enclosures I have the honor, by his particular directions, herewith to transmit. These wou'd have been accompany'd with dispatches from Major General Gould, who commands on the frontiers, had he not been prevented writing by indisposition, from which he is, however, recovering, though at the present it must prove detrimental to the service.

It will be needless to point out to your Lordship the very heavy loss which attended the action of the 8th ultimo, and which, united to the smaller ones that from climate as well as service are daily occurring, has greatly reduced the actual strength of the army operating here, a circumstance the more necessary to be observed as the enemy opposed to it are certainly in superior force.

At present our army is station'd on the plantations this side the Santee, that country being favorable to its procuring provisions and forage, and General Greene has taken a position on

---

[33]   *the extract..*: taken from Balfour's letters of 20th and 21st July, pp 248-50.

[34]   *Stewart's public letter..*: see p 166, note 1.

the other side the river and on the High Hills of Santee, whither he retired after the action at Eutaw Springs.

Your Lordship will be assured I shall regard with anxiety and attention the contending armaments in Chesapeak, as on the land and sea operations there the future situation of this province must greatly depend. On this idea I have neglected no means to establish the magazines necessary to secure this town shou'd any adverse fortune to the King's arms in that part of the world render such precautions requisite here, and from the same motive I have, as far as in me lay, recommended the line of caution and defence as fittest for the advanced corps under the present critical and important aspect of affairs.

In North Carolina some successful efforts have been made by the loyalists, and a considerable body of them have made good their junction with Major Craig after seizing their titular Governor, Mr Burke, and making about 60 of the enemy prisoners, amongst which are thirteen Continental officers. Thus far the prospect is pleasing, but shou'd General Greene detach to that quarter, it is impossible to say how far the measure might affect the fluctuating state of politicks there, but from the judicious line of conduct hitherto pursued by Major Craig many future advantages may be expected.

The powerful eruptions which the enemy of late have made into this country and their having overrun so considerable a part of it must naturally have an influence on the colonies to the southward, and many demands for their support have consequently been made here, but, circumstanced as we are, to part with men wou'd be attended with many bad effects without answering adequate purposes. However, in point of stores and provision both Georgia and East Florida have been supplied as far as our means will admit.

I must now, my Lord, beg leave to rectify a mistake which occurs in my dispatch N° 6, where the investment of the posts at Mott's House and Congarees is mention'd as subsequent to Lord Rawdon's retiring from Camden, whereas the enemy were before them previous to that event taking place.

I have the honor to be, my Lord,
Your Lordship's most obedient and most humble servant

N BALFOUR

Balfour to Germain, 12th October 1781   *109(50): C*

Charlestown
October 12th 1781

Rt Hon Lord George Germain etc etc etc

My Lord

Lieutenant Campbell of the 71st Regiment, being obliged from his state of health to return to Europe, is charged with the dispatches from hence and will have the honor to deliver them to your Lordship, and as there are many circumstances which, tho' necessary for your Lordship to be informed of, might not be proper to commit to writing, I have therefore communicated such to this officer that he may have the honor to lay them before your Lordship.

I have the honor to be, my Lord,
Your Lordship's most obedient and most humble servant

N BALFOUR

§ - §

2 - Between Balfour and Clinton, 1780-1[35]

Clinton to Balfour, 7th November 1780   *4(53): LS*

New York
November 7th 1780

Lt Colonel Balfour

Sir

You will see by the orders that I have appointed Mackenzie Major in the room of poor Mecan. The succession goes on as you wished, I believe.

As the communication between you and Lord Cornwallis may be a little precarious, I send the inclosed dispatches to his Lordship open[36] that you may collect from what is intended for his Lordship's information such as you think necessary and send it in cypher to him, as no doubt you have one.

I am sorry the succession in the 23rd can't go on throughout at present as you recommended, as I find Markland is older than Saltonstall[37], and till I know your reasons for recommending the latter I cannot consent to the appointment, but Innis's son shall have the 2nd lieutenantcy.

---

[35] The papers are in the order in which they were written or received by Balfour.

[36] *the inclosed dispatches..*: of 5th and 6th November, vol III, pp 14-23.

[37] Ralph Markland and Leverett Saltonstall had entered the 23rd, Balfour's regiment, as 2nd lieutenants on 12th and 30th May 1778 respectively. Markland was promoted to 1st lieutenant on 2nd August 1780 and Saltonstall to the same rank one week later. (*Army Lists*)

I am to request you to deliver to the Board of Trustees for Captured Property the inclosed instruction[38], which will be followed by others more ample the instant I can confer with Admiral Arbuthnot.

I have appointed Captain Hatfield[39] of the 43rd Regiment Governor of the forts on Sullivan's Island — a reward for good services.

Tho' I have it not from authority, I understand there were a number of conspirators detected in Charles Town. As it is my intention to let the law take its full course, I beg you will take care in the absence of Lord Cornwallis to direct that all such delinquents are properly secured and brought to trial before a general court martial as soon as well can be and reported to me by the first opportunity, and I shall immediately send execution warrants for such as the law pronounces against.[40]

I am, sir,
Your most obedient and most humble servant

H CLINTON

Balfour to Clinton, 25th January 1781   109(7): C

N° 1   Charles Town
                                                           January 25th 1781

His Excellency Sir Henry Clinton KB etc etc etc

Sir

I am to acknowledge the honor of your Excellency's letter and to thank you on my own part and that of the Welch Fuzileers for the great attention shewn that regiment in the late promotions you have been pleased to make in it.

I am also to acquaint you with the arrival of Lord Cornwallis's aid de camps, Major Ross and Captain Broderick, in a packet from England with the dispatches[41] which Lt Colonel Turnbull will have the honor to deliver your Excellency.

---

38   *the inclosed instruction*: not extant.

39   John Hatfield had spent his entire service in the 43rd Regiment. Entering it as an ensign on 2nd February 1757, he was promoted to lieutenant on 7th March 1762, to captain lieutenant on 25th January 1771, and to captain on 25th May 1772. Posted with the regiment to Boston, where it arrived in July 1774, he commanded its grenadier company, which would have formed part of Howe's wing in the Battle of Bunker Hill. Having taken part in the New York campaign, the regiment went on to form part of the garrison at Newport, Rhode Island. In May 1781 it would arrive in Virginia and be among the corps which capitulated at Yorktown. (*Army Lists*)

40   In expressing himself so, Clinton was no doubt influenced to some degree by the fate of André.

41   *the dispatches*: Germain to Clinton, 9th November, and apparently others. That of the 9th is published in Davies ed, op cit, xviii, 223.

Major Ross having made known to me the very great anxiety of administration to receive advices from this, and as the sailing of the *Camilla* with the Admiral's dispatches for England has been countermanded here, I have taken the liberty to send home the packet with them and Lord Cornwallis's dispatches from hence[42], which, however, I should on no account have done had not a sloop of war been nearly ready to sail for New York, and which affords a safer conveyance there to the dispatches[43], the packet being but slightly armed, to all which considerations was added the *Sandwich* packet, taken in Chesapeak, being here and fit to proceed for New York in about ten days to wait any commands you may have for England, so that I trust from these my motives your Excellency will approve this measure.

By Lord Cornwallis I am directed to represent to your Excellency the great difficulties he labours under in communicating with New York. No trading vessels sailing at this season for the northward and the great want of ships of war here and a resident officer of the navy with authority to make arrangements and disbursements and to superintend the business of this port are at present insurmountable obstacles to this essential part of the service. Nor is this the only bad effect proceeding from the want of such an officer being station'd here. It will be obvious to your Excellency that without one no wants of ours connected with that line can either be supplied or our plans carried into execution, that ships coming in distressed cannot meet that assistance they might otherwise receive, and that the fluctuation of measures consequent to frequent changes in command must be attended with every inconvenience. To this cause I must attribute the *Sandwich*, now supposed to be lost, having been sent to St Augustine, tho' contrary to Lord Cornwallis's requisition for her to remain here to cooperate with the troops and assist in carrying on the service, as also that two frigates have been here repairing these six weeks without any prospect of their being soon fit for sea. I must, however, give every acknowledgement of Captain Gayton's readiness on all occasions, and had he not been order'd so soon to quit us, we shou'd be perfectly easy on this head.

The oat ships would have certainly sailed under convoy of the *Halifax* but for the danger of a winter's voyage, the fear of detaining the dispatches, and the present necessity there is of your Excellency being early inform'd of the state in which affairs are here, and which require that Lord Cornwallis's last letters shou'd be forwarded without delay, but you may be assured, sir, they shall be sent to you by the first good opportunity.

On the 21st instant Major Craig sail'd from hence on an expedition against Cape Fear under convoy of the *Blonde, Otter* and *Delight* men of war and three gallies, having with him the 6 companies of the 82nd Regiment (210 rank and file) with the convalescents of Lord Cornwallis's army and a small detachment of artillery, making on the whole near three hundred men. He has likewise with him two brass threes and two iron six pounders, artillery stores, and frames for batteries in case of taking post, as also three provision and one oat ship for supplying the army whenever the communication is compleated.

---

42 *Cornwallis's dispatches..*: of 18th December and 18th January to Germain, vol III, pp 43 and 47.

43 *the dispatches*: Germain's (see note 41 above) and Cornwallis's to Clinton, 3rd December to 18th January, vol III, pp 24 to 36.

The orders he has receiv'd by Lord Cornwallis's directions are to take post at Wilmington shou'd he find it capable of an easy defence and not attended with too much risque, which at all events he is caution'd as much as possible to avoid and, rather than incur it, to remain at Fort Johnston or some other more secure situation; to open, when the occasion offers, a communication with his Lordship; and above all things to be attentive to procuring of boats and craft and the sending supplies to the army when it reaches Cross Creek.

Colonel Tarleton's unfortunate affair has obliged me for a time to detain Captain Saunders's small detachment of the Queen's Rangers, as it was much wanting at George Town to look after parties of the enemy and, by joining some Provincial dragoons we are attempting to raise, to keep that country in awe, but I am yet in hopes the situation of things may so change as to admit their going in the first ships for Chesapeak, from whence we have yet received no accounts of the expedition under General Arnold.

A fleet for England will sail whenever the *Galatea* is fit for sea, which we hope will be in about ten days, when such transports as are unfit for service, the empty victuallers and oat ships, and a few disabled invalids will be sent home with her.

I must beg leave to refer your Excellency to Mr Simson for whatever respects the civil matters of this country and to express how much I have been obliged to this gentleman's attention and abilities in conducting the police and adjusting much of the very complex business of this town and province.

It will be necessary, before I close this, to observe on the great weight which the number of prisoners here are to us, besides the expence and difficulty of procuring prison ships and supplies for them, but I trust your Excellency will in good time relieve us from this burthen.

I have the honor to be, sir,
Your Excellency's most obedient and most humble servant

N BALFOUR

Balfour to Clinton, 31st January 1781

109(10): C

N° 2

Charles Town
January 31st 1781

His Excellency Sir Henry Clinton KB etc etc etc

Sir

I omitted in my letter of the 25th instant to represent to your Excellency, agreeable to Lord Cornwallis's directions, the great want he is in of money to supply the very many calls of the troops and service on him, his being unable to satisfy which must be attended with the worst consequences and greatly retard the necessary business of this army.

His Lordship is also much distress'd from their being no small arms in store, which must be very disadvantageous to the militia and Provincial establishments and, if not soon supplied, will preclude the raising any more levies of the latter in this district.

In my last I did myself the honor to mention to your Excellency, as a cause for detaining Captain Saunders's detachment, how liable George Town and the country within its vicinity then was to the visits of the enemy. I am now to inform you that in the night of the 25th instant a detachment of cavalry from Greene's army under Marian and Colonel Lee made an attempt on that post and, tho' they failed in their object, made prisoners of Lt Colonel Campbell and one or two other officers of Fanning's corps, who they immediately paroled. In other respects the loss was inconsiderable and nearly equal, two or three being killed on each side.

By the best accounts from Greene's army he was on the 25th to the eastward of Pedee, and I learn his intentions are to distress this country by making frequent inroads of cavalry into it, one of which yesterday morning destroyed the waggons and Quarter Master General's stores at Monk's Corner.

Two very enterprising officers (Lee and Marian) are employed upon this service, but I beg to assure your Excellency I shall do every thing within my power to secure the communication between this and Camden.

The wish of giving your Excellency more full information respecting the army, which by the last accounts was marching onward, has made me keep this open as long as possible.

I have the honor to be, sir,
Your Excellency's most obedient and humble servant

N BALFOUR

Balfour to Clinton, 2nd February 1781   109(11): C

N° 3   Charles Town
                                                              February 2nd 1781

His Excellency Sir Henry Clinton KB etc etc etc

Sir

Since I had the honor to address your Excellency on the 31st ultimo, I have received from Savannah the dispatches of which the enclosed are copies[44], and which the *Halifax* being so long delayed by contrary winds affords me an opportunity of transmitting for your Excellency's information.

---

[44] *the dispatches..*: Clarke to Balfour, 24th January, and Tonyn to Clarke, 22nd January, vol V, pp 329 to 332 and 342.

I shall likewise forward transcripts of them to Lord Cornwallis by the first good occasion which offers and wish in the meantime it was in my power to comply with all Colonel Clarke's requisitions, which, however, the present state of this garrison and the many detachments which the enemy's inroads have obliged us to make from it will on no account admit of, but so far as is possible from hence your Excellency will believe his wants will be supplied.

I have the honor to be, sir,
Your Excellency's most obedient and most humble servant

N BALFOUR

Balfour to Clinton, 5th February 1781   *109(11): C*

Nᵒ 4

Charles Town
February 5th 1781

His Excellency Sir Henry Clinton KB etc etc etc

Sir

I have the honor to inform your Excellency that a fleet from England arrived here yesterday under convoy of the *Chatham* and *Carysfort*, which ships will proceed to New York whenever they are watered, and I shall then take care the oat vessels are sent with them.

The *Halifax* will go to sea immediately, as I am exceedingly anxious to forward the dispatches to your Excellency and am therefore concerned she shou'd necessarily have been delayed so long.

Inclosed are copies of a letter from General Dalling to Lord Cornwallis and instructions to Lord Charles Montagu for raising a corps in this province[45], on the subject of which I beg to receive your Excellency's commands, and, if the measure meets your approbation, how far it is your Excellency's pleasure Lord Charles shou'd be supplied, in case of raising men (of which he seems to have no doubt), with transports and a convoy to Jamaica, and also in what degree you may judge it expedient to furnish his Lordship with money for carrying on this service.

I have the honor to be, sir,
Your Excellency's most obedient and humble servant

N BALFOUR

---

[45] The Cornwallis Papers contain no copies of the enclosures.

Nᵒ 5

Charles Town
February 13th 1781

His Excellency Sir Henry Clinton KB etc etc etc

Sir

In my dispatch of the 25th ultimo I had the honor to mention to your Excellency the expedition under Major Craig and the objects of it, since which I have received from that officer a letter giving an account of his successes[46], the copy of which is herewith transmitted for your Excellency's information.

From Lord Rawdon I have likewise received a letter with pleasing tho' not absolutely authenticated intelligence, an extract from which I now send as it will be no doubt interesting to your Excellency.[47]

Some days since a packet from England arrived here. She left Falmouth the 14th December and sailed in company with one for New York. By her the inclosed circular letter from Lord George Germain has been received and in consequence of it such unemployed transports as are here will be sent home with the *Galatea*'s convoy, which sails the end of this week.

So good a convoy as the *Chatham*'s offering for New York, I have the satisfaction to forward under it the oat ships agreeable to your Excellency's directions.

The necessity for cavalry in this province is daily increasing from the small parties of the enemy which are continually making incursions and threaten generally to distress it unless we can oppose them with horse, for which at present there are no appointments in the public stores.

The Port Master, Towns, has conducted himself so ill in that office owing, as is generally believed, to insanity that I have been obliged to appoint another to do that duty, but as he is honoured with your Excellency's commission, I beg to know your pleasure in what manner I am to proceed with him.

I shou'd have mention'd in my letter of the 5th instant that Lord Charles Montagu's plan for raising a corps was from amongst the rebel prisoners, which is a point on which I must also request your Excellency's commands.

---

[46] *a letter..*: of 4th February, vol IV, p 31.

[47] The Cornwallis Papers contain no copy of Rawdon's letter or of the extract.

As by your Excellency's letter General Du Portail was expressly order'd to Philadelphia[48], he received from hence the fullest directions to proceed there by the way of Wilmington, notwithstanding which he took a round of more than 300 miles in order to call at Greene's camp from no other motive that I can devise than to give all the intelligence in his power to that general, of which I therefore think it my duty to inform your Excellency.

I have the honor to be, sir,
Your Excellency's most obedient and humble servant

N BALFOUR

Enclosure (1)
Germain to Cornwallis, 7th December 1780   *65(15): CS*

Circular   Whitehall
                                                        7th December 1780

Earl Cornwallis

My Lord

The inclosed copy of a letter to me from the Lords Commissioners of the Admiralty will fully inform you of their Lordships' desire respecting the transport and victualling service and of the instructions they have given to the Commander of His Majesty's ships in North America; and as you will from thence see the necessity of giving the quickest dispatch to all victuallers in the delivery of their cargoes, and of being careful that no transports are detained unnecessarily, I think it only necessary to add that I have received the King's commands to signify to you His Majesty's pleasure that you do give the strictest attention to what is desired.

I am, my Lord,
Your Lordship's most obedient humble servant

GEO GERMAIN

---

[48] For Duportail's passport from Clinton, see vol III, p 206.

Enclosure (2)
Lords Commissioners of the Admiralty to Germain,   *65(16): C*
    6th December 1780

Admiralty Office
6th December 1780

The Rt Hon Lord George Germain etc etc etc

My Lord

The Navy Board having represented to us that from the uncommon scarcity of shipping in this kingdom they are under the greatest difficulty to answer the very great and pressing demands that are made upon them from time to time to supply transports for the use of the army, we have directed the Commanders in Chief of His Majesty's ships in North America, at the Leeward Islands and at Jamaica not to detain more transports in those parts than what are absolutely necessary for the use of the army nor to divert the storeships or victuallers which are now with them, or which may hereafter be sent to them, to any other purposes than those for which they were sent out, but to furnish the agents who conduct them with convoys to Europe as soon after they are cleared or discharged as may be practicable; and we submit to your Lordship whether it would not have a good effect if your Lordship were to write to the Commanders in Chief of His Majesty's land forces in those parts not to demand more transports nor to detain the victuallers or storeships longer than may be absolutely necessary, but to permit the surplus shipping to return to England or Ireland as soon as possible.

We are etc

SANDWICH[49]
LISBURNE[50]
H PENTON[51]

---

[49] John Montagu (1718-1792), Earl of Sandwich, had been appointed First Lord of the Admiralty in January 1771, an office he had held in previous administrations. Ex officio he was the leading member of the Admiralty Board, a body concerned, *inter alia*, with tactics, training, discipline, strategy, ship design and the management of the dockyards. In collaboration with Charles Middleton (see vol V, p 100, note 44), whom he had appointed Comptroller of the Navy, he was continuing to pursue what he rightly regarded as the great work of his life, namely a thorough overhaul of the dockyards and of naval shipbuilding policy. Though he was unable to complete these tasks, he had the satisfaction, when he left office in March 1782, of leaving his successors with a fleet larger and in better condition than ever before. He never again occupied an office of state. (*ODNB*)

[50] Wilmot Vaughan (*c*. 1730-1800), Earl of Lisburne in the Irish peerage, was a half-brother of Major General John Vaughan (see vol I, p 11 note 5). He had been serving in the Commons as the Member for Cardiganshire since 1768 and had been appointed a Lord Commissioner of the Admiralty, which carried a seat on the Admiralty Board, in 1770. Like Sandwich, he would resign in March 1782 on the fall of the North ministry and not occupy an office of state again. (Valentine, *The British Establishment*, ii, 887)

[51] Henry Penton (1736-1812) was a barrister who for the last nineteen years had been serving in the Commons as the Member for Winchester. In 1774 he was appointed a Lord Commissioner of the Admiralty and became a member of the Admiralty Board. He would resign with Sandwich and Lisburne and not hold public office again. (Valentine, op cit, ii, 690-1)

Balfour to Clinton, 14th February 1781   *109(15): C*

Nº 6

Charles Town
February 14th 1781

His Excellency Sir Henry Clinton KB etc etc etc

Sir

Since my letter of yesterday's date I have had the satisfaction to receive from my Lord Rawdon the dispatches[52] which I do myself the honor to enclose your Excellency copies of, at the same time congratulating your Excellency on the pleasing accounts they contain.

In order to extend the good effects of Lord Cornwallis's late successes I shall, as soon as every necessary arrangement can be made, move a part of this garrison over the Santee, which I hope will free the country between that river and the Pedee of those parties of the enemy which of late have so much infested it and restore to the lower districts of the province that peace they have for some weeks been deprived of.

I have the honor to be, sir,
Your Excellency's most obedient and humble servant

N BALFOUR

Balfour to Clinton, 24th February 1781   *109(17): C*

Nº 7

Charles Town
February 24th 1781

His Excellency Sir Henry Clinton KB etc etc etc

Sir

As it is as well my wish as duty to render your Excellency every information in my power respecting the situation of affairs in this part of America, I do myself the honor to transmit the copy of a letter from Lord Rawdon of the 15th instant[53] which contains the latest accounts of the army under Lord Cornwallis.

By intelligence brought me yesterday, the post at Congarees had been for three days invested by 7 or 800 men under Colonel Sumpter, but as I learn Lord Rawdon was moving that way, I am in hopes he will be able to accomplish its relief.

---

[52] *the dispatches*: no doubt including Cornwallis to Rawdon, 4th February, vol IV, p 44.

[53] *a letter..*: the Cornwallis Papers contain no copy.

I am sorry to acquaint your Excellency that on the 21st instant Captain De Peyster[54] with an officer and 25 men of Fanning's regiment that had been detached on some service a few miles from George Town, on the approach of a small party of the enemy, took refuge in an house and submitted themselves prisoners of war, the particulars of which your Excellency will be more fully informed of when proper enquiry can be made into it.

On receiving yesterday the letter from General Arnold of which an extract[55] is inclosed, I did myself the honor to lay the same before Captain Barklay, the senior sea officer here, that he might judge what could be done for relieving the fleet and army in the Chesapeak and forcing the French ships from thence (His Majesty's Ships of War the *Chatham, Assurance, Blonde, Carysfort* and *Galatea* being now here), but being informed by Captain Barklay it has been found inexpedient to attempt any thing in this way, the *Chatham* will proceed immediately with her convoy for New York.[56]

By my letter of the 13th instant your Excellency will learn that the *Galatea* and unemployed Government vessels were then to sail for Europe in a few days agreeable to the directions in the circular letter from Lord George Germaine, a copy of which I had the honor to forward to your Excellency with that dispatch and to shew Captain Barkley on his arrival from Cape Fear (where he left every thing in a state of security), but as he thinks it will be best to detain them until the *Camilla* is in readiness for sea, they will then, together with the trade from this, be forwarded under their joint protection.

I have only to inform your Excellency that the fleet of victuallers for New York got in here yesterday and, whenever it is watered, will pursue its destination, and of the arrival of your Excellency's aid de camp, Colonel Bruce, in the *Assurance* after a very long and tedious passage from Cork.

I have the honor to be, sir,
Your Excellency's most obedient humble servant

N BALFOUR

---

[54] James De Peyster (1757-1793) was a brother of Frederick and Abraham (see vol I, pp 104, note 6, and 249, note 14) and a nephew of Arent Schuyler (see vol III, p 299, note 35). When the King's American Regiment was raised in December 1776, he entered it as a lieutenant and was now serving there as a captain lieutenant. He had recently come south with Leslie and had been posted with the regiment to Georgetown. By 1783 he would have ceased to serve in the regiment, but whether he resigned or was cashiered, perhaps as a result of the present incident, is unknown. In 1786 he was commissioned a 1st lieutenant in the Royal Artillery and had the reputation of being one of the handsomest men in the British Army. He was killed near Menin during the Flanders campaign. (*Appletons'*; Sabine, *Biographical Sketches*, i, 374-6; Raymond, 'British American Corps'; WO 65/164(34) (National Archives, Kew))

[55] *an extract*: no copy. See p 213, note 12.

[56] See p 213, note 13.

N° 8

Charles Town
March 3rd 1781

His Excellency Sir Henry Clinton KB etc etc etc

Sir

In my letter of the 24th ultimo I had the honor to communicate to your Excellency the situation of the Congarees and of its being invested by a force under Colonel Sumpter. I have now the honor to inform you that by the good conduct of Major Maxwell of the Prince of Wales's Regiment the rebels were repulsed in their attempts on that post. They next turned their views to Thompson's and were there likewise defeated with some loss. Sumpter then reconnoitred Nelson's but, finding it too strong, passed the Santee 5 miles above that, where he was opposed by some Provincial light infantry under Lt Colonel Watson and obliged to retreat with the loss of eighteen killed, a few taken, and many horses.

This action was brought on by Sumpter's having surrounded Lieutenant Cooper[58] and a small party of the light infantry, on which occasion Colonel Watson mentions with high applause the meritorious conduct and gallant resistance of that officer, and which I therefore think it my duty to communicate to your Excellency.

Having yesterday received by an officer who has been long a prisoner of war at Hillsborough accounts of Lord Cornwallis's rapid advances into North Carolina, and wishing, as they seem to me essential, to give your Excellency the earliest information of them, I have dispatched for this purpose the *Sandwich* packet, which was retaken in the Chesapeak and is now fit for sea.

On the 10th of last month it appears General Greene retired, on the approach of Lord Cornwallis, from Guildford Court House, where it is said he had been previously joined by the corps under General Morgan.

---

[57] Annotated: 'This letter was published entire'. A copy containing no differences appears in Davies ed, op cit, xx, 72-3.

[58] Richard Cooper (1756-?) was not a lieutenant but was in fact an ensign in the 4th Battalion, New Jersey Volunteers. Commissioned on 25th August 1780, he had entered the battalion as a serjeant major when it was raised in Bergen County, New Jersey, at the close of 1776. He was now seconded with its light company to Watson's Provincial light infantry. On 27th February he and twenty of his men had fallen behind the rest of the corps to cover the repair of a broken down waggon. Surrounded by 200 men under Sumter, he refused to surrender but ordered his men to form a loose square behind trees. There they held out until Watson with the rest of the corps came to their relief. For his gallantry Cooper was commended in General Orders. Having returned to his battalion (now renumbered the 3rd), he was promoted to lieutenant on 25th October 1782 and placed on the Provincial half-pay list at the end of the war. Virtually all of the battalion's officers settled on land grants in Nova Scotia. (Nan Cole and Todd Braisted, 'A History of the 4th Battalion, New Jersey Volunteers' and 'New Jersey Volunteers: List of Officers, 1776-1783' (*The On-Line Institute for Advanced Loyalist Studies*, 23rd September 2006); Treasury 64/23(8), WO 65/164(36), and WO 65/165(7) (National Archives, Kew))

On the evening of the 12th he had reach'd the length of Moore's plantation on Country Line Creek, 15 miles from the Dan and 30 to the northward of Hillsborough. This he quitted the succeeding day, when the same ground was taken up by the King's army.

On the 12th I learn General Greene had sent an express to a Colonel Gunby[59], the rebel commander at Hillsborough, ordering him to forward to the army the baggage of the Maryland line, particularly shoes, of which they were in the utmost want. This was followed by another express that evening directing the same to meet him at Taylor's Ferry (on the Roanoke) as he was so closely pursued and harrassed by Lord Cornwallis as to be unable to meet it elsewhere.

In this last express General Greene signified to Colonel Gunby that it had been his intentions to have passed the Dan River at Dixon's Ferry, but the close pressure of Lord Cornwallis had obliged him to change this rout and take that of Boyd's, where he was in hopes of finding the river fordable.[60]

At this time a belief was current at Hillsborough and in the country that Lord Cornwallis had detached a corps on the other side the Dan somewhere near the lower Sawra Town to intercept the passage of the rebels either over that river or the Roanoke.

And it is further confidently asserted that for 2 or 3 days the armies were so near each other that frequent skirmishes pass'd between the rear guard of Greene's and the advanced of Lord Cornwallis's.

As these particulars may essentially affect the corps under General Arnold, I have requested a vessel shou'd be sent without delay to the Chesapeak and by her shall transmit to that officer a copy of this letter to your Excellency, as I am apprehensive least his situation in Portsmouth shou'd stop other channels of information.[61]

I have the honor to be, sir,
Your Excellency's most obedient and most humble servant

N BALFOUR

---

[59] Born into a loyalist family on a farm at Gunby's Creek, Maryland, not far from the present-day town of Crisfield on Chesapeake Bay, John Gunby (1745-1807) had been commissioned a lt colonel in the Maryland Continental line in December 1776 and promoted to colonel four months later. Having come south with Kalb, he had lately been serving on secondment at Hillsborough, charged with forwarding men and supplies to the southern army. He would rejoin the army in time to command the 1st Maryland Continental Regiment in the Battles of Guilford and Hobkirk's Hill, but would be blamed by Greene for the outcome of the latter affair. In September 1783 he was promoted to the rank of brigadier general. Shortly afterwards he retired to his farm near Snow Hill, where, apart from engaging in charitable work, he shunned public life. He died there and was buried in the family plot. (Dr William H Wroten Jr, 'Colonel John Gunby...', *Salisbury Times* (Maryland), 7th September 1959; *The Greene Papers*, vi-viii, *passim*; Boatner, *Encyclopedia*, 471)

[60] For summaries of Greene's letters to Gunby, see *The Greene Papers*, vii, 280.

[61] See Balfour to Arnold, 4th March, p 255.

236

New York
2nd January 1781

Lt Colonel Balfour
Commandant of Charlestown

Sir

I have the honor to enclose herewith an open official letter from me as Commander in Chief to the Trustees of Rebel Property[62], which I am to request you will give to those gentlemen. And as Lord Cornwallis will probably be at too great a distance from Charlestown to give immediate directions to them respecting the business committed to their charge in consequence of the King's pleasure signified in the Minister's letter of the 3rd of August to Vice Admiral Arbuthnot and me[63] (a copy of which I transmit to his Lordship), I think proper to send you my dispatch on this subject to his Lordship[64] unsealed that you may peruse the contents and act (until you receive his instructions) as occasion may require. After you have read the letter for Lord Cornwallis, you will please to forward it to him by the first safe opportunity.

I have likewise the honor to enclose a declaration from the Commissioners to the inhabitants of the revolted provinces, which I request you will be pleased to have reprinted at Charlestown and dispersed.

In my letter of the 6th November to the before-mentioned gentlemen I intimated to them that the Minister's letter was addressed to the Commissioners, but upon reconsidering the matter, the Admiral and myself are of opinion that it was addressed to us as Commanders in Chief of the land and sea forces on this service. You will therefore be pleased to signify this to the Trustees, that no act of theirs may appear to be done by order of the Commissioners.

I have the honor to be, sir,
Your most obedient and most humble servant

H CLINTON

---

[62]   *an open official letter..*: see vol V, p 74.

[63]   *the Minister's letter..*: see vol V, p 72-3.

[64]   *my dispatch..*: see vol V, p 71.

Clinton to Balfour, 9th March 1781[65]

5(109): LS

New York
March 9th 1781

Lt Colonel Balfour

Sir

I was favored with your letters dated the 25th and 31st January and 2nd and 5th of February by the *Halifax* sloop of war on the 16th ultimo.

As the disposal of the rebel prisoners in Carolina is submitted to Lord Cornwallis[66], it is unnecessary for me to trouble you with instructions on that head. And with respect to Governor Dalling's letter and instructions to Lord Charles Montague, I must refer you also for directions from Lord Cornwallis, who is of course the best judge how far it will be for the good of the King's Service in the southern colonies to afford Lord Charles the assistance which General Dalling solicits.

I expect to receive a supply of arms very soon. All those we had to spare were left in Carolina and sent on the expeditions to the Chesapeak.

Captain Amherst of the 60th Regiment, who is so obliging to charge himself with my dispatches for Lord Cornwallis[67], will deliver them to your care.

I have the honor to be, sir,
Your most obedient and most humble servant

H CLINTON

Smith to Balfour, 14th March 1781

5(113): ALS

New York
March 14th 1781

Lt Colonel Balfour
Commandant of Charlestown

Sir

I am directed by the Commander in Chief to acquaint you that as transports are very much wanted at this place, he is extremely sorry to find by your letter of the 13th ultimo you

---

[65] Published with two inconsequential differences in Stevens, *Clinton-Cornwallis Controversy*, i, 346.

[66] See Clinton to Cornwallis, 5th March, vol V, p 85.

[67] *my dispatches..*: see vol V, pp 71-87.

proposed sending all those that were unemployed at Charlestown to Europe with the *Galatea*'s convoy (without waiting for his commands upon that subject) in consequence of a circular letter received from Lord George Germain, which letter his Excellency apprehends you have not conceived in the light he does. If, therefore, any thing should have prevented their departure for Europe, he requests you will be pleased to order such of them as are fit for service to proceed hither with the very first convoy, there not being at this time a single transport in this port.

I have the honor to be with great regard, sir,
Your most obedient and most humble servant

JOHN SMITH
Secretary

Balfour to Clinton, 7th April 1781[68]   *109(26): C*

Nº 9   Charles Town
                                                                        April 7th 1781

His Excellency Sir Henry Clinton KB etc etc etc

Sir

I am honored with your letters of the 2nd of January and 9th of last month, as also with one of the 14th ultimo by your Excellency's directions from Captain Smith.

About a week since, the fleet for England sail'd, and as only such transports as were wholly unfit for service went home with it, I am happy in this respect to have complied with your Excellency's intentions. Those that can be spared from this will be sent with the convoy to New York and only the prison ships remain here.

I took the opportunity of the *Assurance*'s fleet being obliged to water to take out of it the cloathing for the British regiments here and likewise some for the Provincial troops station'd and raising in the southern provinces. And as the want of all kinds of ordnance stores, especially small arms, was great and the demands for them pressing, I have taken the liberty of procuring a small supply from the *Juliana*, the particulars of which will be transmitted by Major Traile, but must, agreeable to the wish of Lord Cornwallis, request in the strongest manner a further quantity of small arms, the consumption of which is very considerable from the frequent loss of them in action and the arming of new levies and militia both here and in Georgia, to which I must add my having been oblig'd to send a thousand stand to Cape Fear and the total unfitness for service of those left at this place.

As Lord Cornwallis is in the greatest want of every supply, I have sent him to Cape Fear what could be procured here, and as he will have many calls on the hospital in consequence of the late marches and action, I have taken care to furnish a supply of officers and stores to

---

[68] Published in Stevens, op cit, i, 392. There is only one material difference, namely 'from England' instead of 'for England' in the second paragraph.

that department at Wilmington, and shall by that way forward to his Lordship your Excellency's dispatches whenever an occasion offers.

The very extensive demands here for money have hitherto been mostly answered by Government bills of exchange, which till lately passed current at the rate of 4*s* 8*d* per dollar, but the merchants are at present unwilling to receive them at a less discount than they bear at New York. However, as their wish is only to have the exchange the same at both places, they have agreed to continue it as usual until this point is adjusted and I can be honoured with your Excellency's commands on this essential subject.

I do myself the honor to transmit your Excellency the copy of a letter from Captain McNemara of His Majesty's Sloop *Hound*[69], by which will be seen the danger which threatens West Florida. On receiving this account I immediately forwarded the same to Governor Dalling and General Vaughn that if possible some aid might be afforded by them to the garrison of Pensacola, and have sent to St Augustine such supplies of ammunition and provisions as we could part with from this, which, together with a strong galley sent there, the presence of Lt Colonel Clarke, and a small reinforcement he takes with him from Savannah, will, I trust, give security to that place.

Subsequent to these advices information has been received by an express to a merchant at Augusta that about the 10th ultimo the Spanish fleet arrived at Pensacola, that the army, nearly two thousand, was landed on Rose's Island, and that the ships of war were cannonading the works on Red Cliffs.

Enclos'd I have the honor to transmit the proceedings of a general court martial held here[70], and which from the occasion of it your Excellency will judge to have been unavoidable.

In some of my former letters I have had occasion to mention to your Excellency the inroads which the enemy were daily making in to the heart of this province and the distresses, both to the people of the country and army, which attended them. I am therefore sorry the occasion still exists for the like information owing in a great measure to the extent of the communications and the want of cavalry (for which there are no appointments here) to cover them from the incursions of small parties, which, tho' singly of no moment, yet produce, when so often occurring, the worst consequences.

Lieutenant Sutherland of the Engineers is now with Major Craig but shall be sent to New York whenever he can be got at, agreeable to your Excellency's directions.

---

[69] *a letter..*: see p 215, note 17.

[70] As is evident from Clinton's letter of 24th May (p 247), the proceedings involved the court martial of Lt Anthony Allaire of the Loyal American Regiment for the wilful murder of Ensign Robert Keating of the Prince of Wales's American Regiment. It was a case of a botched duel. Allaire had shot Keating dead on the streets of Charlestown as he was being beaten by Keating with a cane. The incident stemmed from a drunken argument on St Patrick's Day as to which of them would take the bagpiper of the Volunteers of Ireland to serenade his woman. (Proceedings, court martial of Lt Anthony Allaire, 28th to 31st March 1781 (WO 71/93(287) and WO 71/96(311) (UK National Archives, Kew))

Tho' my Lord Rawdon has the honor to communicate the accounts of Lord Cornwallis's victory over the rebels at Guildford[71], I cannot deny myself the honor of congratulating your Excellency on an event so fortunate in its consequences and so reputable to the army serving under your command.

I have the honor to be, sir,
Your Excellency's most obedient humble servant

N BALFOUR

Balfour to Clinton, 20th April 1781[72]　　　　　　　　　109(28): C

Nº 10　　　　　　　　　　　　　　　　　　　　　　　　　　　　　Charles Town
　　　　　　　　　　　　　　　　　　　　　　　　　　　　　　　April 20th 1781

His Excellency Sir Henry Clinton KB etc etc etc

Sir

I have the honor to acquaint your Excellency that by the letters from Lord Rawdon of the 12th, 13th and 15th instant[73] there is the fullest information that General Greene with his army is advancing into this province and that his light troops have actually pass'd the Pedee. The object of this movement, there is every reason to beleive, is Camden, which at present is but weak, Lord Rawdon having detached Lt Colonel Watson with two battallions from that post, so that in the end it may be expedient for combining the force to relinquish every thing on the other side Santee, a measure, however, which your Excellency may be assured will not be taken but in case of the utmost necessity.

As this movement of Greene's may considerably change Lord Cornwallis's view (who is now at Wilmington), I have judged it fit to lay before your Excellency as soon as possible this intelligence, which is likewise forwarded to Lord Cornwallis by an express boat[74].

I have the honor to be, sir,
Your Excellency's most obedient and humble servant

N BALFOUR

---

[71]　Of Rawdon's letter there is no copy in the Cornwallis Papers.

[72]　Published in Stevens, op cit, i, 418. The only material difference is the omission of 'as soon as possible' in the second paragraph.

[73]　*the letters from Lord Rawdon..*: see vol IV, pp 173-5.

[74]　See Balfour to Cornwallis, 20th April, vol IV, p 170.

Nº 11

Charles Town
April 22nd 1781

His Excellency Sir Henry Clinton KB etc etc etc

Sir

I think it my duty to acquaint your Excellency that a vessel is this evening arrived in 19 days from Jamaica, the master of which informs that when three days out he fell in with a man of war that had been off Pensacola, and which he judges to be the *Ulysses*, that assured him the town of Pensacola was then taken by the Spaniards.

From Lord Rawdon I have receiv'd no further information than what I had the honor to communicate to your Excellency in my letter of the 20th instant, from which circumstance I am rather apprehensive his Lordship may be invested in Camden, and I have certain intelligence that Lee, having join'd his force to Marian's, has been for four or five days before Wright's Bluff, a commanding post on the north side of Santee,[75] from all which I should judge it is the enemy's present intention to strike at Camden and that part of the province, which [is] enfeebled by the absence of Lord Cornwallis, at the same time that I am convinced no exertions will be wanting there to render abortive all views of that kind which General Greene may at this time entertain.

I have the honor to be, sir,
Your Excellency's most obedient and humble servant

N BALFOUR

Balfour to Clinton, 5th May 1781   *109(33): C*

Nº 12

Charles Town
May 5th 1781

His Excellency Sir Henry Clinton KB etc etc etc

Sir

Your Excellency having been pleased to refer the subject of Lord Charles Montagu's corps to the decision of Lord Cornwallis, I had the honor to write him on that head, but the vessel which carried that and other dispatches being unfortunately lost or taken, and the army so soon removing from Wilmington, has precluded my communicating with his Lordship in this respect and obliged me to act in this matter from myself, to which I have been induced by knowing it a measure most consonant to the wishes of Ministry, signified to Lord Cornwallis

---

[75] The rest of this paragraph is annotated: 'omitted in fair draft'.

by a letter from Lord George Germain of the 9th of November last[76], and by Lord Charles's having engaged the men, who by longer delays might have been lost to the service, to further which I have been necessitated at his Lordship's request to furnish the corps with one muster's pay and also several articles of cloathing from the Provincial Stores, accounts of all which I shall transmit to General Dalling that he may send bills for reimbursing the same, and Lord Charles has himself engaged armed vessels for transporting the corps (now compleat) to Jamaica, the freight of which is to be paid there.

The disbursements by public departments here being very considerable and their demands for money consequently great, I cannot but express to your Excellency the concern I feel when obliged to sign warrants to a vast amount without knowing on what account the expenditures have been made or having it in my power to check any improprieties which in this respect may occur, and I therefore hope, as a measure that appears to me of necessity to the service, that your Excellency will be pleased to appoint some person to audit the public accounts here and thereby sanction the grants I am obliged to make of Government money.

Lord Cornwallis having thought it necessary that the proprietors of such houses as are occupied by Government shou'd receive some compensation for the same, I am directed to lay this matter before your Excellency that a rule may be fixed for regulating this business, which I humbly conceive might be done by adopting the rates of rent at some period previous to these commotions, but on this subject I beg leave to refer your Excellency to Captain McMahon[77], the Barrack Master, whose state of health obliging him to quit this during the warm season, he has therefore obtained Lord Cornwallis's leave to go to New York for a few months and, as he is fully inform'd on this head, can answer to any particulars your Excellency may require.

I had signified to Lieutenant Sutherland your Excellency's directions that he shou'd return to New York, but the misfortune of the dispatch vessel being lost has hindered his receiving them and I now learn he is gone with Lord Cornwallis's army.

I have the honor to be, sir,
Your Excellency's most obedient and humble servant

N BALFOUR

---

[76] *a letter..:* see vol III, p 44.

[77] John McMahon (*c.* 1754-1817) was an Irishman of a lowly background who had come out to North America in 1775 as an ensign in the 44th Regiment. Patronised by Rawdon, with whom he maintained a friendship for many years, he transferred to the Provincial establishment as a captain in Rawdon's Volunteers of Ireland. When Charlestown was reduced in May 1780, he was seconded to the office of barrackmaster there. Outwardly unprepossessing, small and pock-marked, he made up for his appearance by obliging manners which went far in conciliating inhabitants of the revolutionary persuasion. Many years later one of his revolutionary opponents would compliment him as being a respected officer of distinguished merit who was characterised by liberality and humanity. He would transfer to the British establishment, rising to the rank of lt colonel, but retire in 1796 rather than serve in Ireland. He went on to enter the Commons as the Member for Aldeburgh but is chiefly remembered as a confidant of the Prince of Wales, whom he served in various capacities, including those of vice-treasurer and private secretary. He was created a baronet one month before his death, by which time he was worth £90,000. (*ODNB*; Raymond, 'British American Corps'; Garden, *Anecdotes* (1st series), 264; Garden, *Anecdotes* (2nd series), 103, 105)

N° 13   Charles Town
                                                                             May 6th 1781

His Excellency Sir Henry Clinton KB etc etc etc

Sir

In my letters of the 20th and 22nd ultimo I had the honor to inform your Excellency that our post at Wright's Bluff was invested by the enemy, and the apprehensions I was then under of Camden being in the same situation.

I am now to acquaint you that the former has since been surrendered. The circumstances which lead to this cannot be more fully explained or with more honor to himself than by Lieutenant Mackay's[79] journal of the siege, which, together with the articles of capitulation, I therefore enclose for your Excellency's inspection.[80]

On the 19th of last month General Greene with about fourteen hundred Continentals and a body of militia came before Camden, where he continued, changing his positions, till the 25th, in the morning of which Lord Rawdon with the greater part of his garrison, upwards of eight hundred, marched out and about 10 o'clock attack'd him in his camp at Hobkirk's Hill with that conduct and spirit which claimed the victory he gained, tho' long contested and against superior numbers, especially of cavalry, the enemy's advantage in which hindered the pursuit being continued further than three miles and enabled them to take off their cannon, which they preserved at first by drawing out of the road into thickets, where they escaped the troops, eager in pursuit of the flying rebels.

To this decided line of conduct, which has produced the best effects, Lord Rawdon was induced by knowing that General Greene was in expectation of reinforcements which in a day or two must arrive, and that he had then detach'd to bring forward his supplies, an occasion which his Lordship's abilities and zeal did not fail to embrace.

The enemy's loss on this occasion is estimated by Lord Rawdon at about five hundred. His own appears (from the returns), as he informs me, two hundred and twenty, in which number is one officer killed and eleven wounded, but not dangerously.

---

[78] Published with inconsequential differences in Stevens, op cit, i, 471.

[79] James McKay was a British American officer who had been commissioned a lieutenant in the King's American Regiment on 30th December 1776. Serving on secondment to Watson's Provincial light infantry, he had been placed in command of the fortified post at Wright's Bluff known as Fort Watson. (WO 65/164(34) (National Archives, Kew); Raymond, 'British American Corps')

[80] A brief extract from the journal appears in *The Greene Papers*, viii, 141, note 1. The articles of capitulation are published in Tarleton, *Campaigns*, 472. For Henry Lee's eyewitness account of the siege and taking of Fort Watson, see his *Memoirs*, 331-2.

The consequences of this defeat of the rebel army gave Lord Rawdon an opportunity of drawing from the country a supply of provisions, of which he was in want, and obliged General Greene immediately to retire to Rugeley's, where he was join'd by the corps under Brigadier Marion and Colonel Lee and from whence he has since moved, but I have not yet learnt in what direction.

By to morrow I am in hopes Lord Rawdon will be reinforced by Lt Colonel Watson with his corps and the 64th Regiment.

But notwithstanding this brilliant success I must inform your Excellency that the general state of the country is most distressing, that the enemy's parties are every where, the communication by land with Savannah no longer exists, Colonel Brown is invested at Augusta, and Colonel Cruger in the most critical situation at Ninety Six, nearly confined to his works and without any present command over that country. Indeed, I should betray the duty I owe your Excellency did I not represent the defection of this province so universal that I know of no mode, short of depopulation, to retain it.

This spirit of revolt is in some measure kept up by the many officers prisoners of war here, and I shou'd therefore think it adviseable to remove them as well as to make the most striking examples of such as, having taken protection, snatch every occasion to rise in arms against us.

I have the honor to be, sir,
Your Excellency's most obedient humble servant

N BALFOUR

Clinton to Balfour, 3rd May 1781   6(35): LS

New York
May 3rd 1781

Lt Colonel Balfour

Sir

I was favored with your letter of the 7th ultimo by the *Amphitrite* on the 22nd, before the receipt of which Captain Tonken had reported to me that six of the transports sent home from Charles Town were the best and fittest for the service required and that Lieutenant Walters, the agent there, intended they should have been sent to this place. I am therefore sorry that Captain Barklay should have ordered these transports to Europe and have to request that the *Lyon* hospital ship and *Success Increase* transport may be sent here with the first convoy.

I approve much of your having taken a supply of stores etc out of the *Juliana* and wish you had taken the whole of the small arms. There is still another ordnance store ship expected, which sailed with the *Assurance*'s convoy but parted company. Should she arrive at Charles Town, you will take all the small arms she has on board, which I believe is about 3,000, if you want them.

As I understand that Mr Towns, the Captain of the Port of Charles Town, is insane, I have appointed Mr Edward Lacey (by my commission bearing date this day) to succeed him in that office, and he goes by the present opportunity.

Mr Sweetland, one of the Deputy Superintendents of the Port of Charles Town, having requested my permission to return to New York for the recovery of his health, you will be so good to permit him to come here by the first opportunity.

I have not time to add by the present opportunity but that I am, sir,

Your most obedient servant

H CLINTON

Balfour to Clinton, 6th June 1781   109(37): C

Nº 14

Charles Town
June 6th 1781

His Excellency Sir Henry Clinton KB etc etc etc

Sir

I am honored with your Excellency's dispatch of the 3rd ultimo and in respect to transports must beg leave to observe that those sent home were such as Captain Barclay deemed unserviceable, but I cannot dismiss this subject without assuring your Excellency it was a measure in which I was wholly unconcerned. The *Lyon* hospital ship and the *Success Encrease* transport are at present at Wilmington, but when they can be got from thence, I shall take care to have them sent to York.

It being impossible to carry on the service with any success in these parts without large corps of cavalry, I have on the requisition of Lord Rawdon been obliged to make large disbursements for horses and other dragoon appointments, which, with the other very considerable expences of this army, has so reduced us in cash that I fear, unless a speedy supply is sent, we shall be under the greatest necessity for want of it.

Lord Rawdon having so fully informed your Excellency of the state of this army and country leaves no room for my adding any thing on that head.[81]

I have the honor to be, sir,
Your Excellency's most obedient and most humble servant

N BALFOUR

---

[81] For an extract from Rawdon's letter of 6th June to Clinton, see Tarleton, *Campaigns*, 481.

New York
May 24th 1781

Lt Colonel Balfour

Sir

I was favored with your letters by the *Speedy* packet on the 22nd instant. Those sent by a merchant vessel which sailed at the same time reached me two days earlier.

I am of course to suppose that Lord Cornwallis will have left orders with Lord Rawdon relative to his evacuating Camden should it be thought necessary, and I take it for granted his Lordship will not hesitate on the measure if it should be judged expedient to adopt it, which may perhaps be the case if his supplies are so precarious and Lord Cornwallis should have quitted the Carolinas.

I must request to have from Lord Rawdon a report of his victory over General Green, which has been most important. His Lordship's decision, in consequence of the intelligence he had received of the detachments the enemy had made, was very judicious and does him great honor.

I am sorry to find that a spirit of revolt should be kept up by the officers who are prisoners at Charlestown. I have proposed an exchange for part of them and I think you should endeavour to rid yourself of as many of them that way as possible.

Being anxious to have Lieutenant Sutherland of the Engineers here, I wish a duplicate of the order for his coming had been sent as it might possibly have reached him tho' the original happened to miscarry.

Having approved the sentence of the general court martial held at Charlestown on the 28th day of March last on the trial of Lieutenant Alaire of the Loyal American Regiment for the wilful murder of Ensign Keating of the Prince of Wales's American Regiment, you will be pleased to signify the same and direct the prisoner to be released from his arrest.

The long delay of the *Speedy* packet since her arrival at Charlestown occasioned an inquiry to be made into the causes thereof, which by the captain's report I find have been various. I request that in future, should it be thought necessary to open at that place the mails directed for New York, the greatest care may be taken of the public dispatches and as little detention as possible given to the packet boats.

I am, sir,
Your most obedient and most humble servant

H CLINTON

N° 15

Charles Town
July 20th 1781

His Excellency Sir Henry Clinton KB etc etc etc

Sir

Since the sailing of the *Warwick* no opportunity has offered of communicating with your Excellency and I am now obliged to trust this to a private and unarmed schooner, Captain Barclay with the *Blonde* having been for some time on a cruise and no ship of war in this harbour.

Lord Rawdon having by the *Warwick* transmitted a state of this country and account of his movements to the arrival of the reinforcement, I now do myself the honor to lay before your Excellency a summary of events, so far as they have come within my knowledge, since that period.

No sooner were the necessary arrangements made than Lord Rawdon proceeded with a corps of about two thousand men to the relief of Ninety Six, on his near approach to which post General Greene took the resolution, rather than risque an action with Lord Rawdon, of storming the garrison, in which, however, he was repulsed by the exertions of Lt Colonel Cruger and the very spirited conduct of the troops under him, with the loss, as acknowledged, of at least seventy five killed and one hundred and fifty wounded, ours being truly inconsiderable both on this occasion and during the siege, which was closely pressed by the enemy.

This event, so fortunate in itself and creditable to Colonel Cruger and his small garrison, took place the 19th ultimo. On the succeeding day the enemy's army retired over the Saluda, and on the 21st Lord Rawdon arrived at Ninety Six.

At this place his Lordship did not rest long but by forced marches followed General Greene to a ford of the Ennoree, where he was within a few hours of coming up with him; but the uncommon fatigues which the troops had undergone (and the direction of General Greene's march over the Tyger and Broad Rivers then pointing at Virginia) not allowing the pursuit to be continued farther, Lord Rawdon returned to Ninety Six and from thence, leaving a part of his force with Colonel Cruger, proceeded to the Congarees.

For this place General Greene, having changed the course of his route, likewise push'd and, by passing over the river a corps of cavalry, surpriz'd a foraging party of ours, of which an officer and three or four were killed and wounded and about forty with their horses are taken.

After this General Greene with his main body passed over with the view of striking at Lord Rawdon, then at Orangeburgh, or cutting off the 3rd Regiment, which was proceeding under Lt Colonel Stewart to join him, but his Lordship's vigilance and skill frustrating these intentions, on his being reinforced by the corps under Lt Colonel Stewart, who accomplished his junction by a march of twenty seven miles in one day, and the troops under Lt Colonel Cruger, General Greene found it necessary to fall back with the greater part of his infantry over the Santee. He, however, detach'd the chief of his cavalry and some mounted infantry against the post at Monk's Corner, where the 19th Regiment and the mounted men of the South Carolina Rangers were stationed.

Before this place the enemy under Colonels Lee, Washington, Marrian and Sumpter appeared in force on the 14th instant, and the next day a party of them came within four miles of this town, having taken near Dorchester several horses in the Quarter Master General's employment and at the Quarter House some dragoon ones belonging to the South Carolina Rangers with a few invalids of that regiment who were left in charge of them and unable to make their escape.

Lt Colonel Cootes[82], finding himself nearly surrounded by the enemy and that their numbers were greatly superior to his, on the 16th instant destroyed the post and stores at Monk's Corner and retreated on the east side of the Cooper towards this, but in his march, being closely pressed by the enemy's cavalry, which were numerous, was obliged to relinquish his baggage and sick, which fell into their hands. The 19th Regiment, however, repulsed in the handsomest manner a charge which was made on it and compell'd the enemy's cavalry to give way.

Thus circumstanced, Colonel Cootes put his regiment in a strong position at Shubrick's House near Hugger's Bridge and sent information to this place of his situation, from which the enemy twice endeavour'd to force him but were driven back with loss.

On receiving this intelligence Colonel Gould with about seven hundred men marched from hence to sustain the 19th Regiment and on his approach the enemy retired, but as Lord Rawdon is come down with a small part of his corps (Colonel Stewart being left in care of the rest) to Goose Creek, I have some hopes he may be able to intercept any parties of them that may attempt to get off that way.

At present it is impossible to ascertain our loss on this occasion, tho' I fear it will prove rather considerable.

These events, the great force of the enemy, especially of cavalry, in which we are vastly deficient, and the general revolt of the province will, I conceive, even with the present force, much circumscribe any future positions we may take.

They will likewise, by throwing on us a great weight of unprovided for militia and refugees, add considerably in these respects to our expence both of money and provisions.

---

[82] John Coates was Lt Colonel of the 19th Regiment, one of the three which had arrived in South Carolina from Ireland at the beginning of June. For a more detailed account of the events in which he had just been involved, see *The Greene Papers*, ix, 13-17.

When a free communication with Lord Rawdon is opened, I shall do myself the honor to inform his Lordship of your Excellency's desire to receive from himself an account of the late action near Camden.

I have the honor to be, sir,
Your Excellency's most obedient and humble servant

N BALFOUR

Balfour to Clinton, 21st July 1781   *109(43): C*

Charles Town
21st July 1781

His Excellency Sir Henry Clinton KB etc etc etc

Sir

I omitted in my letter of yesterday's date to inform your Excellency that Andrew Williamson Esq, formerly a brigadier general in the rebel service, was in the night of the 5th instant taken at his plantation about seven miles from this by a small party of the enemy's militia detach'd for that purpose.

On receiving this intelligence, Major Fraser with the mounted men of the South Carolina Rangers was ordered to pursue and if possible retake Brigadier Williamson as it was fear'd his having reverted to British Government might submit him to the worst treatment.

By avoiding the main roads Major Fraser was enabled to surprize Colonel Haynes's camp of Colleton County militia, where he was inform'd General Williamson then was, and, coming upon it suddenly, killed a Lt Colonel McLaughlan[83] with ten or twelve others, made Colonel Haynes a prisoner, and retook General Williamson.

I have the honor to be, sir,
Your Excellency's most obedient and humble servant

N BALFOUR

---

[83] Like Isaac Hayne, Thomas McLaughlin (?-1781) had served as an officer in the Colleton County revolutionary militia. He was wounded at Beaufort in February 1779. (Moss, *SC Patriots*, 636; Heitman, *Historical Register*, 373)

New York
June 20th 1781

Lt Colonel Balfour

Sir

Captain Tonken, the Principal Agent of Transports, having informed me that it will not be proper to make use of the vessels afterwards as transports which have been employed as prison ships at Charles Town, I am therefore to desire that you will send such of them as are no longer wanted for that purpose either immediately to Europe should there be a proper opportunity or to this place in order that they may be discharged from the service.

I inclose[84] to you herewith an account of expences incurred at St Augustine in shipping ordnance stores for the siege of Charlestown, which you will desire the officer commanding the artillery to pay to the proper persons. You will also receive inclosed a general state of the accounts and expences incurred in the Engineer Department in East Florida as certified by Lt Colonel Moncrief, which you will be pleased to deliver to him and desire that he will pay the amount thereof and charge the same in his account of expenditures as commanding engineer in the Southern District.

I have the honor to be, sir,
Your most obedient and most humble servant

H CLINTON

PS: Having observed in the list of warrants transmitted from Charlestown that the Town Major and Barrack Master have been paid at the rate of ten shillings each per day, I am to desire that they shall receive (from the last payment) only what is customary, viz, 5*s* per day the former and 4*s* the latter.

HC

New York
July 13th 1781

Lt Colonel Balfour

Sir

I am sorry to find by your letter of the 6th ultimo that you are likely to be distressed for want of money, particularly as our funds here are not in a condition to enable us to relieve your wants in this article so effectually as I could wish, but as I understand that ten thousand

---

[84] Of this and the following enclosure there are no copies in the Cornwallis Papers.

pounds which was sent in the *Richmond* and intended for the use of the troops under Lord Cornwallis when at Wilmington has been landed at Charlestown and remains there untouched, I have desired the Paymaster General here to direct this money to be paid over to his deputy with you, which will, I hope, in some degree relieve your wants.

I enclose to you herewith an extract of a letter which I have lately received from Lord George Germain, by which you will see it is his Lordship's desire that as many cannon as Governor Maxwell has occasion for for the defence of the Bahama Islands and can make a proper use of may be sent to him from Charlestown; but as the Governor has only mentioned to me his wants in general without condescending on the particulars I am at a loss to guess the quantity he stands in need of or would require. You will therefore be so good to take the earliest opportunity of writing to Governor Maxwell and desire to know what quantity of cannon, ammunition etc he will require, and when you receive his answer, you will be pleased to order what he wants to be carried to him in some of the vessels in the pay of Government upon your station.

I have the honor to be, sir,
Your most obedient and most humble servant

H CLINTON

Enclosure
Extract, Germain to Clinton, 7th February 1781[85]   *5(71): C*

Lt Colonel Maxwell, Governor of the Bahama Islands, has repeatedly complained of the exposed condition of his Government from the want of heavy ordnance and proper ammunition, and as I understand there is a large quantity of cannon at Charles Town not wanted there, I have directed him to apply to you for as many as he has occasion for and can make a proper use of, which you will order to be carried to him by some of the vessels upon that station in the pay of Government.

Balfour to Clinton, 2nd October 1781   *109(47): C*

N° 16   Charlestown
                                                                    October 2nd 1781

His Excellency Sir Henry Clinton KB etc etc etc

Sir

With your Excellency's letters of the 20th of June and 13th of July last I am honored and shall most minutely comply with the several directions therein contained.

By my last dispatches, of which duplicates are now transmitted, your Excellency will have been informed of the several military transactions here to the period of Lord Rawdon's

---

[85] Annotated: received by Clinton on 27th June.

departure, who left this in a packet for England the 21st of August last, since which I have had the mortification to learn his Lordship has been taken and carried into the Chesapeak by a French 74 gun ship, an event, both from public and private motives, which I cannot too much regret.

The events subsequent to this period will be fully explain'd by Major General Gould's dispatches and the copy of a letter from Lt Colonel Stewart to Lord Cornwallis, which, with its several enclosures, at his particular request I have the honor herewith to transmit.[86]

I shall now observe, because I feel it much my duty, that the number of refugees and militia thrown on our hands by many parts of the province being wrested from us will greatly contribute to exhaust our resources, especially of provisions, as these poor people come to us in the possession of every want.

Nor must I omit representing to your Excellency the many impediments which the service meets with from the want of men of war here either to cooperate with the troops or on an emergency to communicate with the other parts of the Continent. This has been so much the case that for a considerable time no ship of war was in this harbour and the charge of it left to an acting lieutenant who has the command of a galley.

Having mention'd thus much, and confiding entirely in the full information which Captain Nesbit (who will have the honor to deliver this dispatch) has of the affairs of this province, I beg leave to refer to his answers such enquiries as your Excellency may have occasion to make, which I the rather do as the communication is such as does not prudently admit a full *written* explanation in every point. I have therefore made the most confidential communication to this gentleman of such circumstances as I deem absolutely necessary to be laid before your Excellency.

I have the honor to be, sir,
Your Excellency's most obedient and most humble servant

N BALFOUR

Balfour to Clinton, 1st December 1781   *109(51): C*

Nº 17   Charles Town
                                                        December 1st 1781
His Excellency Sir Henry Clinton KB etc etc etc

Sir

I do myself the honor of enclosing to your Excellency the copy of a letter that was lost in the *Hope* sloop of war some time ago, which vessel was sent on purpose to carry dispatches.

---

[86] Of Gould's dispatches there are no copies in the Cornwallis Papers. Note 1, p 166, refers to Stewart's letter.

It is with much regret that I hear your Excellency thinks that little attention has been paid to keeping up frequent intercourse with New York from this place.

Permit me, sir, to assure you that no exertion has been wanting on my part to procure ships for that purpose. I have purchas'd and lost several by the enemy, when I found that it was impossible to procure assistance from the navy, and I feel great reluctance in representing to your Excellency that His Majesty's Service has suffered exceedingly from want of naval assistance in this country, that I have not been able even to procure convoys for provision and stores to the provinces depending on us. Many vessels have been taken of great value within sight of the town almost during the whole summer, and the harbour left without one single King's ship, or any person to give directions concerning naval business, for a considerable time. By this your Excellency will perceive the impossibility of my communicating with New York, Virginia or any other part of the Continent except by private ships, of which we have lost almost every one that was sent by the number of privateers that constantly kept this station.

General Leslie will inform your Excellency of every transaction subsequent to those mention'd in the dispatches that will be sent by the ship of war.[87]

I have the honor to be, sir,
Your Excellency's most obedient and most humble servant

N BALFOUR

§ - §

3 - Balfour to Arnold, 1781

Balfour to Arnold, 7th February 1781[88]   *109(12): C*

Charles Town
February 7th 1781

Brigadier General Arnold etc etc etc

Sir

I have the honor herewith to transmit for your use a number of paroles granted by Major General Leslie to sundry persons in Virginia.

---

[87] Balfour's correspondence with Clinton terminated on Leslie's arrival at Charleston to assume command of land forces south of Virginia.

[88] This letter was conveyed in the *Romulus* but miscarried. See vol II, p 347, note 53.

As you will doubtless have seen thro' the enemies papers accounts of the check which Colonel Tarleton lately met with, and as it is probable it may reach you with the circumstances of our loss on the occasion greatly magnified, I think it necessary to acquaint you that from Lord Cornwallis's and the best accounts hitherto procured our loss does not exceed four hundred killed, wounded and taken. We, however, lost two three pounders and the colours of the 7th Regiment. It is difficult to account for the cause of this misfortune since it is evident the enemy had given way and that the day was nearly ours, when, on receiving an unexpected fire, the troops were seized with a panic which no exertions of their officers could counteract.

After this action Lord Cornwallis moved higher up on the Catawba in pursuit of Morgan and I soon expect to hear of his crossing that river, so that we daily look for some pleasing event, especially as General Greene with his army is on the Pedee and may possibly be tempted to oppose his Lordship's progress.

Before Colonel Tarleton's affair was known here, Major Craig had sailed with about three hundred men for Cape Fear River in order to cooperate with Lord Cornwallis's views on that quarter. We since learn by persons come from thence that he has taken possession of Wilmington and been joined by several inhabitants of those parts, but in these respects it is likely you will procure more certain information than has yet reached us.

This dispatch will be delivered you by Mr Parker, who with Mr Blair and several other refugees wish to join you, and I doubt not, from their characters and zeal, you will find them useful, particularly Mr Parker, whose conduct has been always such that I am persuaded he will merit every attention you may honor him with.

Before I close this I must beg leave to offer you any assistance this part of the world affords and to assure you, in Lord Cornwallis's name, of his hearty wish to further by all in his power the views of the army you command.

I have the honor to be, sir,
Your most obedient humble servant

N BALFOUR

Balfour to Arnold, 4th March 1781

109(22): C

Charles Town
March 4th 1781

Brigadier General Arnold etc etc etc

Sir

Having yesterday received the important advices respecting Lord Cornwallis's movements in North Carolina which are contained in the enclosed copy of a letter to the Commander in

Chief[89], I have thought it necessary to transmit the same to you by an express vessel, which I have now the honor to do as his Lordship's successes may in their operation affect the situation of the army under your immediate command.

I have by two messages attempted to convey to Lord Cornwallis an account of your situation, as contained in your dispatch to his Lordship of the 13th and 14th ultimo[90].

I have the honor to be, sir,
Your most obedient and most humble servant

N BALFOUR

§ - §

4 - Between Balfour and Sir James Wright, 1781

Balfour to Wright, 4th May 1781   *109(32): C*

Charles Town
May 4th 1781

His Excellency Sir James Wright Bt etc etc etc

Sir

I am truly sorry to find by your Excellency's letters of the 17th and 23rd ultimo[91] the distressed state of your province, and the more so, as this being under the same circumstances precludes my affording you any present aid.

I shou'd judge your Excellency is not now to be inform'd that General Greene with his army has advanc'd into this province and is in force before Camden, where, tho' he was attack'd and defeated with considerable loss by Lord Rawdon on the 25th ultimo, yet still the fate of that post is as yet uncertain; and I need not point out the consequences of its falling with the troops there into the enemy's hands, in which case I have directed Lt Colonel Cruger to quit 96 and fall back with his own and the garrison of Augusta to Purysburg or Ebenezer, where he will be able to afford a more immediate protection to your Excellency.

---

[89] *a letter..*: of 3rd March, p 235.

[90] *your dispatch..*: there is no copy in the Cornwallis Papers, but the contents are summarised in Arnold's dispatch of the same dates to Clinton (see Stevens, op cit, i, 324-6).

[91] *your Excellency's letters..*: no copies.

Added to these greater objects of distress, parties of the enemy are actually in every part of the country, and by one of them under Sumpter the post at Buck Head is invested, but I beg leave to assure your Excellency that when we can be freed from our present embarrassments, every thing in my power will be done for the security of Georgia, which at all events shall receive every assistance the state of affairs here puts it in my power to yield it.

Your Excellency's letter to Lord Cornwallis[92] shall be forwarded whenever a communication is again opened with his army, now advancing into the country, and I will by the first occasion send to you the prisoners you mention.

I have the honor to be, sir,
Your Excellency's most obedient humble servant

N BALFOUR

Balfour to Wright, 21st May 1781 — 109(36): C

Charles Town
May 21st 1781

His Excellency Sir James Wright Bt etc etc etc

Sir

I trust your Excellency is assured that only necessity cou'd hinder my sending present reinforcements to Georgia when the occasion for them is so pressing, but such is the state of this province as to require rather than afford assistance, the posts at Wright's Bluff, Buck Head and the Congarees being all taken by the enemy, and Lord Rawdon fallen back to Monk's Corner.

Nor, thus circumstanced, is it in our power to succour the garrisons of Ninety Six and Augusta, which are therefore directed to retreat to Ebenezer, or some safe situation, where they may cover the lower parts of Georgia and be enabled on occasion to reinforce Savannah.

But if it be our misfortune that the enemy should possess themselves of one or both of those garrisons and I find their force afterwards pointed towards you, in such case your Excellency may depend on troops being sent by water to your relief. However, I have the strongest hopes that Lord Cornwallis's movements will soon change the face of things here and give a more pleasing aspect to our affairs than they at present seem to wear.

I have the honor to be, sir,
Your Excellency's most obedient humble servant

N BALFOUR

---

[92] *Your Excellency's letter..*: of 23rd April, vol V, p 326.

Charlestown
August 1st 1781

His Excellency Sir James Wright Bt etc etc etc

Sir

I am honored with your Excellency's dispatch of the 27th ultimo[93].

The operations in South Carolina have hitherto been carried on at such a distance from hence, and the communications been so precarious, that my own informations have been frequently imperfect. Such, however, as came to me and could in any way concern the province of Georgia I regularly transmitted to Colonel Clarke as the officer entrusted with the charge of His Majesty's troops there, and I doubt not, through him, your Excellency got every essential information he was empowered to give.

With your Excellency I regret the loss of the Back Country, especially Ninety Six and Augusta, and the more so, as the manner of it was a general revolt of the inhabitants.

I must assure your Excellency that a full proportion of provisions and stores have from time to time been sent to the troops in Georgia, and I am fearful the Commander in Chief and Lord Cornwallis may be displeased at the very large quantities detained by me for the supply of this, your province and East Florida, and which has always precluded any want.

Such has been the scarcity of guns here that on the commanding engineer's representation of there not being a sufficient number for the works now constructing to defend this town we have been obliged to purchase some. You will therefore see the impossibility of my sending any to Savannah, but I am in hopes you will be able to procure what are wanted in the same way we have done here.

I truly feel the disagreeable state to which many of His Majesty's loyal subjects in your province are at present reduced, which I am the better enabled to judge of from the similar situation of many deserving persons in this.

Not having received from Lord Cornwallis any directions for reinforcing your province, it is Lord Rawdon's opinion as well as mine that it wou'd be improper to do it until we hear from him, but your Excellency may be assured that when such orders come here, there will be no delay in executing of them.

In respect to reestablishing the post at Augusta, I must beg leave to refer your Excellency to Colonel Clarke, to whom I have wrote on the subject and who must be the best judge how far with his present force he is capable of doing it.

---

[93]   *your Excellency's dispatch..*: no copy.

I have the honor to be, sir,
Your Excellency's most obedient and humble servant

N BALFOUR

Wright to Balfour, 16th August 1781   62(26): LS

Savannah in Georgia
16th August 1781

Sir

I had the honor to receive your letter of the 1st instant and am extremely sorry it is not in your power to send the reinforcement I requested untill you hear from Lord Cornwallis, but I am well perswuaded, if you saw and knew the consequence of not taking post at Augusta, you would strain a point to do it, and if you could only send two hundred and fifty, I beleive it might do for the present and probably save this province. And depend upon it, if once the rebells get Georgia, those on each side will not stand long. Possibly Georgia may be considered as of little consequence, but be assured, if America is recovered, it will be one of the first colonys on the Continent, and the consequence and value of it is very well known to the King's Ministers.

On mature consideration of your answer to my letter, and haveing received undoubted information that a body of rebells [is] now at and in the neighburhood of Augusta amounting to about two hundred and fifty, cheifly horse well mounted, and that there are some lesser parties also about, also that they have sent to invite all the rebells who formerly fled from this province to return immediatly to Augusta in order to settle and establish a rebell government, that the[y] avow their intentions of breaking up and plundering every settlement without the lines of the town of Savannah and are endeavouring to raise a regiment of horse and another of foot on the promise of payment by Negroes which they intend to plunder and take from the King's loyall subjects, and that they expect and say — if they are not intercepted — they shall gather like a snow ball and will come down like a torrent against Savannah, on this information being received we were unanimously and clearly of oppinion that every exersion possible should be made immediatly to dislodge the rebells, at least to check, counteract and disconcert them, or be assured they will soon grow formidable, and therefore dettermined to raise a body of milittia and send up the country with as many of the two troops of horses as are raised, say sixty, provided a suitable number of the King's troops could be obtained to go up with them, being of oppinion that the province will be totally ruined and lost if some exersion is not made without loss of time, and I wrote to Colonell Clarke, acquainting him of those matters and desiring to know what assisstance it was in his power to give, who was pleased in his answer, after observing on some matters, to say that, as it was dettermined a movement shou'd be made with the millittia and the two troops of horse, that if four hundred millittia were assembled at Ebenezer and some other matters complied with which he particularly mentioned, he wou'd send two hundred of the King's troops but could not spare any more, and upon the whole we have concluded to prepare for going up the country. I think there is little doubt but four hundred millittia will be collected at Ebenezer, and it is expected two hundred more may join on the march, but this will depend upon circumstances. Certainly it is small force to undertake so long a march and without being altogether clear of the enemy's force, and although we shall be ready by the 25th, yet we shall wait your answer before any movement takes place, as much will depend upon your giveing us some assisstance and also cooperateing, but if nothing is done, I shall expect the consequences I have mentioned, and these, sir, are new matters which (I presume) have happen'd since you wrote Lord Cornwallis and circumstances his Lordship could not know when he might answer your letter, and as I apprehend this to be a very serious affair, *not confined to Georgia* but extending to Florida, South Carolina and the King's cause in generall, therefore I cannot avoid *once more* representing it to you before it may be too late. The objects of the movement are first and principly the takeing post again at Augusta, but this cannot be done without farther assisstance from you, the destruction of the magazine of provisions on Beach Island (This island lyes in Savannah River about five miles below Augusta but is in the province of South Carolina, and I am informed there is now on it fifteen thousand bushells of corn of the last year's growth and a very fine crop on the ground and without which no rebell army can subsist in that part of the country. Therefore, if there is no probability of our repossessing that country again, I presume it ought to be destroyed, but it being in Carolina, the matter is submitted to you. I am informed it is from sixty to seventy miles across from Orangeburgh to Beach Island, and no more, over a fine ridge all the way.), to give the Back Country people an opportunity to collect their familys and effects (if any remaining) and for such of them as may be disposed to do so, or as can do so, to remove this way, and another very essential object is to drive of if possible and disconcert the rebells and prevent there forming their government there and collecting a formidable force, which may prove very serious in Carolina as well as in this province. In short, it is my oppinion that if we suffer them to remain quietly there and collect, they will soon overrun this whole province to the lines of Savannah, and I doubt whether they will not before long drive the King's troops in Carolina on Charles Town Neck. Small begginings in cases of this sort often make a very rapid and astonishing progress.

I must request you will be pleased to communicate what I now write to Lord Roden or any other gentleman in command in Carolina to whom it may be necessary and proper, my correspondence being confin'd to you, sir. I beg you will dispatch the boat as soon as possible because we cannot do any thing any way, either by a march up the country or establishing posts, till your answer is received.

I am with perfect esteem, sir,
Your most obedient servant

JA WRIGHT

Charles Town
24th August 1781

His Excellency Sir James Wright Bt etc etc etc

Sir

I am honored with your Excellency's dispatch of the 16th instant and have detained the express boat three days in hopes the arrival of General Leslie wou'd have enabled me to answer it more satisfactorily, as that officer will no doubt bring with him a new arrangement for the force in the Southern District, when it will be determined what part of it can be allotted to the defence of Georgia. Things therefore in this province are kept much at a stand until the General, who is expected daily, arrives, and I shou'd think the same line of conduct wou'd be best with you. However, in giving this opinion I presume not to interfere with any resolution which may have been taken by your Excellency and Colonel Clarke, who, being on the spot, must be most competent to judge of what is expedient.

I have the honor to be, sir,
Your Excellency's most obedient and humble servant

N BALFOUR

§ - §

5 - Balfour to subordinate officers, 1781

Balfour to Campbell, 1st January 1781   *109(1): C*

Charles Town
January 1st 1781

Lt Colonel Campbell
Commanding at George Town

Sir

You wou'd before this have received particular directions respecting your post had the more general arrangements of the army, with which they are connected, taken place. Till then, when you will hear either from Lord Rawdon or myself, it wou'd be best not to attempt any onward movements but to confine yourself to clearing the roads and communications in your vicinity of such lurking parties of the enemy as may infest them.

Tho' Captain Saunders is at present with the army on business, I wou'd wish you particularly to attend to levying cavalry, which are so essential in your part of the country, and on this head you will be pleased to assure Colonel Cassels that the raising of them has only the good of the province and King's Service for its object.

I have the honor to be, sir,
Your most obedient and humble servant

N BALFOUR

Balfour to Campbell, 19th January 1781   109(4): C

Charles Town
January 19th 1781

Lt Colonel George Campbell
Commanding at George Town

Sir

I am honour'd with your letter of the 14th instant[94] and am sorry to find by it that two serjeants have been taken and one corporal killed in your late action, especially as they appear by your account to have acted a spirited part.

The party of the Queen's Rangers being order'd from George Town, Lieutenant Campbell of the 71st Regiment is appointed to raise a troop of cavalry there and directed to join you immediately. You will therefore be pleased to deliver up to him such horses as have been procured for this service, with the accounts, he having orders to take them under his charge and to be accountable to Government for them.

As it will be necessary for you soon to make forward movements, the redoubt at George Town will consequently become a rear work, and any additional strength to it unnecessary. You will therefore immediately dismiss all the Negroes etc employed on it.

Till such movements as I have mention'd actually take place, you can have no occasion to retain many horses or carriages and may therefore return them to the owners, taking care that they are in readiness when such a call renders them necessary, as by this means the country will be greatly eased and a present saving accrue to Government.

As Colonel Cassells is a person in whom Lord Cornwallis has reposed the greatest confidence and intrusted with the conduct of all matters respecting the inhabitants in your district, you will be so good to consult him in such cases and at all times to consider his advice as directions.

---

[94] *your letter..*: no copy.

I have the honor to be, sir,
Your most obedient and most humble servant

N BALFOUR

Balfour to Campbell, 25th January 1781

Secret

Charles Town
January 25th 1781

Lt Colonel George Campbell
Commanding at George Town

Sir

Lt Colonel Tarleton having in advancing into the country received a check on the 17th instant, I have thought it necessary, tho' the circumstances of it are not yet come to hand, to give you the earliest information possible of this unforeseen event in order that you may provide against the evil effects which exaggerated and malevolent reports of this transaction may have on the minds of the country people, that if any rising amongst them shou'd be attempted you may by timely exertions frustrate such intentions, and finally, by knowing, guard against any bad consequences which this affair might otherwise have on your post.

It will be necessary to acquaint you with General Greene's situation, which is at present in the Cheraws to the eastward of Pedee, tho' I think it not improbable he may now pass over at least small parties to your side of the river and attempt something in that quarter. The utmost caution will be therefore required on your part, and for this purpose I wou'd recommend it to you to push out frequent patroles of cavalry as a measure, both in respect to the inhabitants and enemy, of the greatest necessity. It must also appear to you essential that the communication between us shou'd be preserved, and consequently you will look well to this material point. I have sent 30 regulars to Lenew's Ferry and reinforced the other posts on the Santee, which is now lined with troops.

If you secured within your redoubt a quantity of provisions, it wou'd be a good measure and provide at all events against the very worst which can possibly happen to you.

I have directed Captain Saunders with his party of the Queen's Rangers to return to you. That officer will therefore take on him the command of all the cavalry in your district and I must request your assistance to him in carrying on the recruiting service.

As I am very anxious about the expedition to Cape Fear, which sailed from this on the 21st under Major Craig, I must beg you will procure me all the information you can respecting it, and if possible to let me know if it has made a landing.

Enclos'd is a cypher for your use whenever occasion may require such a precaution.

I have the honor to be, sir,
Your obedient humble servant

N BALFOUR

Balfour to Wigfall, 25th January 1781

109(6): C

Charles Town
January 25th 1781

Colonel Wigfall

Sir

The King's Service requiring it, I am to desire you will immediately on the receipt of this send a detachment of fifty men under a field officer to Murry's Ferry and another of twenty, properly officered, to the lower ferry of Santee. I have sent a party of thirty to Lenew's.

These detachments are to be given by Colonel Ball's and your regiments of militia. You will therefore communicate with that gentleman on the subject and adjust with him the proportions to be furnished by each of your corps for these duties.

As I expect these posts are taken up by Monday next at farthest and look to you as responsible to me and the King's Service for it, I have thought it necessary to empower you, and you are hereby so empowered, to take up and send prisoners to this place all such officers and men of your regiment as shall refuse to comply with the orders you give in consequence of this that they may be dealt with agreeable to their demerits.

I have the honor to be, sir,
Your most obedient humble servant

N BALFOUR

Balfour to McArthur, 10th April 1781

109(27): C

Charles Town
April 10th 1781

Major McArthur
71st Regiment etc

Sir

You will be pleased to proceed this evening with the British troops under your command from hence to Dorchester and, on your getting there, draw to you as soon as possible, if not already arriv'd, Colonel Fenwick's troop of dragoons, taking care by their field officers to embody the militia of that and the near districts.

Should you find that no considerable numbers of the enemy are in those parts, you will then proceed to join Lt Colonel Small at Monk's Corner and put yourself under his orders, sending me advice thereof.

But in case you find that the lt colonel is moved onwards and likely to be opposed by an equal or superior force, you will with all possible dispatch endeavour with your corps to reinforce him, avoiding, in this endeavour, by all means any partial action, which would only weaken, without answering any essential ends or forwarding the chief objects of, this march.

I have the honor to be, sir,
Your most obedient humble servant

N BALFOUR

Balfour to Gray, 20th May 1781   109(35): C

Charles Town
May 20th 1781

Captain Gray[95]
Commandant at George Town

Sir

I am favoured with your three letters of the 17th instant[96] and shou'd before this have given directions for your quitting George Town but for the hope of learning something certain in respect of Lord Cornwallis and his intentions, as also whether Colonel Tarleton with the dragoons may not make your post the route here, in which case the retaining it is of the first moment. I therefore wish it held, if possible, till this point is determined.

But shou'd you find yourself so press'd by the enemy as to make a retreat necessary, you must execute it before it becomes unsafe, for which purpose you will retain the vessel which takes you this and in such event bring off with you all those whose principles may induce them to come with you.

The horses, should you find it impossible otherwise to secure or bring off, may be disposed of as you point out. I will, however, endeavour to send you another vessel to assist in this essential respect.

---

[95] Robert Gray had been serving since 19th October 1777 as a captain in the King's American Regiment, a detachment of which was now forming the garrison of Georgetown. He would continue as a captain in the regiment until its disbandment at Saint John, New Brunswick, in October 1783. He was placed on the British half-pay list. (WO 65/164(34) and WO 12/108(21) (National Archives, Kew))

[96] *your three letters..*: no copies.

As I find Captain Collet[97] only grounds his claim to superior rank on a commission from Lord Dunmore, and his Lordship not having the power to grant such as gave rank over regular ones from the King or Commander in Chief, this claim must naturally be set aside.

I am, sir,
Your obedient humble servant.

N BALFOUR

§ - §

6 - From or concerning Cruden, 1781-3[98]

Cruden to McMahon, 2nd February 1781   *7(8): C*

Charles Town
February 2nd 1781

Captain McMahon

Sir

The repeated complaints I have had made to me from those who have the managements of the estates on which the publick Negroes are employed has obliged me to inform the Commandant that unless they[99] are removed, the estates will prove of no service to Government, and to remove every possible obstacle to the continuance of the Negroes on the estates I have promised to supply the various departments of the army with such commodities as they are able to produce, particularly for the use of Colonel Moncrief's department and yours[100].

---

[97] John Collett had been commissioned by Lord Dunmore as a captain lieutenant in the Queen's Own Loyal Virginia Regiment on 13th February 1776. Making his way, like the deposed Governor, to New York, he raised an independent company in February 1777 and one month later was incorporated with it into the Prince of Wales's American Regiment, being assigned the rank of captain. Later in 1781 he would resign his commission in order to raise two troops of cavalry at Charlestown, but would have his attempt aborted by Leslie. Having resigned his commission, he was not placed on the Provincial half-pay list at the close of the war. He is not to be confused with Captain John Collett of North Carolina, who served in the Royal Fencible Regiment. (Nan Cole and Todd Braisted, 'A History of the Prince of Wales' American Regiment', *The On-Line Institute for Advanced Loyalist Studies*, 19th April 2006; Raymond, 'British American Corps')

[98] John Cruden was the Commissioner for Sequestered Estates in South Carolina.

[99] *they*: the grounds for the complaints.

[100] *yours*: McMahon was the Barrackmaster in charge of the Barrack Office.

I have now, after calculating the value of the wood and the expences of bringing it to town, to offer to supply the garrison of Charlestown with fire wood at the rate of one pound, seven shillings and six pence per cord at the wharves.

And make no doubt, I shall have it in my power to transact the business perfectly to your satisfaction, but at the same time I beg leave to suggest that I have no other motive in this offer than that of improving the estates under my charge to the utmost advantage, Government deriving the sole and whole emolument from the contract. In case of any incursion of the enemy, scarcity of oxen and craft, or any unforeseen events which may possibly prevent me from supplying the whole quantity contracted for, I have no doubt under those circumstances you will think it reasonable that, on my giving you two months' notice of such my inability, that in consequence thereof this contract should cease. I insert this clause not from any apprehension in my own mind in being unable to supply you with the quantity of wood you may want, but rather from an anxious desire that the garrison might not in any respect be disappointed from not having sufficient time to provide from other sources.

If you approve of these proposals, I would point to the first of April as the period from which the contract should commence.

J CRUDEN

Cruden to Balfour, 28th May 1781   7(9): C

Charlestown
28th May 1781

Colonel Balfour etc etc etc

Sir

The vast magnitude of the business with which your time is engrossed makes me anxious to trouble you as little as possible. I therefore take this method of laying such thoughts before you, and of making such application, as the nature of the publick business I have the direction of requires.

I consulted you on the removing of the cattle etc from the estates under sequestration to Daniel's and James Islands, the first of which I inspected myself before any cattle was brought down, and I made my report to you where only danger was to be apprehended. My fears increase, since I had the honor of seeing you, with respect to James Island, where I have collected the best of the cattle and on which my chief dependance is for the supply of the garrison with wood, having been obliged to bring away the people employed in cutting wood at Stono and on the other side of Ashley River. When I spoke to you about a guard for the protection of James Island, you mentioned that the troops could not be spared but that the militia should be thought of for that purpose. If a small redoubt is erected, a body of them with such overseers as have abandoned their homes might prove equal to the defence of the island. If this idea meets your approbation, the sooner your orders are issued for that purpose,

267

I humbly conceive that the security will be the greater. May I request you giving orders that such vessels as I have employed in bringing wood for the supply of the garrison, which is now confined to James Island and this side Ashley River, may not be retarded in the execution of such service, and that the guard at Ashley Ferry may afford such assistance as may be in their power to the people employed in procuring the wood who are very near the ferry.

I have the honor to be, sir, most respectfully
Your most obedient and most humble servant

JOHN CRUDEN

Balfour to Cruden, 22nd August 1781   7(30): C

BY NISBET BALFOUR Esq,
Lt Colonel of His Majesty's Twenty Third Regiment of Foot,
Commandant of Charlestown etc etc etc

TO JOHN CRUDEN Esq

WHEREAS it has been represented to me that there are many Negroes the property of the enemy within our lines in North Carolina[101] which are now unemployed, in order therefore to prevent the said Negroes from becoming a burthen to Government or a nuisance to the community I DO HEREBY authorize and empower you to take the same into your custody and possession and to employ them to the best advantage either in sawing timber for the use of Colonel Moncrief, in making naval stores or in any other manner that may seem to you most advantageous to Government, ALWAYS being certain that such Negroes as you may take into your custody as aforesaid or may be seized by any person acting under your authority are actually the property of the enemies of His Majesty's Government.

And you are hereby directed to make returns to me, or the commanding officer of the Southern District, of all Negroes seized in consequence of this warrant, specifying in what manner the same are employed, the product of their labour to be appropriated to the purposes of Government in the manner directed by Lord Cornwallis in his commission to you as Commissioner of Sequestered Estates.

And for so doing this shall be your sufficient authority.

GIVEN under my hand in Charlestown
22nd August 1781

N BALFOUR

---

[101] The reference to North Carolina is corroborated by a reference to this warrant in *The Commissioner's Narrative*, p 285.

Charlestown

15th September 1781

Captain Thomas etc etc etc

Sir

The hurry of business occasioned by the perplexed state of the important trust committed to my charge has hitherto prevented me from having the honor of being personally known to you, which I trust has been the cause of the obstruction I have this evening experienced in the execution of my duty, as I cannot suppose that you will, when acquainted with the nature of my office, give any orders that will retard me in the execution of it.

I beg leave for your information to inclose you a copy of the proclamation of Earl Cornwallis[102], which will give you an idea of the nature of my appointment, and of the number of vessels necessary to carry on the business, and of the utter impossibility of my conducting it if my authority is not sufficient in all respects to enable those employed under me to pass and repass by land and water within the province.

I have the honor to be
Your most obedient and most humble servant

JOHN CRUDEN

Cruden to Stewart, 28th October 1781   *7(10): C*

Charlestown
28th October 1781

Colonel Stewart etc etc etc

Sir

Indisposition prevented me from having the honor of paying my respects to you when you was in town, from which I was a looser in a double sense: deprived of the pleasure of seeing you and of an opportunity of explaining to you the nature of the very great and important trust reposed in me. I consider it as well my duty as essentially necessary for the interest of Government that you shall be informed by me concerning the nature of my appointment, my progress in the execution of the office and my determinations with respect to the future prosecution of it, and then I will claim most humbly such assistance as you may be able, consistant with the good of the service, to grant me. I take the liberty of inclosing Earl Cornwallis's proclamation of the 16th September 1780, which will fully explain his

---

[102] *the proclamation..*: see vol II, pp 323-4.

Lordship's intention at that time. In consequence of the commission and warrants in my possession I seized many of the most valuable estates in this country. I furnish'd them throughout the province with necessaries of every kind. I appointed overseers to manage the estates and gentlemen in each district to superintend them, but the unlooked for incursions of the enemy prevented me from effecting any of those desirable purposes Lord Cornwallis had in view. Large sums of money had been necessarily expended on taking possession of the property, and instead of being reimbursed from the produce of the estates, expence increased upon me daily. The enemy possessing for a time that part of the country that produced grain deprived me of not only the means of defraying the expences but of food also for supplying the wants of the Negroes on the plantations not far distant from town, most of which, from the commotion in that part of the country lying contiguous to the town, did not raise any crops last season. Humanity and the honor of Government was concerned in preventing the poor wretches from suffering from the want of provision. Besides the Negroes, a variety of people have been dependant upon me for bread: those in particular who were employed as overseers and escaped from the fury of the rebels, and many loyalists recommended to me by Lord Cornwallis. In short, sir, to my very great regret I find myself very much in advance in the prosecution of a measure that I fondly hoped would have been productive of a very handsome revenue to Government. A variety of reasons operate in my mind to make me solicitous for the removal of the crops from such of the sequestered estates as are within our reach, the most powerfull of which is to relieve Government from expences, to fill our magazines with grain, and to prevent the enemy from improving the property to our disadvantage. I am preparing gallies to protect the small craft and am embodying a corps for defence of the estates whilst the people are employed in removing the grain to the landings, and with your countenance and support I hope I may be able to secure the crops on Cooper River and its branches. If you will be pleased to issue orders for the protection of those people employed by me in the business, I shall consider myself very much obliged, and if you should think it adviseable to give orders for waggons to be impressed to bring the produce either to Monk's Corner or Laurens's estate near Strawberry from the sequestered estates in the neighbourhood of the army, it appears the only way to save the property, except you are pleased to order the overseers to deliver it to the commissary for the use of the army, to whom I beg you will be so good as to give an order to account to me for the provisions taken from the sequestered estates, particularly of Henry Laurens, Mount Tacitus, Moultrie Junior[103] near Nelson's Ferry and Maham's, without which account I shall not be able to comply with the instructions of Earl Cornwallis.

If it was consistant with the good of the service, I should be very happy that the army could afford protection for craft in the Santee. By that means the enemy might be prevented from availing themselves of the present crops on the south side of that river, and I would thereby be enabled to bring away the sequestered property, as well as that of our friends, which I am informed the rebels are attempting to move across the river.

---

[103] William Moultrie Jr (1752-1796) had been commissioned a 2nd lieutenant in the second regiment raised by the South Carolina Provincial Congress in June 1775. One year later he took part in the action at Fort Sullivan. Having risen to the rank of captain, he was made prisoner at the capitulation of Charlestown and by now had presumably been released under the cartel with Greene. (Moss, *SC Patriots*, 708)

I beg your forgiveness for encroaching so much upon your time, and have the honor to be, sir,

Your most obedient and humble servant

JOHN CRUDEN

Cruden to Moncrief, 20th November 1781   *7(11): C*

Charlestown
20th November 1781

Colonel Moncrief

Sir

It is impossible for me to carry on the business of my office if those in any other departments have it in their power to take away the people under my direction at their pleasure and without an order from me. Mr Stevens[104] has taken away a number of people employed in cutting wood and logs and in sawing plank for your department without any order from me, and indeed in answer to a letter I wrote him he made no reply but told the messenger that if any of the hands presumed to go away they should be punished. I know you will see the evident impropriety of such behaviour and give Mr Stevens orders to pay that respect to the office I have the honor to hold that I have an undoubted claim to while I am in the execution of my duty. God knows it has only been productive of trouble and vexation to me without the addition of disrespect from my friends.

I have the honor to be, dear sir, respectfully
Your etc

JOHN CRUDEN

---

[104] Stevens was not an officer in the Corps of Engineers. He was presumably a civilian employed in Moncrief's department, perhaps William Stevens, a loyalist of Saluda who had fled the Back Country. For holding a civil office under the Crown he would be subjected to banishment and confiscation by act of the revolutionary assembly at Jacksonborough. (SC Banishment and Confiscation Act 1782; McCrady, *SC in the Rev 1780-1783*, 585)

Charlestown
26th November 1781

Doctor Frazer

Sir

This morning it grieved me to the soul to find that Colonel Balfour thought me blamable for the deficiency of wood in this garrison. I contracted to supply this garrison's wood if the incursions of the enemy did not prevent me, and in that case I was to give two months's notice if I thought it impracticable for me to continue the supply. I did not fail to state my situation and in consequence thereof you had orders to purchase wood and from that very moment I considered the contract at an end; but however much I may be blamed, and notwithstanding the insinuations to my disadvantage, I will not at a time when the service demands the exertion of every individual withhold my assistance, and for two months longer I will strain every nerve to supply this garrison with wood, and from that period you will not have on me any more dependance.

Your most obedient and most humble servant

JOHN CRUDEN

Balfour to Cruden, 20th December 1781   *7(31): C*

BY LT COLONEL NISBET BALFOUR Esq,
Commandant of Charlestown etc etc etc

TO JOHN CRUDEN Esq

WHEREAS certain persons, inhabitants of this province who were taken prisoners in Charlestown at the time of the capitulation, have again joined the enemy either by procuring for themselves an exchange or by a breach of their paroles, and others have become a second time guilty of high treason after having obtained pardon and been admitted to the blessings of British government, and have thereby forfeited all claim to the stipulations made in favor of the inhabitants in general of Charlestown who were actually in town at the time of the surrender, AND as it is repugnant to every principle of justice, of policy or good government, as well as both to the letter and spirit of the articles of capitulation, that any persons of the above description and who are now in open rebellion should be protected by His Majesty's Government either in person or property, I HAVE therefore thought proper to empower you, and *I DO HEREBY* empower and authorize you, the said JOHN CRUDEN Esq, Commissioner of Sequestered Estates, to seize in Charlestown the property both real and personal of all such persons as are above described according to the directions given to you by the Rt Hon Earl

---

[105] Dr James Fraser was an assistant to the Commandant. See vol I, p 25, note 3.

CORNWALLIS and agreeable to the terms of his Lordship's proclamation of the sixteenth day of September one thousand seven hundred and eighty, the said persons by again taking up arms having clearly forfeited any claim to derive benefit from the exceptions contained in the said proclamation.

AND for so doing this shall be your sufficient warrant.

GIVEN under my hand at Charlestown
this twentieth day of December 1781
and in the twenty second year of His Majesty's reign

N BALFOUR
Commandant Charlestown

Cruden to Smith, 5th February 1782
7(12): C

Charlestown
5th February 1782

John Smith Esq
New York

Sir

I have the honor to inclose you a copy of my commission from Lord Cornwallis[106], which I beg leave to request the favor of you to lay before his Excellency the Commander in Chief. I am exerting myself to the utmost of my power to bring the publick business under my direction into such a state as I may be enabled to wait in person on his Excellency.

Most respectfully I have the honor to be, sir,
Your most obedient and most humble servant

JOHN CRUDEN

Cruden to Morrison, 7th February 1782
7(12): C

Charlestown
February 7th 1782

Major John Morrison
Deputy Commissary General

Sir

His Majesty having been pleased to signify his royal approbation to the office which Earl Cornwallis did me the honor to intrust me with, it becomes my duty to transmit without delay to his Lordship a compleat state of my accounts to be laid before the King in Council.

---

[106] *my commission..*: see vol II, p 320.

That I may be enabled to do this in the fullest manner I must call on you as the head of your department, by virtue of the powers in me vested by his Lordship, to furnish me as speedy as possible with an account of all property of every species which have been taken from the enemy by your deputies or agents since the 16th September 1780, the date of my commission, and to pay into my hands the value thereof.

I have the honor to be respectfully, sir,
Your most obedient etc

JOHN CRUDEN

The Commandant and Board of Police in Council,   *110(1): C*
26th February 1782

Charles Town
South Carolina

At a meeting of the Commandant of Charles Town and the Board of Police IN COUNCIL, Tuesday the 26th day of February 1782

Present

Lt Colonel Nisbet Balfour, Commandant of Charles Town
The Hon William Bull Esq, Intendant General of Police

Alexander Wright[107]	)	Intendants of Police
The Hon Edwd Savage[108]	) Esquires	for
James Johnston[109]	)	Charles Town District

The Commandant informed the Board that John Cruden Esq, the Commissioner of Sequestered Estates, was attending in order to lay before the Board for their inspection

---

[107] Alexander Wright was a son of Sir James Wright, the royal Governor of Georgia. A highly respected member of the community, he had resided in Charlestown for many years but was banished from South Carolina in 1777 when he refused to take the oath of abjuration. He was now serving on the Board of Police as a spokesman for the 'planting interest'. Having been subjected to banishment and confiscation by acts of the revolutionary assemblies in South Carolina and Georgia, he would take passage for England when Charlestown was evacuated in December 1782. As late as mid 1786 he was living in London but not long after removed to Jamaica, having presented claims to the royal commission for compensation in respect of confiscated property. (McCowen Jr, *Charleston, 1780-82*, 18; The SC Banishment and Confiscation Act 1782; The Georgia Banishment and Confiscation Act 1782; Coldham, *Loyalist Claims*, i, 69, 537-8)

[108] Before the revolution the Hon Edward Savage had acted in South Carolina as an assistant justice and as a member of HM Council. Now serving on the Board of Police, he was also the presiding judge of the Vice-Admiralty Court, which had been reopened in October 1781. His name does not appear in the Banishment and Confiscation Act passed by the revolutionary assembly at Jacksonborough. (McCowen Jr, op cit, 22, 83)

[109] In pre-revolutionary days James Johnston had served in South Carolina as Clerk of the Crown. He was knowledgeable about the law. The Banishment and Confiscation Act passed by the revolutionary assembly made no mention of him. (McCowen Jr, op cit, 22)

(agreeable to the proclamation of Earl Cornwallis dated 16th September 1780) an account of his management of the said estates, and Mr Cruden, being called before the Board, informed them that, from the unfortunate situation of this province, for a considerable time past he had been prevented from complying with that part of the proclamation which requires him to render his accounts at the expiration of every six months, but that he had now compleated them for twelve months commencing in September 1780 and ending on the 16th day of September last, and produced a general account thereof together with several other papers to the Board, upon which they were of opinion that a committee should be appointed to inspect the said account and to compare it with the books and vouchers of the Commissioner. The following members, being proposed and approved of by his Honor the Commandant and the Board, were appointed a committee accordingly, viz, the Hon Thomas Irving Esq[110] and Colonel Rob[t] W[m] Powell[111] to be occasionally assisted by Colonel Cruger[112].

Cruden's general account, 23rd February 1782   *110(2): C*

THE COMMISSIONER'S GENERAL ACCOUNT DELIVERED IN

Government in account with John Cruden Esq, Commissioner of Sequestered Estates,
D[R]   from 16th September 1780 to 16th September 1781   C[R]

September 16th		£	September 16th		£
To ballance due by the estate of:			By ballance due the estate of:		
John Harleston	per acc[t] n° 1	128-5-3	Henry Laurens	per acc[t] n° 36	1,657-12-11¼
Isaac Harleston	- 2	53-6-6	Ralph Izard	- 37	177-3-5
Thomas Savage	- 3	82-7-4¾	William Moultrie	- 38	29-14-0⅔
John Edwards	- 4	14-2-11⅔	William Moultrie Jr	- 39	230-12-6¼
Arthur Middleton	- 5	80-19-11½	Peter Bocquet	- 40	9-11-4½
Stephen Drayton	- 6	96-18-5½	Stephen Bull	- 41	9-11-4½

---

[110] Before the revolution the Hon Thomas Irving had served in South Carolina as Receiver General of the Quitrents and as a member of HM Council. Now an intendant of police, he too was not included in the Banishment and Confiscation Act passed by the revolutionaries. (McCowen Jr, op cit, 22)

[111] Robert William Powell was a prominent and highly respected merchant who had initially gone along with the revolutionaries, but when a permanent revolutionary constitution was adopted for South Carolina in 1778, he had had a change of heart, refused to take the oath of allegiance, and was banished. Now an intendant of police, he represented 'the trading part of the community' and was also Colonel of the Charlestown royal militia. He additionally presided over the Court of Ordinary with Alexander Wright besides serving as a member of the vestry of St Philip's Church and as an officer of the St Andrew's Society, a stronghold of loyalty to the Crown. Although he was not included in the Banishment and Confiscation Act passed by the revolutionaries, his loyalism is said to have cost him more than £40,000. (McCrady, *SC in the Rev 1775-1780*, 80; McCowen Jr, op cit, 18, 82, 124)

[112] Besides continuing with his military duties, Lt Colonel John Harris Cruger had been appointed an intendant of police now that his battalion was posted in the vicinity of Charlestown. He attended the Board of Police twelve times from January to June 1782. (McCowen Jr, op cit, 19)

Arnoldus Vanderhorst	- 7	186-5-9	Thomas Ferguson	- 42	1,216-16-6¾
William Saunders	- 8	4-19-6¾	Revd Robt Smith	- 43	122-5-8¾
Wm Clay Snipes	- 9	121-19-10½	Thomas Shubrick	- 44	344-14-4¾
John Saunders	- 10	36-9-4	William Parker	- 45	786-18-2¼
Thomas Heyward	- 11	85-10-2	John Rutledge	- 46	1-2-7¼
Joseph Slann	- 12	16-19-2	Pierce Butler	- 47	249-2-8
Samuel Sleigh	- 13	3-13-4½	Christ^r Gadsden	- 48	157-19-7¾
Benj^a Cattell	- 14	633-14-11	John Lewis Jervais	- 49	21-4-10¼
Richd Whithers	- 15	191-7-2	William Flood	- 50	219-18-4
Nich^s Eveleigh	- 16	6-4-0	Hugh Horry	- 51	263-14-9
John Mathews	- 17	92-2-10¼	Alexander Gillon	- 52	270-12-7
Richd Hutson	- 18	270-18-5	James Neilson	- 53	143-14-6½
James Postell	- 19	6-8-11½	Isaac Motte	- 54	95-16-11
Hugh Rutledge	- 20	98-1-4¼	Michael Kalteison	- 55	233-11-10
Joseph Legaré	- 21	36-18-1	James McCall	- 56	54-11-4
Benj^a Singleton	- 22	34-13-8	Isaac Da Costa	- 57	273-10-0¾
Benj^a Guerard	- 23	47-4-10	John Allston	- 58	203-7-11
William Scott	- 24	173-10-1¼	Edward Mitchell	- 59	124-19-6

To ballance due by:

By ballance due the estates in:

The wives and families of sequestered estates	- 25	2,898-10-8½	Camden District	- 60	606-9-1
The ship carpenter acc^t	- 26	40-0-5½	Ninety Six District	- 61	11-8-4¾
The waggon account	- 27	7-17-2	Say, abandoned property	- 62	1,561-13-2½
The shoe factory	- 28	9-3-11	By ballance due:		
Small craft account	- 29	1,525-7-5	The wood account	- 63	474-15-1
Refugee account	- 30	355-4-9	The estate of C C Pinckney	- 64	25-7-3½
House carpenter acc^t	- 31	0-7-9			9,578-1-1¾
Gadsden's wharf	- 32	96-18-9¼	Ballance due John Cruden Esq		6,854-14-10¼
His Majesty's account	- 33	423-10-6¾			16,432-16-0
Account of expences	- 34	1,610-7-6¾	ERRORS EXCEPTED		
Amount of outstanding debts	- 35	6,962-4-10	23rd February 1782		
		16,432-16-0	J CRUDEN		

Charlestown
7th March 1782

Colonel Moncrief etc etc etc

Sir

I have been this day informed that a gang of Negroes, the property of Singleton now in rebellion, that came from the country a few days ago have been taken into your department without any returns made to me or any receipt granted. Being the officer of Government appointed for the care, custody and management of the property of the enemy of every description, I consider it my duty to request that in future you may be so good to give orders that all Negroes that may come into your hands whose owners are in rebellion may be accounted for to me and regular returns made to my office of the names of such people.

I have the honor to be, sir,
Your most obedient and most humble servant

JOHN CRUDEN

Charlestown
20th March 1782

Messrs Booth and Stedman
Mr Anthony Knight[113]
Mr MacDonald

Gentlemen

His Majesty having been pleased to signify his royal approbation of the office which Earl Cornwallis did me the honor to intrust me, it becomes my duty to transmit without delay to his Lordship a compleat state of my accounts to be laid before the King in Council.

That I may be enabled to do this in the fullest manner I must call on you, by virtue of the powers in me vested, to furnish me as speedily as possible with an account of every species of property taken by you or your assistants in the field from the enemy since the date of my commission (the 16th September 1780) and to furnish me with receipts for the same that the Commissary General may pay the amount thereof into my hands that Government may have credit for the same.

---

[113] *Knight*: Knecht.

I have the honor to be, gentlemen,
Your most obedient servant

JOHN CRUDEN

Cruden to Skelly, 8th April 1782   *7(13): C*

Charlestown
8th April 1782

Major Skelly[114]

Dear Sir

I am compell'd by an unfortunate event to be again troublesome to you. I hope the urgency of the case will stand as my excuse.

The inclosed memorial I beg you may peruse and lay it before the General. I am grieved to trouble him but am compell'd to do so in justice to the measure of Lord Cornwallis and to myself.

If the Commander in Chief is pleased to take my office from me and ease me of a load of trouble and responsibility, I give you my honour I will consider myself obliged, and greatly too, but while I have life I cannot sit down and be a silent witness of the dismemberment of my office, and myself deprived of it by inches, and the property I am authorized to keep wrested from me. I say, my dear sir, I cannot sit down easy under these circumstances. I am sure in your generous breast I shall find an advocate.

With sincere regard I have the honor to be, dear sir,
Your obedient and faithful servant

JOHN CRUDEN

Enclosure
Cruden to Leslie, undated   *7(14): C*

TO THE HON ALEXANDER LESLIE Esq commanding His Majesty's forces in the Southern District of North America

THE MEMORIAL of John Cruden, Commissioner for the Seizure, Care and Management of all Sequestered Estates and Property in South Carolina,

SHEWETH

---

[114] Francis Skelly was aide-de-camp to Leslie.

That your memorialist is informed by Lt Colonel Balfour that it is intended to appoint two gentlemen to pay and cloath the Negroes employed in the public departments. That the cloathing of said Negroes, such gratuities or rewards as the heads of departments may choose to allow them for extra services, and also the salaries of the gentlemen to be appointed to the said office are proposed to be paid out of the monies arising from the hire of the Negroes of the enemy.

Your memorialist has already had the honor to state to you fully the nature and extent of the office conferr'd upon him by Earl Cornwallis, which appointment, as well as the measure at large, have met with the royal approbation.

Your memorialist therefore thinks he is called upon in justice to the great trust reposed in him, and in justice to those faithful subjects who are now suffering from the vengeance and preditory laws of the rebels, to present to you that as long as he has the honor to hold his present office he shall consider it his unquestionable right to demand every person to account to him for the property of the enemy in this province of every species whether real or personal, and of which Negroes and of course their labour are the principal.

That he has a right to any advantage that may arise from cloathing the slaves under his charge, a right which from the unhappy circumstances of the country has proved hitherto prejudicial to him, being last season under a necessity of purchasing cloaths, blankets etc in the town at enormous prices and with ready money. That to prevent this inconvenience to himself and expences to his trust in future, he some time ago imported a sufficient quantity of woolens and other coarse goods, particularly a considerable value of Mr Harley's purchased at New York of his agent, Mr Gordon, great part of which articles are still on hand.

That your memorialist considers himself, by virtue of the great trust for which he is responsible, GUARDIAN of all the sequestered property of the enemy for the benefit of the suffering loyalists, who have so fair and so just CLAIM on it for immediate support and future indemnification, and they look to him with anxious expectation and require his utmost care and attention for the preservation and improvement of that fund which at present seems the only one from which they can expect to derive any relief.

In this situation he cannot *silently* look on and see a measure adopted that must obstruct and retard him in the execution of these trusts.

Your memorialist begs to inform you that he is using his utmost exertions to make up his accounts to the 16th of the present month, when he hopes to be able to convince you that if properly supported he may be able to bring the sequestered property of the enemy, even in the present state of publick affairs, to produce a fund of TEN THOUSAND guineas per annum to be applied as above hinted at or in such manner as you shall in your wisdom hereafter [determine].

THE COMMANDANT and BOARD OF POLICE have examined the accounts of your memorialist. If they have discovered that any part of his conduct is reprehensible, they will no doubt make the same known to you and inform you wherein he has not done justice to his trust. If, on the other hand, they report that his accounts are just and that he has faithfully executed his most IMPORTANT OFFICE (an office attended with great anxiety of mind, constant labour and attention and which has hitherto proved the reverse of beneficial to him, HIS HEALTH being much impaired by his persevering application to the duties of it, his private affairs neglected, and in order to support with propriety the consequence of office he has been led into a line of expences far exceeding (as affairs have turned out) the emoluments of it. He has also been detained by it much longer in the country than he intended, having had permission from Lord Cornwallis to leave the province several months ago.) —— if the report of the Commandant and Board of Police is favorable to him, your memorialist hopes, on considering the above stated facts and reasoning, that so far from depriving him of any part of an office which with great labour he has at last brought to a productive state you will be pleased to give him your aid, countenance and support in the execution of it.

AND HE PRAYS that you will give express ORDERS, before any new regulations is made, that the property of the enemy of every kind, particularly the labour of their Negroes, shall be accounted for to him without any deduction whatever.

That each DEPARTMENT shall pay for the cloathing such Negroes as are employed in it as well as such gratuities as may be given by it, and that all cloaths, blankets and necessaries for the Negroes of the enemy shall be supplied by your memorialist.

Cruden to Skelly, 12th April 1782   7(15): C

Charlestown
12th April 1782

Major Skelly

Dear Sir

Conversing with Mr McKenzie[115] yesterday, I found that no alteration had taken place in the arrangement intended with respect to Negroes.

I must again trespass upon your goodness and request the favour of you to inform the General that I shall consider myself compelled, from the justice I owe myself and the trust reposed in me, to demand regular and exact returns of the Negroes, the property of the enemy, from the gentlemen appointed paymasters and as well as full pay, it being assuredly the business of those who employ the Negroes to pay for their cloathing or make adequate allowance for that purpose, and their can be no great hardship in doing so, what I am persuaded the General will think when he is informed that I allow 2/ per day for labourers and 6/ for mechanicks for such assistance as I receive from the Negroes of the enemy in repairing and equipping my own vessels.

---

[115] Perhaps Andrew or Robert Mackenzie. Andrew was a merchant whose loyalism had led him to be included in the Banishment and Confiscation Act passed by the revolutionary assembly in January. Robert was a refugee militia officer, having served as lt colonel in Robert Ballingall's Colleton County regiment of the royal militia. He too had been included in the act of banishment and confiscation. (Coldham, *Loyalist Claims*, i, 202; SC Banishment and Confiscation Act 1782; Clark, *Loyalists in the Southern Campaign*, i, 169, 180, 491-500)

Will you forgive me for troubling you so much. I really am ashamed of myself and earnestly hope that I shall not have any cause to apply to you on a business of a disagreeable nature again, but I hope you will perceive the necessity I am under of stating clearly the nature of my office and of requesting the General to give such orders and directions to those gentlemen who are to have the charge of the Negroes in the publick departments of the army as will prevent any altercation or misunderstanding in future, for till the Commander in Chief removes me from my present office, I cannot allow one iota to be taken from me, and I am determined, the minute that his Excellency Sir Henry deprives me from any part, to give him the whole and lay the responsibility upon him.

Ever most sincerely and faithfully, dear sir,
Your etc

JOHN CRUDEN

The Commandant and Board of Police in Council, 18th April 1782   110(3): C

In Council
Thursday the 18th day of April 1782

Present

His Honor the Commandant
His Honor the Intendant General

Colonel Powell	Mr Irving
Mr Wright	Hon Tho[s] Knox Gordon Esq[116]
Colonel Cruger	Mr Savage

Mr Johnston

Mr Irving from the committee appointed to inspect the accounts of John Cruden Esq, Commissioner of Sequestered Estates, reported to the Board that several of the vouchers and papers appeared somewhat deficient, which they apprehended was owing to the late and present unsettled state of the province. The Board directed them notwithstanding to proceed and make reasonable and necessary allowances on that account.

---

[116] Before the revolution Thomas Knox Gordon (1728-1796) had served as Chief Justice of South Carolina, an office which he had accepted in the hope that it might eventually lead to an appointment as a judge on the Irish bench. Banished from South Carolina in 1777, he took passage to Belfast, from where he set sail for Charlestown in 1780 in compliance with the requirement that all civil officers return. Finding on arrival that the office of Chief Justice had not been re-established, he agreed to serve temporarily as an intendant of police. He died in England. (McCowen, op cit, 21-2; Sabine, *Biographical Sketches*, i, 482-3)

In Council
Friday the 19th day of April 1782

Present

His Honor the Commandant
The Intendant General

Colonel Powell	Mr Irving
Mr Wright	Mr Gordon
Colonel Cruger	Mr Savage

Mr Johnston

The committee appointed to inspect the accounts of John Cruden Esq, Commissioner of Sequestered Estates, delivered in the following report:

In pursuance of a minute of his Honor the Commandant of Charles Town and the Board of Police in Council dated the 26th ultimo[117] appointing Mr Irving, Colonel Powell and Colonel Cruger a committee to inspect and examine the several accounts and papers delivered in to the Board by Mr Cruden, Commissioner of Sequestered Estates, and to report thereon, and likewise of a subsequent minute of the 18th instant, we, the members of the above committee, proceeded to an examination of those accounts, together with the vouchers and other papers thereunto annexed, and are of opinion that the respective charges are vouched in as satisfactory a manner as the nature of the business and the unsettled state of public affairs would admit of, and that the ballance stated in Mr Cruden's account current of six thousand, eight hundred and fifty four pounds, fourteen shillings and ten pence one farthing was justly due to him from the Crown on the 16th of September last.

The committee, before they conclude their report, consider it as a part of their duty, in justice to Mr Cruden, to represent to the Board that it appears to them upon the whole that the Commissioner has not only been at great pains to keep his accounts in as clear and satisfactory a manner as the nature of the business and the unhappy situation of the country would admit of but also to have conducted himself with a laudable zeal to promote the interest of the Crown in such matters as were committed to his charge, and finally that the commission of five per centum charged on the issues of the estates is bearly adequate to the great and necessary expence, labour and attendance in carrying into execution the duty of his extensive and important employment, which will more particularly appear in his narrative delivered in with these papers.

All which is humbly submitted.

Charles Town, 19th April 1782

THOMAS IRVING
R W POWELL
J H CRUGER

---

[117] *a minute..*: of 26th February, p 274.

ENCLOSURE

THE COMMISSIONER'S NARRATIVE

Mr Cruden begs leave to lay before the Hon Board of Police, together with his accounts, the following NARRATIVE and OBSERVATIONS.

In the month of September 1780, when Lord Cornwallis granted his commission and gave orders for sequestering the rebel property in this province, the measure had every appearance of success and of producing a very considerable revenue, as the whole colony was at that time reduced to perfect obedience and offered the pleasing prospect of established and permanent tranquillity.

The Commissioner therefore entered with alacrity on the execution of the trust reposed in him. Upwards of one hundred warrants were granted. Nearly as many plantations and above five thousand Negroes were seized before the present disturbances had become in any great degree alarming.

The extent and importance of this department requiring much assistance, great attention and unremitting exertions, the Commissioner employed several gentlemen of approved loyalty, integrity and abilities as his deputies, allotting to each a particular district. Skilful overseers were engaged and every arrangement made which promised to insure success to the undertaking.

That the charges might be as light as possible, he agreed with his deputies to accept of a commission on the produce which passed thro' their hands in lieu of a fixed salary, excepting only a certain compensation for their extraordinary trouble and expences, which were great, in taking possession, making and returning inventories of the different estates. The most frugal agreements were made with the overseers and others employed.

From these and other arrangements made with the utmost care and attention, there was great reason to expect a clear, permanent and increasing revenue of fifty to sixty thousand pounds per annum to be applied to the service of Government, had the country remained in a state of tranquillity.

The Commissioner, however, received almost all the plantations in very bad condition. They had been either deserted or neglected by the proprietors during a war carried on for two campaigns in the heart of the province and had suffered exceedingly from the devastations of both armies as well as from many other circumstances attending the rebellion. None had in the former year produced any considerable crop, very few had even yielded provisions sufficient to support the slaves until the ensuing harvest, and many were *totally destitute of that most indispensable necessary*. The slaves in general were almost if not altogether naked, very scanty supplies of cloathing having been attainable for many years. The estates were likewise destitute of all sorts of plantation tools and implements of farming, and but very ill supplied in general with horses, cattle or stock of any kind.

In order to preserve the slaves and carry on the business all these wants must be supplied. Cloathing and food for the Negroes, horses, cattle and plantation necessaries must be provided. This has exhausted a very large sum of money. Another great and equally unavoidable expence has been incurred. The small pox and a malignant camp fever raged in general over the country. It was therefore necessary to assist with advice and medicine those already seized with either disorder and to inoculate those that had not had the small pox. The expence of this article alone is very great.

To defray all this expence from the produce of the crop 1780 was never expected by the Commissioner, but there were several funds from which he had reason to think that sums nearly, if not altogether, sufficient for that purpose might be drawn.

Besides the small crop of rice and some indico made in the lower settlements, large quantities of wheat, indian corn and pease, also stocks of cattle, sheep and hogs, were found on the sequestered estates about Congaree, Wateree and Ninety Six Districts, which over and above providing for the families and slaves on the estates would have furnished a considerable supply for other plantations that were in want and also for the King's troops in that neighbourhood. Some tobacco, indico and hemp was also found in that part of the country. But a greater and more productive article promised a speedy and constant resource — lumber and firewood.

On some of the estates there were good saw mills. Others were to have been erected in proper situations where plenty of timber offered itself. From the great and almost inexhaustible demand for this commodity and its high price both here and in the West Indies vast sums might have been drawn had the country remained open and quiet. One estate alone was capable of furnishing ten hundred thousand feet per annum, worth above £6,000 sterling, without interfering with or reducing the quantity of its other produce. Add to this the labour of at least two hundred Negroes employed by Colonel Moncrief on the public works, for which, agreeable to Lord Cornwallis's regulations, he ought, *but has not*, paid the Commissioner according to the usual rates.

By means of these funds the Commissioner reasonably expected that the department would at least have supported itself the first year and defrayed all the expences incurred by putting the plantations into good order, and that the crops and other products of the year 1781 would have yielded a large sum.

Those prospects were unfortunately soon changed, almost immediately after the unexpected misfortune of the 17th January 1781 and Lord Cornwallis's movement into North Carolina. The frontiers and great part of the interior of this province became scenes of confusion, robbery and murder.

In the month of March Sumpter with a large body of cavalry broke into the northern and western districts and ravaged the whole country from Ninety Six to Santee, whilst Marion, Clarke and Mackay overrun and destroyed the eastern and southern parts. On this occasion all the settlements at Ninety Six and on the Congaree and Wateree were broke up. Many overseers were murdered, and several Negroes having been carried off, the rest were secured at the different posts until they could be removed to places of more security. By this and the subsequent incursions of the enemy vast quantities of provisions and cattle and a great deal of tobacco, indico etc were lost and the plantations destroyed. Great part of the Negroes were saved and brought nearer town and might yet have been employed to advantage, but the invasion of the province by General Greene, the evacuation of Camden, George Town and other outposts, with the general revolt of almost the whole country, have frustrated all the Commissioner's measures and cut off not only all prospects of a crop but even all communication with the estates, the greatest part of which are actually in the enemies possession. These misfortunes have not only destroyed all the Commissioner's resources but have also involved him in a very heavy additional expence: several overseers and other persons employed by him on these estates have been murdered, to support whose distressed families he is called on both by humanity and the honor of Government. Many others with their wives and children have been obliged to fly to the British lines for protection and must also be maintained, but the heavyest charge is a vast crowd of loyal and helpless refugees, who have lost their all and been driven from their habitations by the rebels on account of their attachment to Government. The Commissioner has received express orders from Earl Cornwallis, Lord Rawdon and the Commandant to maintain and provide houses for many of these. To this purpose several valuable places in safe situations near Charles Town have been appropriated which would otherwise have yielded considerable profit, and he is under the necessity of purchasing provisions to feed these people as well as great numbers of the sequestered Negroes driven from the estates, who must otherwise perish. The incursions of the enemy are now so frequent and so near our lines that the procuring firewood for the use of the garrison, which the Commissioner had contracted for and would under more favourable circumstances have been very able to have performed, has been greatly obstructed and rendered exceedingly expensive and precarious, and several vessels employed by him in that service have been burned or otherwise destroyed by the enemy. By Earl Cornwallis's instructions the wives and children of sequestered persons were directed to be supported out of the produce of the estates and certain portions thereof were allotted for that purpose with a discretionary power in the Commissioner to supply further sums if the said portions should prove inadequate to the purpose, which, from the many misfortunes above set forth, has too often happened and has required very considerable sums.

From such a series of calamitous events, which have reduced this country to its present miserable situation, it grieves the Commissioner to be under the necessity of observing that, contrary to all appearances at the time of adopting this measure, it has, instead of yielding a very considerable revenue to Government, brought on it a heavy but unavoidable expence, to defray part of which he has been compelled to apply to the Commandant for a supply and has received the sum of four thousand pounds, which is very short of his advances, to reimburse which a much larger sum will still be necessary. He has also the mortification to find that the valuable property of some gentlemen employed and acting under him has been materially injured and in some parts of the province entirely destroyed by the enemy in revenge for their having assisted in this business, the rebels threatning, and when in their power (which is too extensive) constantly executing, vengeance on all persons acting in this department.

From the above short narrative it will appear what difficulties the Commissioner has had to struggle with, and that notwithstanding all his exertions very little can *now* be expected this year from these estates even if the enemy should be driven away, and the communications opened, in the winter season, the crops being everywhere much injured and in many places entirely destroyed etc.

Charles Town
June 1st 1781

The foregoing narrative contains the substance of a memorial drawn up last summer by Mr Cruden for the information of His Majesty's Ministers concerning the state of his department at that period, and which he now communicates to this Hon Board for the same purpose. It is needless for him to trouble the Board with a recital of the tragical events which have happened since that date or to point out the distresses of our present situation. These are matters but too well known.

It will be sufficient to observe that his apprehensions at the above date have been too fatally reallized and that from the increase of public calamity very little has been since received by him from any of the funds of the department, the expences of which were unavoidably continued till very lately. Even the estates in the vicinity of Charles Town have not been protected, and a very considerable value in cattle and other stock, in grain and in gardens, particularly on James Island and Charles Town Neck, has been destroyed by the ravages of the militia, vagabond refugees and others, to prevent which every endeavour in his power was used but without the desired effect.

The Commissioner requests the Hon Board to pay particular attention to the following observations, which he thinks it necessary to make on his accounts.

By the warrants produced and the returns of his deputies it will appear that the principal estates belonging to rebellious subjects in this province have been regularly seized agreeable to Lord Cornwallis's proclamation; that, by virtue of one general warrant for the seizure of all abandoned property in this province and another for that of the Negroes of the enemy in North Carolina, he is vested with full power over all property of every kind belonging to the enemy which *has been* or may be taken possession of by any person or persons under His Majesty's Government in these provinces.

It is therefore evident that every department in the service ought to account to him for all the property that may have come into their possession, of which the labour of Negroes makes a very material article. The Commissary General acknowledges to have received in cattle and provisions to the amount of [*blank*], which should certainly be paid over to the Commissioner, who is possessed of Lord Cornwallis's positive orders to the commissaries of captures to give him vouchers for all such property, and the Board will observe that the chief engineer, Lt Colonel Moncrief, owes him a very large ballance on account of the labour of Negroes furnished by the Commissioner and for lumber. This ballance alone would reimburse to the Commissioner his advances, and *both* would enable him to pay over to the Paymaster General a handsome sum for the King's Service, agreeable to the original intention of his commission.

The complicated business of this department could not be carryed on without a number of small vessels. To hire such upon every emergency was always uncertain, often impracticable and the expence very great. It became therefore necessary to purchase or build a sufficient number. The same misfortunes that have ruined the other branches of this business have occasion'd a considerable loss under this head. Some vessels were burned or otherwise destroyed by the enemy in their first incursions, and several were lost in the gale of wind on the 10th of August last, a list of which will be produced.

The variety of matter, the confusions and desolations of the country, with the long train of losses and disappointments, occasioned by the untoward events of last year, have rendered it impossible for the Commissioner to make up his accounts at the precise dates directed by his instructions and also to state exactly the sums due to all the overseers for wages, as some have been murdered, some drove off, and others have joined the enemy without coming to any settlement, but the sums paid them have always been short of the amount of their salaries.

At the time the Commissioner entered on his office it is well known that all sorts of plantation necessaries were scarce and dear, especially woollens. Blankets of the most moderate quality could not be purchased under nine or ten guineas a piece, and the common kind of Negroe cloth still dearer in proportion, and even not to be procured at any price, in the begining of the winter. There was therefore a necessity for cloathing many of the Negroes with a kind of coloured coarse duffel, which, altho' costing more per yard than common plains, was not in fact dearer, as being double the wedth and of much better quality. The shoes, plantation tools and other necessaries, altho' charged in the name of John Cruden & Co to prevent a number of cross useless entries in the public books, were purchased of the various importers and shop keepers in town on the lowest terms and charged at the same prices which were actually paid.

The Board will also be pleased to observe that in Lord Cornwallis's commission to Mr Cruden the rate of poundage to be charged by him is left blank, and that, considering how little the estates have yielded owing to the calamities occasioned by the war, no rate of commission on such trifling sums can be adequate to the expence and trouble attending the prosecution of this business, the labour, anxiety and attention to which increased as the profits diminished; but as he had mentioned to Lord Cornwallis (before we were deprived of the possession of the country) that, altho' *five per centum* would not be considered by merchants as a proper compensation for the supplying and managing the estates and the sale of the produce, yet the great extent of the object might render it an equivalent, he has therefore charged no more. But the very small amount of the produce has rendered *that* commission such a trifle that it is scarsly sufficient to pay his clerks and other necessary assistants, much less to defray the very heavy *additional* expence which the Commissioner has been involved in by such a public line of life, to say nothing of his own labour and detention in this country to the great detriment not only of his health but of his large concerns in other parts of the world, which have suffered much by his constant residence here, which nothing but the distress of the country, which so embarrassed his department as to render his own presence absolutely necessary, could have induced him to submit to, his concerns in England demanding his presence there, as is well known to Colonel Balfour as well as to Lord Cornwallis, whose leave of absence he had obtained. The Commissioner therefore expects that the Hon Board will pay due attention to these circumstances in their report on his accounts.

The report of the committee and the Commissioner's Narrative being read, the Board proceeded to the consideration of the said report and, after mature deliberation thereupon, unanimously agreed with the committee on the same.

Thereupon ORDERED that the Secretary to this Board do prepare for and furnish the Commissioner of Sequestered Estates with a copy of the proceedings upon his accounts, together with the following certificate[118] to be signed by the members of the Board:

We do certify that, agreeable to the direction of Earl Cornwallis contained in his proclamation of the 16th of September 1780, we have inspected the accounts of John Cruden Esq, the Commissioner of Sequestered Estates, commencing on the said 16th day of September and ending the 16th of September last, and that the same appears to us to be just and right and there was justly due to the said Commissioner from Government on the day last mentioned the sum of six thousand eight hundred and fifty four pounds fourteen shillings and ten pence ¼ sterling, money of Great Britain.

	R W POWELL	)
N BALFOUR	A WRIGHT	)
Commandant of Charles Town	J H CRUGER	) Intendants of
	THO IRVING	) Police
W^M BULL	THO KNOX GORDON	)
Intendant General of Police	EDWARD SAVAGE	)
	JA^S JOHNSTON	)

Cruden to Ballingall[119], *27th April 1782*   *7(16): C*

Charlestown
27th April 1782

Robert Ballingall Esq

Sir

Mr Gordon presented me this moment a note of yours desiring him to furnish you with the names of the Negroes in my department that they may have passes from you. I am willing to hope you did not consider the nature of the demand, as I cannot suppose that you would make a requisition that must hurt me as holding an office as honorable as it is important; and I have from you that while I have the honor to be at the head of it, I will not allow any Negroe seized by me to go with any pass but my own unless such as I have hired or may hire to publick departments.

I should hold myself unworthy of the trust reposed in me (a trust, sir, approved of in the fullest manner by my Sovereign) if I did not immediately express how keenly I feel on this subject, and to inform you that I shall consider any incroachment upon me in my office as obstructing and retarding me in execution of it and make an immediate representation thereof to the throne.

I have the honor to be, sir,
Your etc

JOHN CRUDEN

---

[118] *the following certificate*: according to 7(41), it was signed on 4th May.

[119] Ballingall was one of three commissioners of claims. Among other things, they issued certificates to 'friendly' owners of slaves employed in the public departments. On presenting the certificates, the owners received compensation. (McCowen, *Charleston, 1780-82*, 101n)

Charlestown
17th May 1782

Robert McKenzie Esq

Sir

In consequence of the letter I had the pleasure to receive from you I waited twice at your house but had not the good fortune to find you at home.

I beg you may believe that I am fully sensible of your personal attention to me and I retain a proper sense thereof and have for you that regard which I am persuaded nothing can remove, but I must confess to you I am at a loss to conceive what possible reason either Mr Perroneau[120] or you can have to justify you for not answering my letter. As an individual I have a right to that respect, but as a *highly responsible* officer of Government I have an undoubted right to expect immediate attention whilst in the execution of my office. And I beg leave to inform you that unless I do receive a very pointed answer to my publick letter, I shall be compelled to take steps that will give me pain because they may prove injurious to you and Mr Perroneau, for whose characters I have great respect, but when I have reason to apprehend that it is intended to encroach upon my office and obstruct and impede me in the execution of it, I owe it to myself and my noble patron to take immediate steps to do myself justice.

With sincere regard I have the honor to be, sir,
Your etc

JOHN CRUDEN

---

[120] Perhaps Robert Peronneau, a physician and prominent citizen of Charlestown, who had taken protection and sworn allegiance to the Crown. For his sin he had been included in the act of banishment and confiscation passed by the revolutionary assembly at Jacksonborough. Like his brother Henry, who had been Joint Public Treasurer of South Carolina before the revolution, he would become exiled in England. (Lambert, *SC Loyalists*, 293; McCowen Jr, *Charleston, 1780-82*, 52-3; The SC Banishment and Confiscation Act 1782)

Office of Sequestration
Charlestown
28th May 1782

Samuel Bean[121] Esq

Sir

I find myself compelled to trouble you for an immediate interference in your publick capacity.

The appointment conferred upon me, which has received the royal approbation, renders all heads of departments solely accountable to me for property of every species seized from or abandoned by the enemy and as much of the said property [as] has been in particular seized of the deputies and assistants of the Commissary General from the troops being landed previous to and since the reduction of this province, and tho' I have made reiterated sollicitation for returns of the same, they have been withheld. I must therefore beg leave to request your being pleased forthwith to interpoze the authority of your office with Major Morrison that he direct all within his department to render for your inspection the most accurate, unreserved return of every kind of seizure respectively made, particularly for the cattle, forage and other articles taken for the army on the march from Savannah, a large quantity of various property by Mr Clarke[122] while acting with the army in the Back Country, and by deputies and others upon the Wateree and Congaree Rivers. My early departure makes me urge your earliest, most summary and effectual means of inducing this settlement, which if declined to you, be pleased to represent to Lt General Leslie the urgent necessity of it for adding to those publick accounts I shall have the honor to submit to the Commander in Chief and to enable my lodging the amount of the same with the Deputy Paymaster General in conformity to the express letter of my commission.

I have the honor to be, sir,
Your etc

JOHN CRUDEN

---

[121] There is reason to suspect that Samuel Bean may have been the person of that name who was once a commercial agent in Kingston, Jamaica. If so, he arrived at New York from England in 1781 and attempted to enter into correspondence with Robert Morris, the so-called 'financier of the revolution', but Morris declined as they were on opposing sides. Bean may have gone on to hold a public office at Charlestown in which his commercial expertise was of use. (Marko Junkkarinen, 'Living an American Lifestyle in 18th Century Philadelphia – Robert Morris, Prosperous Merchant and Family Man', *EurAmerica* (Institute of European and American Studies), xxxv, N° 3 (September 2005), 459-499)

[122] As indicated in Cruden's next letter, Clark(e) was an assistant commissary.

Office of Sequestration
31st May 1782

Samuel Bean Esq etc etc etc

Sir

I have the honor to acknowledge receipt of your letter of yesterday. Permit me to return you my humble thanks for your attention to my request [and] polite tender of assistance in your publick capacity to enable my prosecuting the business of an office in which I have the mortification to suffer, in addition to that which the distraction of the country occasioned, difficulty and obstruction where I had every right to expect countenance and support. I think it incumbent on me, reverting to the subject of my last to you, that I inform you of having received from Major Morrison a short and accurate but, I firmly believe, just and true account of the cattle received by his department since 24th April 1781. I have also seen returns from Messrs Knecht and McDonald, assistant commissaries, which tho' I will not presume to say were otherways than just, I am certain and do affirm they cannot comprehend all the property taken for the supply of that part of the army furnished by them that was not paid for to the inhabitants, and beg leave to declare as my opinion that all doubtfull property should be accounted for to my office.

And as 'tis difficult to discriminate rebels from those who are not, whatever the final result of the contest may be, those who are admitted to enter claims would find a more certain resort in my office than in having recourse to any assistant or deputy of the Commissary General, who are so liable to change of situation from the arrangements of the army. Upon this idea I beg your leave to submit such intelligence relative to the property unaccounted for as the peculiar distractions of the period since my being in office has afforded me the means to obtain.[123] During the march of the army from Savannah untill the appointment of commissaries of captures here, Mr Clark, an assistant commissary (new in the issue of forage), possessed and expended to the army property to large amount. From that period to that of the march of Earl Cornwallis, when the appointment of commissaries of captures became extinct, to the arrival of the army at Cambden untill their return to this place, afterwards when Lord Rawdon commanded, and from the action of the 16th August to the march of Earl Cornwallis in North Carolina, during all which periods to my certain knowledge either the commissary of captures or the deputies of the Commissary General consumed or carried off from estates of the enemy, sequestered or abandoned, an amazing quantity of grain, horned cattle, sheep, hogs, stock and forage, in so much that you will observe, by the copies of those letters from Earl Cornwallis and Lord Rawdon[124] I have the honor to convey, the army while at Wynnesborough subsisted by the supplies I have mentioned. And besides the supply furnished to the main body of the army, the out posts and detachments received their principal support from the sequestered estates contiguous, especially at Cambden and George Town,

---

[123] The manuscript suggests that rest of this letter may have been subject to some miscopying.

[124] *those letters..*: Rawdon to Stedman, 31st October 1780, vol II, p 288, and Cornwallis to Stedman, 15th December 1780, vol III, p 450.

[together] with the flying corps [of] Colonel Watson and the detachments commanded by Colonel McArthur, as also at the Cheraws, Ninety Six, Congarees, Mott's House, Nelson's Ferry, Wright's Bluff, Wapetaw, Pocotaligo, Dorchester, John's Island, Port Royal, Monk's Corner with other posts I cannot perhaps recollect. The posts in Georgia, especially Savannah and Augusta, were afforded supplies from the estates of this province. The settlement of all the property so taken and issued Major Morrison does not choose to undertake, at which I am not surprized, but unless he takes cognizance of the business of this nature relative to the departments previous to the 24th April 1780[125], a representation must of necessity be made to the Commissary General of requisition that a full and final adjustment of the same be assumed by him, as imposing the necessity of my calling upon the deputies in that line of the various degrees would be a deviation from the rules of office prescribed. Whereby recourse is only had to the head [of] the departments, from which, in the case I have had the honor to state to you in much detail, the principal either in appointment or on the spot should collect the returns of all in subordinate capacity and be solely rendered accountable to me for all property of the description I have mentioned, the proceeds of which ought ultimately to center in my office.

With perfect respect I have the honor to be, sir,
Your etc

JOHN CRUDEN

Bean to Cornwallis, 12th June 1783   7(55): C

12th June 1783

My Lord

I beg leave to inclose Cruden's two accounts as received from his father, also several certificates reffered to in my report[126], as well as his own Narrative and the Board of Police's report on his first account previous to the time of my arrival. There is an intermediate account wanting, which is also passed by me, and which his father says is already given in to the Treasury, but be that as it may, in case of need I have it copied in my books.

With all these testimonials, together with your Lordship's certificate and General Leslie's, I hope and wish the purpose may be fully answered and the poor man get his money, which he is well entitled to.

I have the honor to be with profound respect, my Lord,
Your Lordship's much obliged and most obedient servant

SAM BEANE

§ - §

---

[125] *1780*: 1781, as evinced by the earlier date in this letter.

[126] The Cornwallis Papers do not contain copies of the later account, the certificates or the report.

7 - Miscellaneous papers, 1781-4

Lady Charlotte Madan to Cornwallis, November 1781[127]   *277(14): ALS*

Peterbro'
November 1781

My dearest Brother

As I find my health declines very fast and am fully persuaded I shall not long continue in this world — perhaps may never have the comfort of seeing you again, I cannot help leaving a letter behind me to express some sentiments with which my heart is full.

I have, my dear brother, ever since you was born, loved you with the most perfect affection, which every action of your life has encreased. I never met with a character that appear'd to me so completely amiable (you will not accuse me of *flattery*, as I don't propose you shou'd see this till I am *no more*). Your noble, generous, disinterested, affectionate disposition I think can scarce be *equal'd*, I am sure not *exceeded*. I really look upon you with a degree of admiration which I think does not proceed from partiallity, as I have the satisfaction of finding Dr Madan[128] and many others have exactly the same idea of your character that I have ever had, and if I knew of any faults in it, I shou'd take this opportunity of mentioning them, as my concern for your *happiness* does not meerly extend to the short period of this transitory life (where it's seldom *enjoy'd*, and never without much alloy[129]), but I trust your felicity will be hereafter complete and endure to all eternity, for tho' I have never heard you talk on the subject of religion, I think it's impossible any body can uniformly act in the manner you have always done without a just sense of the several dutys it enjoins, and I hope, when you have more leisure, you will dedicate more time to that most important study, where you may be *sure* of *meeting with your reward*. I can from experience assure you it's the only comfort in adversity, the only support in pain and sickness, and the only effectual cordial in the hour of death. I am persuaded I shall find it.

---

[127] While describing certain circumstances of his family, this private letter is interesting mainly for the light it throws on the character of Cornwallis.

[128] The Reverend Dr Spencer Madan (1729-1813), the husband of Charlotte, was a son of Martin Madan, sometime Colonel-in-Chief of the Dragoon Guards in Ireland. Presently a prebendary and king's chaplain at Peterborough Cathedral, he was being helped financially by Cornwallis, who, as Constable of the Tower of London, had appointed him to the sinecure of gentleman porter at the Tower. In 1792 he would be appointed Bishop of Bristol, from where he would translate two years later to the Lord Bishopric of Peterborough, an office he would hold until his death. He is buried in the Cathedral's new building. His son Charles, a captain in the 76th Regiment, served as an aide-de-camp to Cornwallis in India while his daughter Charlotte married a son of General George Warde, Commander-in-Chief in Ireland from 1791 to 1793. (Wickwire, *Cornwallis*, 36-8; The Reverend W D Sweeting, *The Cathedral Church of Peterborough* (London, 1926), ch vi)

[129] *alloy*: debasement.

But my design in writing this letter was neither to advise you, which I think you don't want, nor to praise you, which I know you don't love, but to acquaint you with some circumstances relating to myself which I have long wish'd you to know and which I flatter myself wou'd vindicate my conduct in your opinion, and it's impossible for me not to wish to appear in the fairest light to one I so entirely love and perfectly esteem, and tho' your innate goodness has made you ever behave to me with the strongest fraternal affection, yet, as you were totally ignorant of my motives for marrying, I am sure you must have thought me at least very *imprudent*, but indeed, my dearest brother, it was not a violent girlish affection (which wou'd have been scarce excuseable at the age of 29) that bias'd me. I love Dr M a hundred times better now than I did when I marry'd him, but I had some very strong objections to the continueing to live with my uncle[130], which you know I then did, and of such a nature that it was no reflection to *me* to dislike my situation. In this distress I acquainted my mother with it, who likewise told my father, at a time that upon my honor I had not seen, corresponded, or even heard whether Dr M was dead or alive, marry'd or single, for three years before.

We *had* been acquainted and he had shew'd a partiallity for me at the Dean of Durham's (Dr Cowper[131]), his near relation, about 5 years before, which the Dean then encouraged him to think, when he got better preferment, might take place, but I never gave him any promise, as indeed I look'd upon it as a thing my parents wou'd never consent to and was determined never to dispose of myself without their approbation, and upon my Aunt Cowper's[132] discovering his attachment and telling my father of it, who thought it (as I imagined he wou'd) not a proper match for me, both Dr M and I gave him our word we never wou'd hold any correspondence together without his knowledge and, I assure you, strictly kept our promise to him.

And till I accidentally met him about 2 months before we marry'd, I did not know, as I before assured you, the least what was become of him, and after I had this short conversation with him, in which he only told me he was still single and ask'd me whether I thought my father equally averse to our union, I told my father the very next day all that had pass'd, when to my great surprise he listen'd very favorably to it and even ordered me to write to him to know what his friends wou'd do for him and what addition he cou'd make to my fortune to settle upon me. I am persuaded my dear father's motive for this was owing to his tenderness both to me and my uncle and not knowing how any other way to extricate me from the painful situation I was then in, as I frequently saw the uneasyness it gave him to dispose of me (what the world calls) *so ill*, which went to my heart and made me often, during the

---

[130] Charlotte's marriage took place early in 1756. Of her uncles by that time, two (Richard and Stephen) were dead, one (Edward) was serving in the Mediterranean as Lt Colonel of the 24th, and another (Frederick) was Bishop of Lichfield and Coventry. Of the rest, the one to whom Charlotte refers has not been established.

[131] The Reverend Dr Spencer Cowper had been appointed Dean of Durham in 1746 and had continued in office until his death in 1774. He was a younger brother of William, 2nd Earl Cowper (1709-1764) and a cousin of Judith Cowper, the wife of Colonel Martin Madan and the mother of Dr Spencer Madan. For more about him, see *Letters of Spencer Cowper Dean of Durham 1746-74* edited by Edward Hughes (Surtees Society, 1956).

[132] Charlotte is apparently referring to Dorothy Cowper, wife of Dr Spencer Cowper and daughter of Charles, 2nd Viscount Townshend.

time the settlements were drawing, beg he wou'd put an end to it and I wou'd freely give it up, but this he wou'd not consent to, only proposed to me to marry without his knowledge, which he say'd wou'd excuse him to the world, but this I cou'd not agree to, as I thought it wou'd be such a reflection both on my own and Dr M's character that we cou'd never support, so my dear father, whose tenderness I never reflect on without a mixture of pleasure and pain (as I wou'd have dyed to have given him any comfort and cou'd not bear to live to give him any pain), went on with the busyness of the settlements, named himself the trustees, and sign'd and seal'd before we did. He made me a long visit the day before we were marry'd to take leave of me, and then promised me, if we behaved prudently, a continuance of his affection and that he wou'd see me when an opportunity offered, and, a little while before he dyed, wrote to me to come to London, but I most unfortunately was then very big with child of Charles and cou'd not undertake so long a journey at that time. And alas! he dyed when I had only been brought to bed a week, so I never saw him again, but I had been before twice in London at the same time he was, when he was *influenced* (I am sure it was not his *own wish*) to take no notice of me, and this I imagine was the reason why both Dr M and I have met with so much barbarity from some, and so much coolness from most of my relations.

How my mother, who knows the truth of every word I have advanced in this account, and to whom I wou'd willingly appeal *to vouch it*, can answer it to her conscience to behave in the manner she has done to me and my children I cannot guess, as I always look'd upon her as a very conscientious woman and am not sensible I ever gave her any offence in my life, whilst I lived at home, she always say'd I was a dutyful, affectionate daughter. Since our separation, now near 26 years, I don't know how I can have misbehaved to her, and if she wou'd have permitted it, I shou'd have given her every possible proof of the continuance of my love and duty, with the greatest satisfaction. I earnestly and dayly pray to God that she may not suffer for her unkindness to me, for I cannot help calling it *unkind* and *unjust*.

Both Dr M and I have, I am sure, behaved in the most prudent manner it was possible ever since we married, tho' it has often been with the greatest difficulty we have been able to support a genteel appearance, but we have never indulged ourselves in any unnecessary expence and *his* care and prudence from the first was beyond what I ever saw in any other young man. Alas! I think he ought to have been better rewarded for that and his unremitted tenderness to me! Notwithstanding the cruel behaviour of most of my family to him, I am sure his character has ever been not only unexceptionable but merritorious in every respect, his family and connections such as can bring no disgrace on any alliance with the highest nobility, his education the best any can receive, and the proficiency he made both at Westminster and Cambridge, and the esteem he was held in at both those places for learning and ability, such as any body wou'd have great reason to be proud of, and tho' my relations have appear'd so little desirous of his company, he is reckon'd by the best judges not only a sensible but a most pleasant companion, but his spirits of late years have suffer'd very much from the numberless disappointments and mortifications he has endured, which has also injured his health.

I flatter myself, my dear brother, you will continue after my death the goodness you have ever shewn to him and my children. You are the only relation or friend I have on whom I have any dependence, and if you could read my heart, you would find it replete with gratitude and thankfulness, but all the returns I can make are my earnest prayers, which I shall with my last breath offer up to God for the felicity both transient and eternal of you and your dear children. Farewell for ever, my dearest brother. Remember with some regard, but no *concern*, I beseech you, a sister who was ever

Your most truly affectionate

CHARLOTTE MADAN

[*Endorsed*:]

I request my dear husband to send this letter to my good brother as soon as he can conveniently after my decease, unopen'd.

Digby to Cornwallis, 23rd December 1781   *94(1): ALS*

New York
December the 23rd

My dear Lord

I have not been able to read half your papers, but as the time draws near that the *Europe* must sail, I am unwilling to run any risk of forgetting to send them by this opportunity. They are made up in five parcels and I have wrote to Captain Childs[133] to desire in case of accidents he will take care that they don't fall into the ennemy's hands. I think you heard of the arrival of the *Mulgrave* at Charles Town before you sail'd. No news of any consequence from thence, except in Mr Rivington's paper.

The *Charles Town* and *Vulture* are just sail'd with a convoy for that place and I have taken care to send your packets with directions to provide against accidents. The Marquis is, I hear, gone to Boston to take a passage, so that we shall have no chance of meeting with him.

I have the honor to be with great sincerity
Your Lordship's very obedient servant

R DIGBY

---

[133] Commissioned a lieutenant in the Royal Navy on 7th November 1755, Smith Child (?-1813) had been promoted to commander on 30th October 1777 and to post-captain some two and a half years later. As captain of the 64-gun man of war *Europe* he had recently taken part in the Battle of the Chesapeake Capes on 5th September. He died an admiral of the blue. (Syrett and DiNardo eds, *The Commissioned Sea Officers*, 81; 'Sailing Navies 1650-1850: Officers — Great Britain (Royal Navy)' (Internet, 2nd August 2006))

Richmond to Cornwallis, 15th February 1783   *7(5): ALS*

Whitehall
February the 15th 1783

Earl of Cornwallis

My Lord

I have this moment receiv'd your Lordship's letter of to day expressing your approbation of Captain Rochford's behaviour on several occasions and of that of the corps under his command in the defence of York Town.

Your Lordship's commendation does them much honor and I beg leave to assure your Lordship that I shall be happy in any opportunity that may offer of shewing the respect I have for it.

I have the honor to be
Your Lordship's most obedient and most humble servant

RICHMOND[134]

Board of Agents for the American Loyalists to Cornwallis,   *94(7): C*
5th March 1783

*Comments objected to by the Board of Agents for the American Loyalists,
as published in Cornwallis's Answer to Clinton's Narrative*

Pages 3 and 4

Our hopes of success, in offensive operations, were not founded only upon the efforts of the corps under my immediate command, which did not much exceed three thousand men, but principally upon the most positive assurances given by apparently credible deputies and emissaries that, upon the appearance of a British army in North Carolina, a great body of the inhabitants were ready to join and co-operate with it in endeavouring to restore his Majesty's Government.

Page 5

The unexpected failure of our friends rendered the victory of Guildford of little value. I know that it has been asserted or insinuated that they were not sufficiently tried upon this

---

[134] A forceful opponent of the North ministry and an early convert to the idea of American independence, Charles Lennox (1735-1806), Duke of Richmond, Lennox and Aubigny, had been appointed Master General of the Ordnance, with a seat in Cabinet, on the fall of North in March 1782. Apart from one fairly short break, he would occupy the office until January 1795. (*ODNB*)

occasion, but can any dispassionate person believe that I did not give every encouragement to people of all descriptions to join and assist us, when my own reputation, the safety of the army, and the interests of my country were so deeply concerned in that junction and assistance? All inducements in my power were made use of without material effect, and every man in the army must have been convinced that the accounts of our emissaries had greatly exaggerated the number of those who professed friendship for us, as they must have observed that a very inconsiderable part of them could be prevailed upon to remain with us or to exert themselves in any form whatever.

Pages 5 and 6

This disappointment, and the wants and distresses of the army, compelled me to move to Cross-creek, but meeting there with no material part of the promised assistance and supplies, I was obliged to continue my march to Wilmington, where hospitals and stores were ready for us.

Page 15

But I trust it will appear from the correspondence now laid before the public that our failure in North Carolina was not occasioned by our want of force to protect the rising of our friends but by their timidity and unwillingness to take an active and useful part.

Cornwallis to Wright etc, 8th March 1783   94(9): Df

Mansfield Street
March 8th 1783

Sir James Wright Bt, President, and the other members of
the Board of Agents for the American Loyalists

Gentlemen

I have received the honour of your letter of the 5th instant[135] and I am extremely concerned to learn that some expressions in my Answer to Sir Henry Clinton's Narrative have given pain to a body of men so respectable and so peculiarly circumstanced as the unfortunate American loyalists.

My services in North America gave me numberless opportunities to observe the undoubted loyalty of a great body of people, and I hope that the whole tenor of my conduct has proved not only that I was ever sensible of their merits but that, if at any time my friendship and protection has not come up to their expectations, the want of ability has been the sole cause of their disappointment.

---

[135] *your letter..*: not extant.

When I found myself called upon by Sir Henry Clinton's Narrative to publish a vindication of my own conduct during the campaign of 1781, it was as far from my intention as it would have been cruelly unjust to convey a doubt of the loyal disposition of a great number of the inhabitants of North Carolina. Convinced of their loyalty, it was with reluctance, even when disappointed, that I complained of their inactivity, as it proceeded from causes which will save them from censure with all generous minds.

North Carolina being, in proportion to its immense extent, but thinly inhabited, and our friends being not only much dispersed but mixed in every district with people of opposite principles who had possessed themselves of the powers of government, their efforts to manifest their loyalty had been made under great disadvantages and had been attended with many fatal consequences previous to our march into that province. Many had lost their lives and numbers had long languished in confinement or had been driven out of the country in consequence of the rising in the year 1776. The premature rising at Ramsoure's, Colonel Bryan's junction with us in South Carolina (both directly contrary to my recommendation) and Colonel Ferguson's defeat on King's Mountain in the year 1780 had occasioned the ruin of many families and had furnished pretexts to exercise cruelties upon individuals to a degree neither believed nor conceived in this country. Those rigours, joined to a long series of former oppressions, had in my opinion totally broke the spirits of the greatest number of our friends before our arrival among them. Hopes of relief naturally induced their emissaries (perhaps not sensible of it) to conceal this from me and I could only discover it from experience when I called upon them for assistance. I will freely confess that I was then convinced that we had been too sanguine on both sides: our expectations had been too high of co-operation and assistance, and our friends had expected too much from the appearance of a British army in the province. To account for some parts of my own conduct it was necessary to state this disappointment, but when the situation of these unfortunate people is fairly considered, I am persuaded I cannot have excited any emotion but compassion for them in the breasts of all liberal men. The characters and principles of a great body of loyalists at present in this country or with our army in North America can be still less affected by misconstructions of any expressions of mine. Many by gallantly taking arms in the common cause, some by acting in civil capacities, and others by abandoning their families and properties in America have proved their loyalty and attachment to this Government beyond all possibility of being controverted, and have therefore the best founded claims for compensation upon the generosity and justice of Britain.

I beg leave to assure the Board of Agents that I am truly sensible of the high value of the favourable opinion that they have been pleased to express of my conduct during this calamitous war, and I shall ever lament that my endeavours were so ineffectual to promote the interests of individuals and the reunion of the British Empire.

I have the honour to be with great respect, gentlemen, etc

[CORNWALLIS]

Halifax
April 9th 1784

My Lord

I have troubled your Lordship with a great many letters since my arrival here. I am now, I hope, to close all back accounts between the colonel and the regiment. The men not having received half mounting[137] at the time they were cloth'd at York Town from the clothing of the northern army, I have directed the pay master to credit them that are with us for it, which amounts to £36 4s 6d, no clothing having been sent from England since 81. Credit to serjeants for their half mounting and the differance between their clothing and private at York Town, to man discharg'd, and servants not cloth'd: £54 19s 6d. I fear your Lordship is much out of pocket by mismanagement, but I am sure you would condemn me were I not faithfully to give every man his due, particularly to those men who were the companions of your service. I have great pleasure in repeating that they go on as well as you could wish them, in defiance of every other house in Halifax being a rum shop, and we are now in high health.

If there is no prospect of our going home, I should be glad of our Yorkshire recruits. They certainly will be better here than at home. The 33rd are the most incomplete regiment in Nova Scotia. The absent subalterns must join us as soon as possible; we have hardly sufficient to do the duty and one or two present want to go home.

We have had nothing regular from England for near five months. Extracts from English papers by the way of Boston mention a change in the Ministry and that your Lordship has given up the Tower[138]. I hope it is for something better.

The Governor[139] sends his compliments. I believe he is rather alarm'd least a change at home should remove him.

I have the honor to be with great respect, my Lord,
Your Lordship's most obedient and most humble servant

J YORKE

§ - §

---

[136] Cornwallis and John Yorke were respectively Colonel and Lt Colonel of the 33rd Regiment.

[137] *mounting*: the shirt, shoes, stock and hose, or stockings furnished by the colonel of a regiment every year.

[138] Cornwallis was Constable of the Tower of London.

[139] Edmund Fanning (see vol III, p 113, note 86) had been sworn in as Lt Governor of Nova Scotia on 23rd September 1783 and would remain in office until 1786. (*DCB*)

Index[1]

Abercromby, Robert (III, 444), 126, 128-9
Affleck, Edmund, 33n, 42
Allaire, Anthony (III, 460), 240n, 247
Amherst, Jeffrey, Lord (II, 21), 163
Amherst, Jeffrey (V, 315), 238
Amiel, Henry or Otho (V, 166), 14, 25
Andrews, Samuel, 177n
Andrews, William, 135n
Aplin, Peter (V, 117), 45, 47
Apthorpe, Charles, 129n
Arbuthnot, Marriot (I, 7), 162, 225-6, 237
Archer, William, 86n-8
Armistead, Moss (V, 253), 92
Armstrong, Thomas, 127n
Arnold, Benedict (III, 55), 213, 234, 236, 254-6
Ars, ——, d', 68
Augusta, surrender of British post at, 64, 66

Balfour, Nisbet (I, 35-7), 12, 65-6, 71, 73-5, 79-82, 94, 172, 187, 267-8, 272-5, 279, 281-7 —
    relates to Germain and Clinton events of 1781, principally in the Carolinas, 209-254;
    states in January that many of the principal inhabitants of SC and some who held chief offices under the revolutionary government have reverted to their loyalty to the Crown, 210;
    his problems with the navy, 226, 253-4;
    mentions the great burden of the prisoners at Charlestown, 227;
    sends unemployed naval transports to England, much to Clinton's displeasure, 230-2, 234, 238-9, 245-6;
    his need of horses and cavalry appointments, 230, 246;
    his want of all kinds of ordnance stores, especially small arms, 239;
    seeks directions on the payment of rent for houses occupied by Government, 243;
    relates the almost universal revolt in SC after the arrival of Greene, together with the great force of the enemy, especially in cavalry, 218, 245, 249, 258;
    reports the loss of the vessel conveying his

and other dispatches to Cornwallis at Wilmington, 242;
    his instructions in January and May to the officer commanding at Georgetown, 261-3, 265-6;
    regrets the loss of the Back Country, 258;
    stresses the need to make striking examples of those who have sworn allegiance to the Crown but take up arms against it, 245;
    recounts events from Rawdon's march to relieve Ninety Six to mid July, 248-250;
    points out that the Battle of Eutaw Springs, the climate, and daily service have greatly reduced the actual strength of the army in SC, 222;
    adverts to the great expense of providing for refugees and displaced militia, 249, 253;
    reports that sea communications are plagued by revolutionary privateers, 254;
    his correspondence with Sir James Wright, 256-261
Ball Sr, Elias (I, 51), 264
Ballingall, Robert (II, 75), 287n
Barkley, Andrew (III, 49), 76, 209, 212-3, 234, 245-6
Barras, Jacques-Melchior Saint-Laurent, Comte de (V, 129), 4, 121
Barrett, Thomas (III, 156), 64
Basden, ——, 20
Battle of the Chesapeake Capes, 4, 102
Bean, Samuel, 289n-291
Benson, George (I, 172), 221
Blair, ——, 170n
Blair, George (III, 57), 255
Board of Agents for the American Loyalists —
    objects to comments in Cornwallis's Answer to Clinton's Narrative, 296-7;
    Cornwallis's response, 297-8
Booth, B—— (II, 243), 109-111, 277
Bose, Carl von, 66n
Branson, Eli (I, 186), 51n, 157
Brodrick, The Hon Henry (I, 22), 76, 163, 188, 210, 225

---

[1] The letter 'n' after the number of a page indicates the presence there of biographical or identifying information. Such information appearing in another volume is indicated in brackets immediately after a person's name.

reports the occupation of Yorktown and Gloucester, together with progress on fortifying them and evacuating Portsmouth, 19, 24, 27-8;

looks to Clinton to command in the Chesapeake when solid operations recommence there in October, 27;

recommends that Clinton's commands relating to South Carolina be directly transmitted to Leslie, 27;

reports that a great number of loyalist refugees have come from Portsmouth to Yorktown, 27;

mentions that the consumption of provisions at Yorktown is considerably increased from feeding former slaves employed in the public service as well as loyalist refugees, 28;

orders on 9th August the inhabitants of surrounding counties to repair to Yorktown, deliver up their arms, give their paroles, and bring their spare provisions, for which they will be paid, 108;

needs more heavy guns and many artillery and engineer's stores, 28;

his regiments are in dire need of their paymasters, clothing, and necessaries, 72, 76;

reports the arrival of de Grasse's fleet and the disembarkation of French naval troops, 29-31;

has provisions for six weeks, 31, 35;

refers to the return of de Grasse's fleet after the Battle of the Chesapeake Capes, 34;

advises Clinton on 16th September that he would risk an action were there no hopes of relief, but relief needs to arrive very soon, otherwise Clinton must be prepared to hear the worst, the posts being in no state of defence, 35;

agrees on 26th September that inhabitants may leave Yorktown and that former inhabitants may remove their families and effects, 91;

sends word on 29th September that he will retire within the works during the night and that he can hold out if relief arrives in any reasonable time, 36;

reports on 3rd October that the siege has begun, sees no means of Clinton's forming a junction with him but by York River, and asserts that a diversion would be of no use, 38, 40;

intimates on 15th October that his situation

is now becoming very critical and recommends that the navy and army run no great risk in endeavouring to save him, 40-1;

recounts on 20th October the siege and capitulation, 125-9;

his correspondence with Washington on the form of paroles, 129-130;

his parole, 131;

obtains a French guard on his flag vessel at Yorktown to prevent revolutionaries from disturbing him, 136-7;

explains that Yorktown and Gloucester were occupied against his better judgement and were not abandoned in view of the hopes of relief held out by Clinton, 153-4;

his passage from Virginia to New York, 164-5;

his passage from New York to England, 7, 188-9;

his exchange for Henry Laurens, 182-4;

his dormant commission to succeed Clinton in the event of the latter's death or incapacity, 202-3;

directions for his health, 203-5;

his character as related by his sister, together with information about his family, 292-5

Tarleton, Banastre (I, 154-7), 21, 44-5, 47-8, 59,
74, 86, 88n, 180, 210-1, 214, 227, 255, 263 —
        is promoted by brevet to the regular rank
        of lt colonel, 163
Thomas family, 97n-8
Thomas, William (V, 35), 269
Tonken, Thomas (V, 98), 189, 245, 251
Towel, Mark, 93-4
Towns, ——, 230, 246
Trail(e), Peter (II, 72), 239
Traverse, ——, 178n
Tuck, John, 101n
Tucker, Thomas Tudor (III, 441), 95-6
Turnbull, George (I, 138), 225

Vallancey, George Preston (IV, 153), 60
Vaughan, The Hon John (I, 11), 240
Vaughan, Wilmot, Earl of Lisburne, 232n
Vaugirauld, ——, de, 84-5n

Waldegrave, George, Viscount Chewton (II, 119),
189
Wallace, Gustavus Brown, 88-9n, 90
Walter, Richard (V, 98), 245
Washington, George —
        his force on the Hudson, 22, 24;
        his march to Virginia, 3-5, 31-3;
        his force at Yorktown, 3, 6, 33
Washington, William (I, 46), 167-8, 249
Watson, John Watson Tadwell (II, 199), 11-2, 217,
235, 241, 245
Wayne, Anthony, 28, 45, 47, 59, 220
Weeks, Amos, 105n
Weir, —— (III, 154), 47
Weir, Daniel (II, 118), 149
Wigfall, John (II, 64), 264
Williamson, Andrew (I, 77), 250
Wormeley, The Hon Ralph, 109n
Wright, Alexander, 274n, 281-7
Wright, Sir James, Bt, 256-261 —
        is informed by Balfour in May that no
        reinforcements can be sent for the time
        being except the recall of the garrisons of
        Augusta and Ninety Six to the Low
        Country, 256-8;
        is of opinion in mid August that the
        province will be lost unless some proposed
        exertion is made without loss of time, 259-
        260;
        is advised by Balfour that matters are at a
        stand until the arrival of Leslie, 261

Yorke, John (IV, 111), 299
Yorktown and Gloucester —
        occupation of, 19;
        fortification of will be a work of great
        time and labour but not very strong, 72;
        siege of, 4-6, 29-41, 125-9;
        correspondence between Cornwallis and
        Washington about the proposed
        capitulation, 112-6;
        the articles of capitulation, 117-121

§ - §